TERROR
OF THE LOST
TOKUSATSU
FILMS

By John LeMay
Edited by Ted Johnson
Foreword by Colin McMahon
With Contributions by
Allen A. Debus
Peter H. Brothers
And
Mike Bogue

BICEP BOOKS
Roswell, New Mexico, U.S.A.

BICEP BOOKS

Roswell, New Mexico, U.S.A.

For Mark Jaramillo, a great discoverer of lost projects...

TABLE OF CONTENTS

Acknowledgments

If it weren't for the following this book would have been a lot shorter. If they didn't contribute an essay or share a movie with me, then they likely suggested I include a rare film that I had yet to hear of in this book. Thanks Martin Arlt, Mike Bogue, Allen A. Debus, Colin McMahon, Justin Mullis, Josef Meditz, Peter H. Brothers, Joshua Sudomerski, Henning Straub, Kevin Derendorf, Don Glut, Kyle Byrd, Matt Parmley, Andres Perez, Ed Godziszewski, Steve Ryfle, Nicholas Driscoll, Neil Riebe and anyone else from Facebook Monsterland who helped. An especially big thank you to Ted Johnson for editing this book like you did the last one!

FOREWORD
BY COLIN McMAHON

When I was a kid growing up in the 1990s, I remember looking forward to going to the mall. My excitement wasn't fueled primarily by toy stores or arcades or even the book shop. No, the main attraction was Saturday Matinee, a local video store that had everything—at least in my young mind.

I would dash by the new releases, skip the romance section, pause briefly at animation before heading for the back. That was where Saturday Matinee stocked their foreign films. For me, it was Godzilla. I had to see if there was anything new in stock.

I was a collector of Godzilla films, even then. I wanted to own every single one. And I don't mean taped off the TV onto a recordable VHS. The quality wasn't as good on those, plus they could be taped over accidently. Oh, don't forget the commercials.

So yeah, it was official VHS release or bust. But honestly, the collecting was only part of the fun of visiting Saturday Matinee. What I remember more was the incredible sense of discovery every time I set foot in the store. I had no idea what was waiting for me back in that mysterious foreign film section.

Could it be *Godzilla vs. the Cosmic Monster*? *Godzilla vs. the Bionic Monster*? Oh, how about *Godzilla vs. The Thing*? As a kid, I thought these were all unique movies. After all they had their own titles and own covers. Yeah some of them looked similar and the pictures on the back of *Cosmic Monster* reminded me a lot of *Mechagodzilla '74* but hey, video distributors got a lot of stuff wrong back then. Take a look at Paramount/Gateway's *Terror of Mechagodzilla* VHS cover from 1995 if you don't believe me. It's entirely gorgeous and completely from the wrong movie. It's especially perplexing considering Paramount's 1980s VHS release featured the movie's international poster art. Likewise, most VHS slips of *Godzilla vs. the Cosmic Monster* showed Mechagodzilla on the front and Jet Jaguar on the back.

It wasn't until I discovered the internet that I finally knew the truth. Cosmic Monster, Bionic Monster and Mechagodzilla were all the same creation. The King of the Monsters never duked it out with Howard Hawks' outer space creation. Similarly, there was no remake of *King Kong vs. Godzilla* that used the 1976 Kong suit (blame GoodTimes Home Video's 1998 VHS for that one; again, their 1980s VHS release featured actual Toho stills).

5

From a collecting standpoint, my job got a lot easier. On numerous websites, I found the truth. Exactly 22 films (at the time)—some available in the States, some not. No, there was no alternate ending to *King Kong vs. Godzilla*. *Bambi Meets Godzilla* did exist but only as a short cartoon. It seems silly now to think otherwise.

However, there was a dark side to the internet. For the first time I knew everything and it was... kinda dull. I didn't look forward to my trips to Saturday Matinee anymore. Why would I? I knew exactly what could and could not be on those shelves. Actually, with the internet I didn't even need to keep going. I had all of the movies that were released internationally and I had ordered bootlegs of those that weren't.

I believe Saturday Matinee closed a short time after. The end of an era.

Don't get me wrong; the early internet time was great! Not only did I know every movie but sites like Toho Kingdom gave me so much more, including a list of films that weren't even made. Finally, there was more Godzilla to digest! I read through the list and checked for others and, well, I didn't find a ton. Most were baseless rumors discussed on forums or just misinformation from someone trying to impress the growing throngs of internet audiences craving new knowledge.

I think the loss of mystery is part of growing up. There are so many things we don't understand as children, that's what makes the world seem like such a magical place. Then we grow older, grow "wiser" and learn the rules one by one.

I had a microcosm of this lesson from the internet. I got what I wanted at the expense of something I didn't know I'd miss. My sense of discovery was gone. Yeah, there were new movies to look forward to but it wasn't the same. Everything, released or not, was known. I could see the complete picture and—while I appreciated this—I missed the days of Saturday Matinee.

Then last year, I read a *G-Fan* that introduced me to John LeMay and the work he was doing. John had done something I didn't know was possible. Using the internet and the tools it provided, he had found dozens of previously unreported abandoned Godzilla projects and was writing a book, *The Big Book of Japanese Giant Monster Movies: The Lost Films*. The G-Fan article teased *Bride of Godzilla?* —a work of such improbable fantasy that it was immediately obvious why the film wasn't made.

And I loved every bit of it, feeling that spark of discovery reignite after years of dormancy. My excitement only grew until G-Fest XXIV, when I was fortunate enough to meet John and hear firsthand about more of the abandoned projects. I had to wait until later to actually get my copy (sold out at the event—popular item!).

6

I love my copy of *The Lost Films*, it represents the best of both worlds. The enhanced knowledge base of the internet combined with the dedication of a passionate fan. The result is something truly special: a book that made me feel like I was back in Saturday Matinee, pulling VHSes off the shelves to get a glimpse at something I had never seen before.

Mystery survives in this world. The great deception of the internet is putting everything so simply that we forget that our knowledge is still incomplete. Wikipedia contains more articles than I can count but each one is a constant work in progress–we're always refining what we know. The best of us will look past what is given and wonder at what more there could be.

That's why I'm so glad that John has decided to continue his research into this book. Godzilla is not the only monster hiding secrets. Every industry in cinema across the globe has films that didn't quite work out, and others which have been lost to time. Some of these stories are completely gone; nothing of them exists.

However, for every deleted project, another remains in fragments, tantalizing audiences still. Will we ever find *London After Midnight* or the missing spider pit sequence from the 1933 *King Kong?* Only time will tell. I do know this for certain, though: if these countless hidden works are ever brought to light, it will be because of people like John.

Sit back reader, and prepare for a fascinating trip through film history. I hope that you will be transported back to the time of wonder and mystery in the same way that I was.

Colin McMahon
January 2018

INTRODUCTION:
OR, HOW DOES ONE DEFINE A LOST FILM?

"No more, I'm sick of Godzilla!"

The above line was spouted off by Ichiro Arishima in Toho's seminal 1962 box office hit *King Kong vs. Godzilla*. And, although the Godzilla series has become Toho's flagship franchise, it sometimes overshadows many of their other stellar special effects films without giant monsters. Some good examples include *Matango* (1963), about mutated mushroom people, and *Submersion of Japan* (1973) where, as the title suggests, Japan sinks into the ocean. The book you now hold in your hands serves two purposes. Firstly, it functions as a sequel to *The Big Book of Japanese Giant Monster Movies: The Lost Films* featuring the unmade, non-giant monster movies[1] of Toho, Daiei, and their brethren—sequels to films like *The Human Vapor* (1960), *Submersion of Japan*, and original scripts like *Adam of the Stars*. Secondly, this book also exists to educate the uneducated (or the educated but still curious) fans of tokusatsu movies unfamiliar with produced films such as *The Invisible Swordsman* (1970), *Blue Christmas* (1978), and the many other non-giant monster tokusatsu movies of Japan.

How this tome came about initially is simple. You see, whenever an author finishes writing a book, it is almost always inevitably that it leads to a related volume or sequel of some sort. Often, one finds information that is tangent to the subject of the book they are working on, although it just doesn't quite seem to fit the scope. In reading *Toho Tokusatsu Unpublished Works* I saw several non-giant monster tokusatsu films like *Frankenstein vs. the Human Vapor* which was limited to human-sized monsters. Though tempted, I didn't feel Toho's first aborted Frankenstein film fit the giant monster scope of *The Lost Films*. Likewise, though a spiritual sequel to *Atragon*, I didn't feel that *The Flying Battleship* qualified as a lost monster film either.[2] So it seemed like a no-brainer then to devote a sister volume to the non-giant monster tokusatsu films that were never made. But would it be as interesting?

I thought for sure none of the ideas in these non-kaiju films could be as good—or as crazy—as the ideas presented in scripts such as *Bride of Godzilla?* (1955). But once again I underestimated the pen of Shinichi Sekizawa and the other great sci-fi script writers of Japan. Have no fear, if unique crazy scenarios are your bag, you will find more of that here. *Frankenstein vs. the Human Vapor* in particular had some ambitious scenes that amazed me (how would you describe the Frankenstein monster parachuting out of an airplane?). Similarly, readers may be surprised to learn that portions of Sakyo Komatsu's ideas for his sequel to *Submersion of Japan* take place in outer space! Toho's aborted 1974 *Human Torch* likewise intrigued me with its twists and turns throughout its narrative. Had it—or its second iteration, *Invisible Man vs. the Human Torch*—been produced it may well have rekindled a 1970s era continuation of Toho's Transforming Human series that began in the 1950s.

Like *The Lost Films*, this book details projects that began life as treatments and scripts but never actually went before cameras—the lone exception being *The Flying Battleship* (1966) which developed into the Tsuburaya Productions TV series *Mighty Jack* (1968). Scripts like *Frankenstein vs. the Human Vapor* ended up paving the way for *Frankenstein vs. Godzilla* which itself became *Frankenstein Conquers the World* (1965). Just imagine, had *Frankenstein vs. the Human Vapor* been made, Toho likely never would have had the idea to make a movie about a giant Frankenstein monster. This, in turn, means that Sanda and Gaira, the Frankenstein Brothers in Japan, from *The War of the Gargantuas* (1966) would never exist! And as to what we have to thank for the cancellation of *Frankenstein vs. the Human Vapor* is supposedly the failure of *Matango* at the box office. Essentially, *Matango* spelled out the doom for human-sized monsters and from that point forward, Toho mostly stuck to giant monsters.

Then, in the 1970s, when films from Toho's Transforming Human Series began airing on television to high ratings, the concept was briefly revived and Tomoyuki Tanaka considered launching a new series. As stated earlier, it would have begun with *Human Torch*, which was passed over in favor of the more ambitious *Invisible Man vs. the Human Torch*. Ironically, giant monsters would lead to the cancellation of these films as well. Problems with the Hammer/Toho team-up *Nessie* delayed production on *Invisible Man vs. the Human Torch* and the Godzilla Revival Meeting of 1978 essentially killed the project for good.

The other entries in this book deviate somewhat from what many may define as a "lost film" and covers rare but released films that many in the west have yet to see, such as Toho and Daiei's Invisible Man films. So again, while they are not lost films in their native country, chances are many in the west have heard of these films but have not actually seen them. I will admit that chances are if you are reading this book you are a super-otaku who has seen many of these films. However, I also wrote this book in mind for the all-around American Tokusatsu fan who probably hasn't seen said films.

This is probably also as good a spot as any to explain that "tokusatsu" refers to Japanese special effects movies. However, that does not necessarily mean it has to refer to a sci-fi/fantasy film, hence why I also include a film like Daiei's *Buruuba* (1955)— essentially a Japanese version of Tarzan with a few special effects scenes.[3] That does not mean, however, that this book covers every single tokusatsu film not released in the U.S. as that would be exhaustive (Toho's war films, with special effects by Eiji Tsuburaya and Teruyoshi Nakano, are also tokusatsu). So no, this book is by no means comprehensive and comprises of films that the author has seen and also thinks English speaking toku-fans will find of interest.[4]

Now, to return to the matter of just how one defines a rare film, *Submersion of Japan* (1973) is a good example. The film is easily obtainable in Japan, but it has never seen a home video release in its uncut form in America.[5] Instead, it was re-edited *Godzilla, King of the Monsters!*-style by having Lorne Greene (best known for the TV series *Bonanza*) shoehorned into the film, which was retitled *Tidal Wave* and released in 1975. Though *Tidal Wave* played on television into the 1980s, today it is nowhere to be found. It's not on YouTube, and even bootleg DVD releases are scarce. So yes, *Submersion of Japan* was released to the west in a way, but it is still a very rare film for westerners and "average fans" who don't go to the trouble to track it down via bootleg or buy a region free DVD player.

Toho's "mutant trilogy" (*The H-Man, The Secret of the Telegian* and *The Human Vapor*) is another good example, as all films in said trilogy have at one point had an official U.S. release—even if that release was confined only to television. However, today only *The H-Man* has seen a DVD release in America.[6] On the other end of the spectrum, similar films like Daiei's *Invisible Man vs. the Human Fly* (1957) have never seen a U.S. release of any kind whatsoever. Actually, the only reason that films like *The H-Man* were released in America at all, as opposed to similar films like Toho's *Invisible Avenger* (1954), was that they were made after movies like *Godzilla, King of the Monsters!* (1956), *Rodan* (1957) and *Gigantis, the Fire Monster* (1959)[7] became hits in America. As *Invisible Avenger* was made before Toho films became popular in the U.S. it has never seen a release in this country or been dubbed into English.

Similarly, Daiei Studios actually churned out a great many effects films before the creation of *Gamera* (1965). But, even with the success of *Gamera*, Daiei special effects films—even post-Gamera ones like the Daimajin and Yokai films—never did receive U.S. theatrical releases and were lucky to even go to television. This is why many tokusatsu fans in the west have yet to see many fantastic

Daiei films such as *Invisible Man Appears* (1949), *The Whale God* (1962), and *The Invisible Swordsman* (1970). Fans may be even more surprised to learn that Eiji Tsuburaya did effects work for Daiei in the late 1940s when he had briefly left Toho. So, bottom line, if a film was released in Japan but not the U.S. (like *Invisible Avenger*) it gets its own review in the book. If it was released in some form to theaters or television in the U.S., but is still rare (like *The Human Vapor*), it will be covered in a "special section"—often with related films from the same genre or series—apart from the main body reviews.

And if you've read *The Lost Films*, you know I also love appendices, and here, there are four. As in *The Lost Films*, Appendix I details other unproduced films which lacked sufficient information for inclusion in the main volume. And though tokusatsu war films (like 1953's *Eagle of the Pacific*) were not covered in the main part of this work, they are covered here as fans may still find what was planned, but not produced, of interest. Appendix II includes details on existing films and how they differed in their inception. Appendix III details yet more Japanese tokusatsu films that have never been released in the U.S., many of which come from Daiei. While this list is selective[8] rather than exhaustive, it does cover various horror, sci-fi and fantasy films that this author feels Godzilla, Gamera, and tokusatsu fans will find of interest. Appendix IV even covers the now lost U.S. edits of movies like *Half Human* (1957), *Tidal Wave* (1975) and *High Seas Hijack*—the 1978 version of *Conflagration,* which inserted Peter Graves into the film and re-edited the storyline.

Whatever your opinion may be of my criteria, as with the last book, I hope you enjoy yet another journey into the unknown of what might have been—and what was, but many still have yet to see. I know I did.

Section Notes

[1] "But, John, didn't you include *Abominable Snowman* (1955), a non-giant monster movie, in *The Lost Films*?" you ask. You are indeed correct my astute reader, I did. But at the time I had no idea I was going to write *this* book next. If I did, I would have rightly saved *Abominable Snowman* and 1974's *Great Prophecies of Nostradamus* for this book. As they say, "If I knew then what I know now…"

[2] A giant plant monster briefly appears in the initial treatment, though it was excised from the first draft script.

[3] By the same token, Appendix I includes unmade films like the aborted Japanese version of *Those Amazing Men in Their Flying Machines*.

[4] This also includes an American TV precursor to *Matango* made in 1958. Though it's obviously not Japanese, it's unreleased to VHS and very rare. It is this book's lone exception as far as non-Japanese films go.

[5] The Japanese version was released in theaters in California circa 1974.

[6] Apparently MGM's materials for *The Human Vapor*—and *Gorath*—are deteriorated too badly to be useable.

[7] The author is using the U.S. release dates for said films. In Japan *Godzilla* was released in 1954, *Rodan* in 1956, and *Godzilla Raids Again* in 1955.

[8] This section covers a few select Daiei samurai films with a supernatural element (like *The Ogre of Mount Oe*) but not all of them as there are enough of those to warrant an entire volume of their own.

12

1.
INVISIBLE MAN APPEARS

Release Date: September 25, 1949

Directed by: Nobuo Adachi **Screenplay by:** Nobuo Adachi, Akimitsu Takagi (story) & H. G. Wells (novel) **Special Effects by:** Eiji Tsuburaya **Music by:** Goro Nishi **Cast:** Kanji Koshiba (Shunji Kurokawa/Invisible Man), Daijiro Natsukawa (Kyosuke Segi), Chizuru Kitagawa (Machiko Nakazato), Ryunosuke Tsukigata (Dr. Kenzo Nakazato), Takiko Mizunoe (Ryuko Mizuki), Teruko Omi (Kimiko Chosokabe), Kichijiro Ueda (Otoharu Sugimoto), Shosaku Sugiyama (Ichiro Kawabe), Mitsusaburo Ramon (Matsubara)

Academy Aspect, Black & White, 82 Minutes

SYNOPSIS Dr. Nakazato has recently developed a serum for invisibility, but hides this fact from his two protégés: Dr. Kurokawa and Dr. Segi. Instead, he creates a competition between the two to see who can create the invisibility formula first. The prize will be his daughter Machiko's hand in marriage. A group of jewel thieves, led by Ichiro Kawabe, kidnap Dr. Nakazato, fully aware of his invisibility serum. The same thieves trick Kurokawa into taking the professor's invisibility serum under what he thinks are the professor's wishes. Kurokawa gladly obliges thinking this will win him Machiko's hand in marriage. The jewelers then reveal to Kurokawa that before they will give him the cure to restore his visibility, he must steal a famous necklace belonging to his sister called the Tears of Amour. Kurokawa reluctantly agrees as the invisibility serum begins to affect his mind. Kurokawa's sister, Ryuko, works with a police inspector to protect the necklace from the invisible man, unaware it is her own brother. Kurokawa goes to visit Segi, revealing to him what has happened and how he has been deceived. Machiko walks into the room, unaware of Kurokawa's presence, and declares her love for Segi. This enrages Kurokawa who runs away, now more determined than ever to steal the necklace. Ryuko disguises herself as the invisible man and infiltrates the jewelers' hideout to free Dr. Nakazato. It is there that Kurokawa learns there is no cure for his condition. Kurokawa engages in a gun battle where he kills Kawabe, and then is gunned down himself by the police.

COMMENTARY Recognized as Japan's oldest surviving tokusatsu film, Daiei's *Invisible Man Appears* is an overlooked film for many reasons.[1] Of course, the biggest reason it remains relatively unknown is the fact that it came out before *Godzilla* (1954) which put Japanese effects films "on the map" so to speak. In fact, *Invisible Man Appears* special effects director was none other than Eiji Tsuburaya, who had left Toho at the time in the middle of a dispute to go to Daiei. Sadly, more people are aware of Tsuburaya's later Invisible Man film for Toho released shortly after *Godzilla* than they are this one.

Right away the film's opening sets itself up as a smarter thriller than its successors, Toho's *Invisible Avenger* (1954) and Daiei's later effort *Invisible Man vs. the Human Fly* (1957). Firstly, the film begins with these words: "There is no good or evil in science but it can be used for good or evil purposes." The first scene then introduces the main characters in a scientific discussion about the color black in the color spectrum[2] (and how it could be used to render an object invisible) that is far ahead of the aforementioned later two films which don't spend much, if any, time discussing how their titular Invisible characters were rendered such. The film also benefits from a well done love triangle—which predating *Godzilla* can't be called a copycat of the Serizawa/Emiko/ Ogata story.

In this case, our titular protagonist is Dr. Kurokawa—a tragic character that is manipulated into becoming the invisible man by crooks. When the elder Dr. Nakazato goes missing (in reality, he has been kidnapped), Kurokawa thinks he is testing out Dr. Nakazato's invisibility serum at the doctor's insistence, but he is actually being manipulated by the crooks who kidnapped him. The crooks, led by the typical mustache-twirling villain Kawabe, are using the doctor's invisibility formula in an elaborate ploy to steal the Tears of Amour. The effects of this formula are irreversible, a fact they purposely neglect to tell Kurokawa. They promise to give the doctor a nonexistent antidote after stealing the necklace for them.

To make matters worse, when Kurokawa tells Dr. Segi (his rival for Machiko's affections) his tragic tale, Machiko walks in and, not knowing Kurokawa is there, professes her love to Segi. Kurokawa understandably becomes enraged. As the serum causes psychotic mood swings in those who take it, Kurokawa is pushed further and further towards the edge until he becomes a complete menace to society. Though, his goal of becoming visible again is understandable.

Kurokawa's death in the climax is well-handled. After being shot by police, his footsteps appear in the sand and are soon washed away by the tide. Minutes later, his form rematerializes under the waves and the film ends with the same words that it began with:

"There is no good or evil in science but it can be used for good or evil purposes."

Character touches aside, this film is of merit for being Eiji Tsuburaya's first major fantastical film as director of special effects. Tsuburaya's first trick is making a guinea pig turn transparent. Interestingly, the hair briefly turns black, then back to white, before becoming a ghostly image that fades away, implying an imaginative chemical reaction going on within the animal. There's also an invisible pet cat that runs around, though we don't see its transformation. The scene is played for shock as much as it is humor, as Machiko is unaware that her father has turned the cat invisible (let alone invented an invisibility formula) as it walks through the house, tipping over vases and causing some minor mayhem.

As for the film's invisible man, his design is directly inspired by the original Universal Studios Invisible Man with iconic bandages, sunglasses, hat, and trench coat look. The famous unveiling scene in this film happens 25 minutes in when Kurokawa walks into the jewelry store and requests to speak to the manager in private. When he makes his demands to the manager known, he tells him that he is an invisible man and first takes off his glasses, revealing the absence of eyes. Next, he unravels the bandages around his head which is an excellent effect on par with the Universal films. He then strips off all his clothes until only his gloved hands remain.

At the same time, later unveiling scenes also become somewhat gimmicky. At one point, the Invisible Man (naked and completely invisible) accosts an old drunk for his clothes, which he steals. However, all this does is draw attention to himself as he now has the appearance of a headless man in a trench coat! A cop spots him, causes a ruckus, and soon the Invisible Man has discarded the clothes he has only just stolen from the bum as he runs off into the night.

Later, the Invisible Man (in his bandages and trench coat) forces his sister Ryuko's car to stop so that he may steal the Tears of Amour. As it turns out, it was an imposter that Kurokawa forced to pose as him by wrapping his face in bandages to steal the necklace. The police arrest the impostor, and as they question him about the invisible man's identity, Kurokawa comes and stabs him in the back! He then steals the necklace from the inspector (though it turns out to be a decoy). The fact that Kurokawa must steal from his sister is a bit of a plot hole. One has to wonder why instead of trying to steal the necklace, he doesn't just explain his situation to his sister who would likely hand it over to him. At the film's end, rather than simply drop the gun that gives away his position, Kurokawa shoots at the cops who are able to pinpoint his position as a result. Obviously, he would have been better off dropping the gun and running away. However, both of these lapses in logic could be explained away by the fact that Kurokawa has become crazy since taking the serum. Another slight detriment to the film is a sequence where the Invisible Man follows Machiko on a motorcycle which can't help but be comical—so much so that it might've been better off to have the Invisible Man appear at the final meeting place sans any explanation.

Apart from that, the film succeeds both as a science fiction film and a 1940s-era caper. It even has a dance club scene perhaps making it the true precursor to Toho's transforming human series that would begin with their own *Invisible Avenger* in 1954.[3] The film is also well-directed by Nobuo Adachi[4] who utilizes several excellent POV shots from the Invisible Man's perspective. This lets the viewer know where Kurokawa is and also instills some creepiness into the proceedings. A good example is a POV shot from Kurokawa as he watches a group of people searching for him inside of a hotel. Overall, Kurokawa is a sneaky, devious invisible man with a good sense of menace, particularly in a scene where he returns to terrorize the jewelry store owner. The owner is telling another man of his terrifying ordeal as the other man makes light of his story. Soon, a door comes creaking open and both men are sure it is the invisible man. In walks a stray cat, putting them both at ease. Their conversation returns to the invisible man, with the skeptical man remarking that he'd like to meet him. At that point, Kurokawa speaks, revealing he came into the room with the cat and soon begins terrorizing the two men.

Though some may be tempted to classify this as a Japanese imitation [read: rip-off] of the Universal Studios' Invisible Man films, it too is a quasi-adaptation of the H.G. Wells story which, like the Universal film, transports the action into the present day.[5] The Japanese version does specifically lift one plot aspect unique to the Universal film wherein the invisibility formula causes the user to become psychotic. Conversely in the H.G. Wells novel, the Invisible Man is psychotic before becoming invisible.

Overall, *Invisible Man Appears* isn't a terribly entertaining film but tokusatsu fans will find it worth a watch for its historical significance. And for a film of its time, it is a quality production all around.

Chapter Notes

[1] Those that want to argue that Daiei's *The Rainbow Man* was the first should be aware that the effects footage was very minor compared to *Invisible Man Appears*.

[2] Black isn't necessarily a color. In fact, a black object absorbs all the colors of the visible spectrum but reflects none of them to the eyes. So in a sense, black is all colors combined and yet the absence of color at the same time. The film's scientific discussion is about how if an object were to be rendered completely black it therefore couldn't reflect light and would be invisible.

[3] Almost all of Toho's "Transforming Human" films seem to involve dancers/singers in some way and often had scenes set in nightclubs or dance theaters.

[4] Adachi directed several other tokusatsu films for Daiei such as *The Iron Claw* (see Appendix IV).

[5] *The Invisible Man* was published in 1897. The 1933 adaptation by Universal was fairly faithful to the book keeping the characters' names and overall premise.

2.

INVISIBLE AVENGER

Release Date: December 29, 1954
Alternate Titles: *Invisible Man*

Directed by: Motoyoshi Oda **Screenplay by:** Shigeaki Hidaka & Kei Beppu (story) **Special Effects by:** Eiji Tsuburaya **Music by:** Kyosuke Kami **Cast:** Seizaburo Kawazu (Takamitsu Nanjo/Invisible Man), Miki Sanjo (Michiyo), Yoshio Tsuchiya (Komatsu), Keiko Kondo (Mariko), Minoru Takada (Yajima), Kenjiro Uemura (Ken), Kamatari Fujiwara (Mariko's grandfather), Haruo Nakajima (Invisible Man hit by car)

Academy Aspect, Black & White, 70 Minutes

SYNOPSIS An accident on a busy Tokyo street reveals the existence of an invisible man when he is hit by a car. A suicide note explains that the man was part of a top secret program during the war that turned him and several other men invisible. Now that he is dead, the note says only one other survivor of the group remains. Hysteria takes over Japan for fear of the invisible men when this is revealed by the press. A gangster takes advantage of the situation by having a faux gang led by an invisible man (in fact just a normal man wearing bandages). The real invisible man, Nanjo, now works as a clown in order to hide his appearance. When the gangsters murder the grandfather of a young girl that he has befriended, Nanjo goes on the offensive to take down the gangsters. Nanjo chases down the gangster boss to a Tokyo oil refinery where both men fall to their deaths.

COMMENTARY In late October of 1954, after *Godzilla* had been screened for Toho executives, a meeting was held to determine what film would serve as the New Year's release.[1] After Toho executives became understandably impressed by *Godzilla's* effects scenes, another effects film was pitched to them—albeit a much less ambitious one. Surprisingly, this pitch didn't come from producer Tomoyuki Tanaka, but an art director/production designer named Takeo Kita.[2] Even stranger, Kita was promoted to the position of producer on the film![3] As such, *Invisible Avenger* is one of the few Toho special effects films to not be produced by Tomoyuki Tanaka.

Reportedly, the story proposal was submitted on October 21st and by the 25th, the production was greenlit to be the December 1954 New Year's release. Although the script's developmental process was short (the film would begin shooting in November), there are some differences in the three drafts. For instance, in the first draft, Nanjo's love interest Michiyo was the daughter of a flower shop owner rather than a nightclub performer. Also, she and Nanjo's blossoming romance was better handled and not as abrupt as it is in the finished film.

Godzilla fans might find the film of particular interest because it was done by much of the same principal crew behind *Godzilla Raids Again*—director Motoyoshi Oda, writer Shigeaki Hidaka, actor Yoshio Tsuchiya, and, of course, special effects director Eiji Tsuburaya. The film finished its shooting and effects work on December 21st, and was released one week later on the 29th making it one of Toho's tightest deadlines ever. Luckily though, Tsuburaya already had experience with invisible men having helmed the effects for Daiei's *Invisible Man Appears* only five years earlier. However, always one to top himself and try new techniques, Tsuburaya upped the ante on this Invisible Man film. Whereas Daiei's film had the titular character more or less copy the Universal film's method of stripping out of his face bandages, Tsuburaya wanted to try a technique where Nanjo disappears as he wipes off his clown makeup. To do this, Tsuburaya had the actor rub black makeup over his face rather than rubbing the white makeup off. When combined with the separately shot background, Nanjo seems to disappear before our eyes. Similarly, rather than using piano wires for the scene where Nanjo throws various objects at the gangsters in the club, a stuntman[4] in an all-black suit threw the objects against a black backdrop. When combined with the separately shot backdrop of the club, it really does appear as if an invisible man is picking up the objects. The film even used one miniature for the climax where an oil refinery catches fire.

The film gets off to a promising start in the way that it sets up its concept and presents the idea of the invisible man—or men. In the opening scene, a man driving his car suddenly stops in the middle of the road, convinced he has hit something even though nothing is there. A crowd gathers, and soon blood begins to spread from under the car and a man's body begins to materialize. There to witness the act is reporter Komatsu,[5] who finds a suicide note revealing the man's past. The note states that the man was part of a top secret government project during the war that turned him and several others invisible—a process that is irreversible.[6] As most of the men met their doom during the 1944 Battle of Saipan, the note states that he (the suicide victim) and one other mystery man are the lone survivors. Immediately after, a news report is released about the Invisible Man program and the Japanese populace reacts with fear and shock.

Though the audience doesn't know it yet, they are introduced to the lead invisible man right away. As the news plays on TV, Nanjo is standing on the sidelines dressed as a clown along with another clown who quips about how much he would like to meet this invisible man. Nanjo then makes a comment that you can't see what isn't there and the two go about their business. Though the audience must surely suspect it, confirmation that Nanjo is the invisible man isn't given until exactly halfway into the film when he takes off a glove revealing nothing underneath—or nothing that we can see. From there we get our first look at the real Invisible Man as he wipes the makeup off his face for Tsuchiya's reporter character who has concluded that Nanjo was the invisible man.

Overall, Nanjo makes for a very likeable lead character as played by actor Seizaburo Kawazu. Kawazu would also have minor roles in other Toho effects films such as *Mothra* (1961), *The Last War* (1961), *Gorath* (1962) and played the gangster boss in *Space Monster Dogora* (1964). He manages to wrangle the audience's sympathies very well. In an odd departure for the era, Nanjo reveals that he is a Christian, or at least that he tries to honor his mother's Christian faith which drives his compassion for others. The heart of the film is the relationship between Nanjo and a blind girl, Mariko, whom he watches over while her grandfather is out. Though Nanjo is poor, he does his best to buy her a special music box she wants that will play "Jennie's Theme"—something that comes into play prominently in the film's final moments.

As for the villains, they are the standard Toho gangsters and there really isn't much to say about their individual characters. However, there is an interesting twist in that the gangsters take advantage of the Invisible Man hysteria by wrapping their faces in bandages and shouting that they are the Invisible Men while robbing a bank!

As in *Godzilla Raids Again*, *Invisible Avenger* features a significant nightclub sequence, so either writer Hidaka or director Oda were fond of this aspect. The nightclub sequences showcase a fairly risqué dance scene as well, at least for 1954 standards. Even more edgy is a scene where one of the scantily clad dancers is hung up by her wrists and has her legs whipped as punishment for stealing from the gangsters. Reportedly, some even racier footage from this scene was cut though. It's also interesting to note that the first of Toho's "Transforming Human Series," 1958's *The H-Man*, also contains several scenes set within a nightclub including a risqué dance scene.

If one compares Toho's *Invisible Avenger* to Universal's Invisible Man series, Toho's version is actually quite innovative. The fact that they chose to make their invisible man a clown is something the Universal films never did before and also allows for the actor's face to be seen for most of the film rather than being obscured behind bandages or a disembodied voice like Vincent Price was in *The Invisible Man Returns* (1940). When comparing the film to Daiei's *Invisible Man Appears*, there are naturally some similarities—notably the floating gun scene. Also, just like in Daiei's film, Nanjo drives a scooter to chase down the villains in what is undeniably a funny scene.[7] In fact, it's so funny it's somewhat at odds with the more serious nature of the film. It's enough to make one wonder if perhaps the film would have been better off as a light action comedy. The climax is a bit underwhelming as the various gangsters pretend to fight Nanjo (or "shadowbox") and fall down.

The final climactic battle between Nanjo and the gangster boss at an oil refinery is particularly disappointing. It's enough to make one wonder if a more elaborate ending was planned but wasn't possible due to the rushed production period. As was predictable in Toho films, Nanjo dies while fighting the villain when both fall to the ground. However, Nanjo's final moments are touching and well-handled, and the music box that plays "Jennie's Song" as the film fades out couldn't be better.

Chapter Notes

[1] In Japan, the entirety of December is considered "New Year". As *Godzilla* was released on November 3rd, it was far too early to be considered a New Year's release.

[2] Kita served as an art director on nearly all of Toho's effects films all the way up to 1970's *Space Amoeba*.

[3] *Invisible Avenger* was Kita's lone producer credit and supposedly this all came about due to the actions of a local union which caused Toho to promote several other staff members to full-blown producers.

[4] Likely Godzilla suit actor Haruo Nakajima, though he has never been credited as such.

[5] Yoshio Tsuchiya, who actually wanted to play the titular character but wasn't cast. This would not be the last time Tsuchiya requested an odd part with limited face time. During filming of *The Mysterians*, Tsuchiya chose the role of the helmeted Mysterian leader over that of the hero, eventually played by Kenji Sahara.

[6] This idea that the men were part of a secret military unit is intriguing, though Universal's 1942 film *Invisible Agent* also played with the concept.

[7] In *Invisible Man Appears*, the Invisible Man steals a police motorcycle.

3.
BURUUBA

Release Date: October 25, 1955

Directed by: Shigeyoshi Suzuki **Screenplay by:** Hideo Oguni & Yoichiro Minami (story) **Special Effects by:** Yonesaburo Tsukiji **Music by:** Akira Ifukube **Cast:** Yoshihiro Hamaguchi (Buruuba), Yuko Yashio (Reiko), Bontaro Miake (Dr. Watanabe), Frank Kumagai (Daisuke), Osamu Maruyama (Kenkichi Yamada), Woody Strode (Native Chief)

Academy Aspect, Black & White, 88 Minutes

SYNOPSIS A father and daughter duo, Dr. Watanabe and Reiko, travel to Kilimanjaro, Africa searching for Dr. Shiba, lost there 20 years ago where he reportedly found a lost diamond mine. Along for the expedition are big game hunter Daisuke and insect collector Yamada. Instead of the long lost Dr. Shiba, they find Shiba's fully grown son Joji, or Buruuba, who saves Reiko from peril. When the party finds Reiko, Daisuke shoots Buruuba who darts off into the river. Buruuba nurses his wound while the expedition continues their search for the lost diamond mine. When they arrive at their destination they are accosted by a hostile tribe. Buruuba leads a rescue mission comprised of himself and wild animals to rescue them. Once again, Daisuke tries to kill Buruuba but is attacked and killed by a lion. In the end, Reiko decides to stay in Africa with Buruuba rather than return to Japan with her father.

COMMENTARY The origins of this Japanese version of Tarzan lie in the year 1949. That year Yoichiro Minami wrote *The Adventures of Buruuba,* the first of six popular juvenile novels. At the same time, Daiei president Masaichi Nagata successfully began negotiations with Walt Disney and MGM to distribute their films in Japan. Then, in 1955, Nagata greenlit the production of a live-action film adaptation of Yoichiro Minami's Buruuba stories. Due to his distribution deal with MGM, Nagata was able to actually film the movie on the same jungle sets that the original *Tarzan, the Ape Man* (1932) were filmed on in Los Angeles!

23

Really, the film's story is an adaptation of the 1932 MGM Tarzan film more than it is either Edgar Rice Burroughs's books or even Minami's Buruuba stories. The only significant deviation, in keeping with Minami's stories, is that Buruuba shares a connection with lions rather than apes.[1] Also, instead of the elephant graveyard, the main expedition is searching for a diamond mine—presumably King Solomon's mines or something similar. Otherwise, the film might as well be a near shot-for-shot Japanese remake of *Tarzan, the Ape Man*. This certainly isn't a swipe at the film though. It is quite well made, and it isn't unusual for American studios to readapt Japanese properties themselves.

The success of the Johnny Weissmuller Tarzan films[2] even influenced the casting of Buruuba. Like Weissmuller, lead actor Yoshihiro Hamaguchi was a swimmer who had won the silver medal at the Helsinki Olympic Men's 800-meter freestyle relay in 1952. And indeed, Hamaguchi (who wears a wig for the role) spends lots of time in the water, though there is no underwater camerawork. Like Weismuller, Hamaguchi has a distinct yell created for the character—actually "Buruuba!" is literally what the character yells every time and also where he gets his name. Like any yell that isn't the iconic Weissmuller yell, it ends up being rather comical. Other than that, Hamaguchi admirably holds his own against comparisons to Weissmuller. Hamaguchi does an excellent job swinging from the vines, and in most instances, it appears to be the real actor rather than a stunt double. In one scene, Hamaguchi—not a stunt double—wrestles a real, live python! At one point, the large snake very nearly strikes him. And last but not least, Hamaguchi's Buruuba even has a chimpanzee side-kick akin to Cheeta.[3]

As stated earlier, the story is structured exactly as the 1932 MGM film with its own versions of Jane (here Reiko), her father, and a big game hunter villain of sorts.[4] As in *Tarzan, the Ape Man*, the titular character doesn't show up right away and Buruuba doesn't appear until about 24 minutes into the film. The occasion is that Reiko is kidnapped by the infamous *Gorilla at Large* (1954) suit![5] Buruuba shows up to battle the gorilla with his knife and it runs off. As in *Tarzan, the Ape Man*, the next portion of the film consists of Reiko and Buruuba getting to know one another and trying to communicate.

When the expedition reconnects with Reiko, the villainous Daisuke shoots Buruuba who dives into a river and swims away. Stock shots of crocodiles darting into the water follow—presumably setting up a fight between Buruuba and the crocs that was either deemed un-filmable or cut for some reason. The action shifts back to the expedition and when we next see Buruuba, he is riding atop a crocodile prop. Due to the prop's inanimate nature, it is unknown

24

if the crocodile is Buruuba's friend giving him a ride back to shore or if the croc is dead from an off-screen fight between the two and Buruuba is merely riding its corpse. In any case, the stock shots of the crocs chasing Buruuba prove confusing and should have been cut.[6]

Oddly, during the climax, the main characters never do enter the diamond mine they are searching for and only spy the location from afar before being kidnapped by a hostile tribe. The tribe is headed by none other than actor Woody Strode, later to be famous for supporting roles in numerous westerns. When they are captured, rather than inciting an elephant stampede, Buruuba calls an army of lions to his aid (though he does ride atop an elephant). This film also doesn't see Reiko's father die like Jane's does. He lives to watch his daughter abandon society to live in the wilds with Buruuba. The film even ends with the same shot as *Tarzan, the Ape Man* with the two romantic leads standing atop a cliff together.

As was often the case of jungle films of the black and white era, *Buruuba* is stuffed full of African wildlife stock shots. They blend in seamlessly half of the time, which all things considered is pretty good. At other times, the older footage sticks out like a sore thumb. One of the better stock shots involves the film's comic relief, Yamada, encountering a panther. He passes out and a monkey drops a coconut on his head from a tree to wake him and the editing is quite good.

As for other production values, the film was scored by the great Akira Ifukube, who had only recently scored *Godzilla* the previous year. Ifukube uses the same instruments, and even composes a similar melody, for his jungle scenes here that he would reprise in *King Kong vs. Godzilla* seven years later. That being said, most of the picture actually goes unscored. Overall, *Buruuba* and *Tarzan, the Ape Man* would make for a very intriguing double feature.

Chapter Notes

[1] In the books, Buruuba was raised by a chimpanzee. Later on, he saved the life of a lion who, along with other lions, became his faithful ally. Though not raised by lions in the books, Buruuba has a connection to lions similar to the allegiance Tarzan has with apes.

[2] Weissmuller's last Tarzan film was *Tarzan and the Mermaids* in 1948, and by this time Weissmuller was playing the fully clad "Jungle Jim" character in a series of the same name.

[3] Cheeta was not in Burroughs books and was a creation of the MGM films.

[4] The Minami novels apparently lacked the element of a Japanese expedition searching for Buruuba in Africa, so this was likely lifted from the Tarzan stories.

[5] That suit was created by George Barrows, who inhabited it in films such as *Gorilla at Large* (1954) and *Robot Monster* (1953). The suit was later loaned out for the shooting of *Konga* in 1961.

[6] There was one deleted scene from the script deemed too difficult to film where Buruuba was to spar with a lion which would end in the lion regarding Buruuba as his better.

26

4.
FEARFUL ATTACK OF
THE FLYING SAUCERS

Release Date: November 7, 1956

Directed by: Shinichi Sekizawa **Screenplay by:** Shinichi Sekizawa
Special Effects by: Yoshiyuki Kuroda **Music by:** Satoshi Kusakawa
Cast: Tadao Takashima (Masao Hayashi), Junko Ebata (Kaoru
Hoshina), Taiji Tonoyama (Dr. Otsuki), Junji Masuda (Dr. Kuroi),
Shigeru Amachi (Osugi), Hiroshi Sugi (Dr. Hoshina)

Academy Aspect, Black & White, 80 Minutes

SYNOPSIS A mysterious U.F.O. seen around the world lands atop a
TV tower in Tokyo where it launches its robot emissary into the
streets below. Dr. Otsuki tries to communicate with the robot, but
when a helicopter flies too close to it and the U.F.O., they attack.
Soon the U.F.O. begins attacking Japan and the rest of the world.
Dr. Otsuki and his reporter friend, Masao, track down the reclusive
scientist Dr. Hoshina who has created the super weapon Rocket R-
1. The robot attacks and kills Hoshina at his secret lab in Izu, but
Masao and Otsuki manage to launch Rocket R-1 which defeats the
U.F.O.

COMMENTARY Inspired by the same year's *Earth vs. the Flying
Saucers*, and perhaps also *The Day the Earth Stood Still* (1951),
Fearful Attack of the Flying Saucers is noteworthy for being the
directorial debut of famous writer Shinichi Sekizawa.[1] The hows and
the whys of the film's inception are unknown, but considering
Sekizawa wrote and directed it, one could assume it was a passion
project. And considering he had yet to link up with Toho, that would
be the reason why Toho had nothing to do with the film. In fact,
Fearful Attack of the Flying Saucers was produced by National Film
Production and when Toho and Daiei both refused to distribute it,
Shintoho, which had a hand in the film's special effects work,
released the film.[2]

Scene from **Fearful Attack of the Flying Saucers.**

At the time of the film's production, Japan was experiencing a fascination with the phenomena of U.F.O.s and their alleged alien occupants as were many other places across the world. 1956 had already been a big year for sci-fi movies, with Daiei's *Warning from Space* and Toho's *Rodan* which made it easier to convince competing studios to try their hands at sci-fi films and Sekizawa's first draft for National Film Production was called *Target Earth*.[3] However, when it came time to release the film, Shintoho decided upon a more sensational title.

Though thought to be lost entirely after its 1956 release, in February 2010, a 16mm print of the film surfaced on Yahoo! Auctions. A bidding war soon erupted and when bids reached heights of over ¥200,000 it was withdrawn and relisted with a suggested bid of ¥3 million. In the end, the print was sold for ¥2.1 million. The editor of *Tokusatsu Hihou* tracked down the winner and managed to see the film and reported on its contents in Volume 2 of the book. The editor said he was impressed with the film's quality despite not coming from Toho or Daiei. Happily for fans, the film shouldn't remain lost much longer and is in the process of being restored for a DVD release in the near future.

So now, thanks to *Tokusatsu Hihou*, more information about this mysterious film is finally available including images and a full synopses. Though this author obviously can't judge the film itself having never seen it, the images available tell an interesting story. First of all, the robot is obviously inspired by Gort from *The Day the Earth Stood Still*, though in this case neither the alien nor the robot are

The film's alien robot.

benevolent. Also, this alien robot is undeniably silly when compared to Gort as it has an oversized, insect-like head, and pinchers for hands. The U.F.O.'s design is excellent though, and has a few nice variations from the usual flying saucer. Rocket R-1, the first of many superweapons in Sekizawa's career, is a fairly standard 1950's era rocket ship.

As usual, Sekizawa's hero is a reporter, here played by Tadao Takashima who would go on to become a star popular for the Toho salaryman series with Yu Fujiki.[4] And of course there is the perennial scientist character, Dr. Otsuki, who has an interesting backstory in that his son was killed in the Tokyo air raids of WWII. He has since become a foster father of sorts to Kaoru Hoshina, as her father has gone underground to develop a new superweapon.

Dr. Hoshina is clearly inspired by *Godzilla's* Dr. Serizawa as he is missing his left eye and also his left arm due to an injury from the war. Like Serizawa, he fears his research falling into the wrong hands and so keeps it a secret in a hidden underground lab in Izu. He is also a precursor to Captain Jinguji from *Atragon* (1963) in that he invented a superweapon and is estranged from his daughter. Considering the fact that said superweapon rises from a secret underwater silo, it's clear that Sekizawa later reused these ideas for his screenplay for *Atragon*[5] and perhaps even the unproduced *The Flying Battleship*.

Overall, it would seem the film contains plenty of action and special effects scenes that precede similar scenes from future blockbusters. The scene where the U.F.O. lands atop the TV Tower in Akasaka sounds similar to a scene in *Godzilla 2000* (1999) where the alien craft perches itself atop a skyscraper. There is also a confrontation between the U.F.O. and a helicopter not dissimilar to *Independence Day* (1996). The U.F.O. also battles U.S. jet fighters not long after. All of Hong Kong is destroyed—though in all likelihood, this probably took place off screen via a radio report. The film also naturally copies some scenes from *Earth vs. the Flying Saucers*, notably when this film's saucer destroys the Diet Building.

Though the film was a success for Shintoho[6]— other than one of their last productions, *Jigoku* (1960)—they didn't dabble again in special effects films, perhaps considering them too costly. *Fearful Attack of the Flying Saucers* was no small production, and encompassed miniature work, underwater photography, and the suit for the robot. Despite its positive reception, the film strangely disappeared not long after its release.

Chapter Notes

[1] Starting with 1958's *Varan*, Sekizawa became one of Toho's premiere writers scripting classics such as *Mothra* (1961) and many entries in the Showa Godzilla series.

[2] Shintoho was founded by a group of Toho workers that left the studio after a dispute, hence the name "New Toho". The company began in 1947 and produced around 800 films before going bankrupt in 1961.

[3] Or, literally in Japanese, *Earth is Being Targeted*.

[4] And, as fans know, Takashima would one day star in several of Sekizawa's penned Godzilla films.

[5] Though based on a novel, 1899's *Undersea Battleship*, much of Sekizawa's screenplay for *Atragon* comes from his own imagination. The estranged father and daughter, and Manda for that matter, were not in the original novel, for instance.

[6] It may have influenced an unproduced Daiei treatment from 1965 called *Giant Space Monster Elegin and Command Robot*.

5.
INVISIBLE MAN VS.
THE HUMAN FLY

Release Date: August 25, 1957

Directed by: Mitsuo Murayama **Screenplay by:** Hajime Takaiwa **Special Effects by:** Toru Masumi & Toru Mizuma **Music by:** Tokujiro Okubo **Cast:** Ryuji Shinagawa (Dr. Tsukioka/Invisible Man), Yoshiro Kitahara (Chief Inspector Wakabayashi), Junko Kano (Akiko Hayakawa), Ichiro Izawa (Kokichi Kusunoki/Fly Man #2), Ikuko Mori (Mieko), Shizuo Chujo (Yamada/Fly Man #1), Joji Tsurumi (Sugimoto), Shozo Nanbu (Dr. Hayakawa), Yoshihiro Hamaguchi (Detective Hayama)

Academy Aspect, Black & White, 96 Minutes

SYNOPSIS On a flight to Tokyo, a man is found murdered mysteriously while in the bathroom—and there is no sign of the culprit. Sitting next to the murdered man on the flight was Dr. Hayakawa. Chief Inspector Wakabayashi wonders if perhaps the killer was invisible and asks Dr. Hayakawa if this is possible. To his shock, Dr. Hayakawa takes him to his secret lab to show him that he has an invisibility ray, though neither he nor his assistants, Dr. Tsukioka and Sugimoto, are the culprits. As more mysterious murders occur, Wakabayashi pieces together the clues and finds that all victims heard a mysterious buzzing before they were killed. Wakabayashi goes to visit the employer of one of the victims, Kusunoki, but finds him to be quite amiable. As it turns out, Kusunoki holds the strings of Yamada the Human Fly, whom he has given a formula to that can make him shrink down to miniature size and fly! As the murders continue, Wakabayashi beseeches Tsukioka to use the invisibility ray on him to help solve the case. Tsukioka refuses, thinking it too dangerous, but when the Human Fly kills Dr. Hayakawa, he turns the invisible ray on himself. Tsukioka spies on Kusunoki and discovers he and the Human Fly are in cahoots. Soon afterward, Yamada is found dead and Tsukioka helps Wakabayashi arrest Kusunoki. However, Kusunoki takes the fly potion and flies away to escape. Kusunoki then bombs a bullet train as a testament to his power and demands that he be given the invisibility ray or he will set off another bomb. A trade is set between Wakabayashi and Kusunoki atop a building at midnight. Meanwhile, Akiko, Dr. Hayakawa's daughter and Tsukioka's fiancé, sets the invisibility ray upon herself. Kusunoki arrives in a helicopter and despite Tsukioka and Wakabayashi's best efforts, absconds with the invisibility ray. To their surprise, it turns around and lands. An invisible Akiko has forced Kusunoki to land. Kusunoki tries to escape but is shot by Wakabayashi.

COMMENTARY Unfortunately, one's expectations for *Invisible Man vs. the Human Fly* can be skewered right away due to the title itself. If one were to go into the film based off of the title alone, they would no doubt get the impression that they were going to see something akin to the classic, bandaged invisible man duking it out with something similar to David Hedison's fly-man from 1958's *The Fly*. Instead, this film's Human Fly is just a tiny man who somehow has the ability to fly.

In the film's defense, it predates *The Fly* by one year. A better title for the film might have been "The Invisible Man vs. the Incredible Shrinking Man". As it is, *The Incredible Shrinking Man* (1957) is the true influence for this film's Human Fly who retains a totally human appearance despite the fact that he can somehow fly—an ability that is never adequately explained (nor is the reason that he buzzes like a fly)! The film does offer an explanation that the man becomes so light that he can float, though this really isn't satisfactory.

While the Human Fly is a deadly assassin that can sneak up on victims, the truth of the matter is that all the Invisible Man needs to defeat him is a simple flyswatter or rolled up newspaper. When the Human Fly reverts back to normal size there is nothing special about him to make for an interesting physical confrontation. Actually, there are two Fly Men, the first being the homicidal Yamada[1] and the second being the big boss Kusunoki. Likewise, there are also three invisible humans in the film.

The invisibility scenes are lackluster, and there is no classic unraveling scene with the bandages as in the 1949 Daiei *Invisible Man Appears*. This could have been due to Eiji Tsuburaya being back at Toho and perhaps the film's effects director was unable to pull off the technique. Instead, the invisible humans are brought to life solely through piano wires operating objects. That said, in the case of Sugimoto the secondary Invisible Man, he is only partially invisible due to how he exposes himself to the invisibility ray. As such, his head and one of his hands are still visible. The scene were Sugimoto reveals his invisible self to his friends by sitting down at the dinner table and picking up some of the amenities is quite humorous. As to the effects for the Human Fly, they are a little too transparent and ghostly to be convincing.

As for the million dollar question, how is the titular battle between the transforming humans? In short, the battle isn't terribly spectacular. As stated earlier, it's difficult for a battle between a shrinking man and an invisible man to be very interesting. And yet, the ending of the film does have its merits—even if an army of soldiers lying in wait to take on the Human Fly is a ludicrous idea. In a moment of Bond-ian flare, Kusunoki lands atop a high-rise building in a helicopter wearing a business suit. Before this happens, to give him some added menace leading up to the climax, Kusunoki becomes a bomber when he blows up a bullet train killing hundreds![2] Now, if Kusunoki isn't given the invisibility ray, he will blow up another mystery target.[3]

Surprisingly, Kusunoki never does revert to his fly form for the climax (though he does try at one point) and instead, the heroic inspector and the invisible Dr. Tsukioka wrestle about with him before he manages to board his chopper and fly away. The next scene may well be the picture's saving grace. Suddenly, the chopper turns back around and lands. As an invisible man holds the gun on Kusunoki, the villain marches out of the chopper with his hands up. It's not Dr. Tsukioka, but the female lead Akiko, who earlier turned the ray on herself. However, the film's creators couldn't let Akiko get away with being the hero and Kusunoki escapes once again, then is shot by Inspector Wakabayashi and falls from the roof of the building to his death.

The epilogue is also nicely done as Dr. Tsukioka and Akiko address a group of reporters at the police station regarding Dr. Hayakawa's invisibility ray. The couple informs the press that the ray will be turned over to the government as per the late doctor's wishes and then, they turn the ray on themselves. They disappear before the reporters eyes and then sneak out of the office.

Overall, *The Invisible Man vs. the Human Fly* is a film where the parts are better than the whole. Though it has its clever moments, the film has a few too many plot holes and lapses in logic to be taken seriously. However, this would not have been a problem if the film were directed in the manner of say—Disney's *The Absent-Minded Professor* (1961). Even though the film has some light, comical moments, it also has too many serious ones—like the murders at the hands of the Human Fly—to classify it as a comedy. And as stated earlier, there are some wonderful comedic scenes—chief among them when Kusunoki turns into his fly form to escape the police, flies into an air conditioner vent, and one of the cops flips on the AC, blowing him back out!

As for the film's other merits, it manages to be constantly surprising. For example, all signs point to Chief Inspector Wakabayashi becoming an invisible man so it is rather surprising when Dr. Tsukioka turns the invisibility ray on himself instead. Akiko turning the ray on herself towards the film's end is another welcome twist—even if it does clue more clever viewers into guessing the ending. That Kusunoki, a very likeable character when we first meet him, turns out to be the main villain is another twist. Viewers will also no doubt be surprised when the first human fly, Yamada, takes a dive into a vat of chemicals in his fly form and perishes well before the climax, leaving Kusunoki to become the next Human Fly.

In short, with a little script-doctoring to clean up the plot holes, and perhaps a lighter tone, *The Invisible Man vs. the Human Fly*[4] could have been a classic on a par with entries in Toho's own transforming human series that would begin with *The H-Man* the next year.

Chapter Notes

[1] Yamada's murders mostly have to do with an attraction he has to nightclub dancer Mieko. Kusunoki uses him for the odd job, but the murders, as stated earlier, revolve around Mieko, whom he eventually kills in a jealous rage.

[2] This well-done sequence even involves miniature work.

[3] It is never explained why Kusunoki wants the ray other than being evil.

[4] Though never released in the U.S., Daiei shopped the film around under the title *The Murdering Mite* according to Stuart Galbraith IV in *Japanese Science Fiction, Fantasy and Horror Films* (pp.312).

MUTATIONS, MADNESS, AND MUSHROOMS: THE HORROR FILMS OF ISHIRO HONDA
BY PETER H. BROTHERS

Mainly remembered today for directing monster movies populated with gigantic creatures, incredible destruction, and mass panic, Ishiro Honda was a true "master of the Apocalypse." Because of this, he is typically listed in cinematic studies as a "genre" director, a designation which would have irked him since he was actually a mainstream director and while he did direct 25 fabulous fantasy films, he also helmed social dramas, war epics, love stories, and even an occasional comedy (though the last of these would be 1966's *Come Marry Me*).

In one of cinema's true incongruities, Honda's epochs of violence and terror were directed by a gentle and self-effacing man of good taste, modesty, and humor who greatly respected his audience and because of this, is sometimes criticized as one reluctant to "go the distance" in horrifying movie-goers.

However, when one examines his three horror films—*The H-Man* (1958), *The Human Vapor* (1960), and *Matango* (1963)— this proves not to be the case, as each is an uncompromising exercise in nightmarish imagery to be counted among the director's most daring works. All are distinguished by their own unique style yet have much in common, such as the unsettling special effects of Eiji Tsuburaya and Hajime Koizumi's lush cinematography (interestingly, none were scored by Honda's most-prolific fantasy film composer, Akira Ifukube, as Masaru Sato wrote the music for *The H-Man*, Kunio Miyauchi for *The Human Vapor*, and Sadao Bekku for *Matango*). More significant still, the screenplays for all three were written by the same man: Takeshi Kimura (later known as Kaoru Mabuchi). A cynic by nature and radical by choice, Kimura's scripts are discourses on bureaucratic meddling, public indifference, and people who are not what they seem.

Honda's horror films evoke derelict ships, vacant clothing, the pursuit of money, women and drugs, heroes and hallucinations, extreme violence, cruel cops, forbidden passions, corpses (both alive and dead) with knockout endings alone worth the price of admission, and only one with what could remotely be considered as a happy ending. More creative than graphic and more subtle than

35

scary, they paradoxically contain moments of dancing, singing, and elements of eroticism not found in Honda's other fantasy films.

Edgar Allan Poe is often incorrectly considered as a master writer of supernatural tales yet never wrote a ghost story and the same holds true for Honda in that none of his films included supernatural creatures such as goblins or ghouls; the apparitions in *The H-Man* were affected by radiation, the islanders in *Matango* were created by eating an unknown type of mushroom, and the Human Vapor achieved his paranormal powers due to a scientific experiment gone terribly wrong.

THE H-MAN (1958) Released in June of 1958, *The H-Man* (*Bijo to Ekatai-Ningen* or *Beauty and the Liquid People*) is the director's most flamboyant genre film, implied by an imaginatively expressionist trailer showing intense and shadowy close-ups of the main participants. A *tour-de-force* of lighting, color, cinematography and editing—with memorably creepy shots of undulating slime accomplished via high-speed photography and traveling mattes—it pre-dated two films with similar monsters: Irvin Yeaworth and Russell S. Doughton Jr.'s *The Blob* released three months later, and Mario Bava and Riccardo Freda's *Caltiki, the Immortal Monster* (1960). However, Honda's effort is superior in terms of overall production value, acting, score and the creative use of sound, such as background traffic heard during early scenes in the police station and the echoing of feet sloshing through slimy sewers. Additionally, Honda does not make overt attempts to horrify, but creates instead a turgid environment of suspense, irony, and vapid sexuality.

The H-Man is a macabre mosaic of mass evacuations, car chases, smuggled drugs, gang violence, Inferno Squads, and its seedy atmosphere of creepy dampness is extremely pervasive. Dialogue-driven, some viewers find it tedious to watch, but this is an indication of impatience more than anything else as Honda knew frenetic action and fast editing makes it difficult for viewers to become involved with the story and its characters.

While having horrific moments, the film is less about revulsion than respect between two professionals, junior professor Dr. Masada (Kenji Sahara), who is valiantly trying against authority to prove his incredible theory, and Inspector Tominaga (Akihiko Hirata), a man attempting to crack an incredible case, as well as the misguided loyalty of a good girl gone wrong, Chikako Arai (Yumi Shirakawa), who is finally given a chance at redemption. *The H-Man*'s greatest set piece is a sailor's nightmarish flashback of the discovery and boarding of a (not quite) crewless ship in a sequence ranking as one of the finest of its kind ever recorded on film.

It is interesting comparing *The H-Man* to the April 1960 release of Toho's *The Secret of the Telegian* (*Dengo Ningen,* or *The Electrically-Transmitted Man*). Directed by former Honda assistant director Jun Fukuda and written by Shinichi Sekizawa (another long-time Honda collaborator), *Telegian* is composed of clever camera angles, brisk editing and a novel use of sound, yet despite a unique commencement involving a mysterious murder in an amusement park's "Thrill Cave," it does not engender a great deal of suspense or fear.

The film borrows a number of elements from Honda's film such as an outsider infringing on a police investigation (with the outsider also being a friend of one of the policemen), an exotic dancer in a nightclub, a criminal element, the discovery of loose clothing and yet another a car chase, but at the end has something quite different and totally unnecessary: a volcanic eruption. The film lacks *The H-Man*'s subtlety and instead opts-out for the blunt statement with nudity, blood, ghastly makeup, a legless man falling out of his wheelchair and the world's worst cops spending much of their time pursuing their quarry *en masse* without any success. This constant hiding-and-seeking becomes monotonous and almost comical. Once again, the leading lady is Yumi Shirakawa (this time as Akiko Chujo), but she is given much less to do other than engage in a brief and syrupy romance with reporter Kirioka (Koji Tsuruta) and in fact, has no real reason for being in the film at all. Tadao Nakamaru is moderately effective as Sudo the Telegian (aka Goro Nakamoto), but his one-note performance lacks an empathy we would later feel for the Human Vapor; nor does it help that he is just a bad person trying to kill other bad people, and when they die—unlike the fatalities in Honda's horror films—their deaths don't affect us.

Part of the problem is that while the plot of *The H-Man* involves people affected by the effects of radioactivity (a theme Honda was obsessed with), *Telegian* is a straight-forward and fairly predictable revenge story, although Fukuda does manage to pepper the film with an occasional surprising moment. This was only his second feature-length effort and seems to have been partially influenced by his former supervisor—at one point, Fukuda quickly dollies from a medium shot to a close-up of a seated individual—but whereas Honda filmed his sensual dancers from a respectful distance, Fukuda focuses on a gold-painted dancer's bikini-covered breasts.

The film lacks *The H-Man*'s disturbing and arousing power and is quite conventional in its execution, and while at times interesting, is not terribly compelling. There are also various lapses in logic, such as how Sudo was able to survive a cave-in after being shot in the face, why he invited Kirioka and Akiko to his hide-out, how the murderer knew the remaining members of the gang would be hiding on an island, and how Professor Niki never knew about a "secret room" in his own lab the Telegian used for his teleportations.

All-in-all, *The Secret of the Telegian* was a modestly successful entry into the Toho horror-film canon and a worthy endeavor. The final scene where the dying doctor disables the teleportation device causing the Telegian to suffer horrific consequences recalls a moment nearly 20 years later in *Star Trek: The Motion Picture* (1979) when two individuals must endure the awful effects of "forming" due to a malfunction with the *Enterprise*'s transporter.

There are two other analogies to Honda in *Telegian*: at one point Detective Kobayashi (Akihiko Hirata) states that "All human life is precious," a principle the director heartily approved of, and actor Yoshio Tsuchiya (Detective Captain Okazaki) became so intrigued with the Telegian's character he asked Honda if he could one day play a similar part. As it turned out, he got his wish sooner than he could have imagined.

THE HUMAN VAPOR (1960) Released in December of 1960, *The Human Vapor* (*Gasu ningen dai ichigo,* or *Gas Human Being No. 1*) is the most moving of the director's horror films, yet it seems a shame calling it a horror film since there is more to it than mere shock. As with Honda's *Farewell Rabaul* (1954)—categorized as a war film—it is more precisely a love story with a heartrending intensity, a bravura theatricality, and a depth of human emotion rarely seen in such films. Kimura runs wild with commentaries on cold-blooded killers achieving celebrity status, science gone wrong, insensitive officers, inept bureaucrats, the cost of non-conformity, thrill-seekers, imprisoned prostitutes, raucous theatre patrons, an opportunistic press, a reverence for the arts, a set-up and a sacrifice, and ultimately a love so measureless it could never be fulfilled on Earth.

The characters are unforgettable: the impetuous Kyoko (Keiko Sata), the elegantly afflicted Fujichiyo Kasuga (Kaoru Yachigusa), an agonized police sergeant who must make the fatal decision to throw a detonating switch (Yoshifumi Tajima), and the withdrawn intensity of Mizuno, the Vapor Man (Yoshio Tsuchiya). All of the acting is outstanding—including the supporting players and extras—and among the highlights are Yachigusa displaying her dancing skills as well as Tsuchiya's curiously affecting performance. An eccentric man who never hesitated taking chances as an actor (playing everything from aliens to oddballs), Tsuchiya was the only feature player to appear in all three of Honda's horror films, portraying a rookie cop in *The H-Man* as well as *Matango*'s corruptible "captain."

The director is in complete control with characteristically human touches: Fujichiyo's shocked expression during her police grilling (quick reaction cuts were a favorite Honda technique), reporter Kyoko's look of embarrassment after the dancer points out the journalist's love for Detective Okamoto (Tatsuya Mihashi), the sobbing bank manager upon learning of his employee's death, and even when Okamoto skeptically scratches his nose. When Fujichiyo is shown sitting quietly alone in her cell during a full-blown prison riot, this discordant sight-and-sound image was another *modus operandi* of Honda's, seen in *Godzilla* (1954) when Yamane and his team are forlornly sitting in the Diet while off-screen politicians scream at each other.

Kimura's plot-driven script intentionally leaves elements up for the viewer to decide—such as why Fujichiyo ended up in a sanitarium and who disconnected the detonator wires *(editor's note: it is heavily implied Fujichiyo found them and disabled them for Mizuno)*—while Honda brilliantly utilizes Hajime Koizumi's cinematography with canted angles, tracking shots, and (rare for the director) intense close-ups. No less effective are Tsuburaya's startling effects, utilizing animation, human form inflatables, wireworks, multiple exposures, reverse photography, and good old-fashioned dry ice.

The film contains many memorable images such as Mizuno's limp clothes falling onto a misty floor, his subsequent revelation in the rain, and his embrace with Fujichiyo during a lightning storm. As with *The H-Man*, it is really about relational conflicts and contrasts, such as between the studious Okamoto and his overenthusiastic girlfriend Kyoko and the unconditional love between the Vapor Man and his *inamorata*.

MATANGO (1963) The grandest, grimmest and most fully-realized of Honda's horror films is the August 1963 release of *Matango* (aka *Attack of the Mushroom People*) and the only one where the majority of the action takes place in a fictional non-urban setting. Inspired by William Hope Hodgson's short story "The Voice in the Night" with an assist from William Golding's book *Lord of the Flies*, Kimura's character-driven plot is considered his signature work. Beginning and ending with a patient confined in a psychiatric ward, *Matango* has an entirely different quality than *The H-Man* or *The Human Vapor* and is an example of the director's astonishing versatility.

Since the film was filled with hallucinatory images— Kenji Murai (Akira Kubo) seeing his fractured reflection in shards of glass, two ghostly figures in a hallway approaching Kenji and Naoyuki Sakuta (Hiroshi Koizumi), and the appearance of a giant, red-faced apparition in the captain's quarters—many have interpreted *Matango* as a warning to Japanese youth regarding mind-altering substances such as LSD, while others see a thinly-veiled reference to Japan's atomic bomb survivors. However, Honda himself stated that his intent was to highlight (if that is the word) the loose morals of yachters, whose free and frivolous lifestyle stood in direct opposition to the director's regard for decency, dedication, and hard work. Unencumbered by social standards and setting their own rules, these "society yachters" have simply shirked their land-bound responsibilities and squandered away their moral fiber and their humanity.

Honda surrounded himself with a splendid ensemble of experienced actors playing wonderfully off of each other in physically and emotionally-demanding roles, with several cast against established "types," giving them the opportunity to display their versatility. As a result, many turned in some of the finest performances of their careers, perhaps none more so than Kumi Mizuno (Honda's favorite actor) as the incandescent Mami.

Whereas man's tinkering with nuclear weapons produced the H-Men and a crazed scientist created the Human Vapor, *Matango*'s participants bring about their own destruction. Captain (in-name only) Kasai (Yoshio Tsuchiya) insists they continue sailing despite appalling conditions even as the boat's actual skipper Sakuta opposes him, and so a discussion among the passengers ensues eating-up valuable time, and by the time the decision is finally made to turn back, it is too late.

But was it too late? The director and screenwriter offer up a true "Honda's Choice" to those marooned on the accursed island: either live a squalid existence filled with the constant staving-off of starvation by eating rotting roots onboard a rusty hulk and continuously weather attacks from the Mushroom People or enter into their existence empty of pain, hunger, and loneliness. Koizumi's vibrant cinematography puts us right in the picture and predicament: when Senzo (Kenji Sahara) picks up a red berry and Kenji fights with the fully-grown Mushroom People, we see it from their perspectives. Hajime Koizumi utilizes a hand-held camera for confining scenes onboard the derelict ship—a masterpiece of set-design by Shigekazu Ikuno—and as a result, we also feel imprisoned and Honda spends nearly five minutes of screen time following the shipwrecked survivors exhaustibly exploring the island so as to further accentuate our involvement with them. As a result, we can almost sense the humidity, the heat, and the anxiety both internal and external. Eventually we too are given the same choice and ask ourselves: what would *we* do?

There are many terrific scenes, with Mami's spiritual seduction of Kasai a highlight of Honda's career, and if *The H-Man*'s persistent element was rain, *Matango*'s is that plus fog, slime, rust, cobwebs— and especially mold—skillfully supplemented with Sadao Bekku's poignantly haunting music. We identify with some characters and sympathize with others, watching them trying to adapt and respond in their desperate struggle to survive. Some surrender to long-suppressed desires, some commit crimes, and others become traitors. Some give up and some give in, while others try remaining strong, yet all are doomed.

In a scene during a stroll on the beach, Murai asserts people must work together in order to survive, and this cooperation motif was one Honda stressed on a global stage with his science fiction films *The Mysterians* (1957), *Battle in Outer Space* (1959) and *Gorath* (1962). At one point the film's writer character Etsuro Yoshida (Hiroshi Tachikawa) states "You can only trust yourself," a comment in such direct opposition to Honda's most-valued ethical code that his ultimate fate should come as no surprise.

Honda knew the more realistic reactions people had to the monsters they encountered, the more believable the films would be. And to be sure there were plenty of monsters: gangsters in *The H-Man* and callous cops in *The Human Vapor*, whereas the individuals in *Matango* had only themselves to blame for their perdition—yet there was always a chance for redemption, however slim. Chikako's decision to renounce the gangster lifestyle finds favor with the gods so she doesn't get slimed in the sewers, and one may reasonably assume that Fujichiyo and Mizuno will find bliss in the afterlife. As for the "Ship of Fools" in *Matango*, had they immediately set about repairing the yacht while searching for sustenance, they might have escaped the accursed island...

It is always tempting to read biographical references into a director's work and this is an intriguing concept when examining Honda's horror films sequentially, as they seem to reflect a certain mindset. He directed *The H-Man* when he was 47 and still in the early stages of his feature-length directorial career, enthralled with the magic of movie-making while still relatively young, aggressive and daring to take risks, and two years later with *The Human Vapor*, his work appears more polished and personal.

Early in his film career, Honda made movies which were clarion calls regarding everything from humanity's intrusion on the environment to thermonuclear war, but as his career progressed he became much more interested in looking inward, and his subsequent fantasy films reflected this change. *Mothra* (1961) and *Gorath* show him as an optimist, yet a number of films he made during the mid-to-late 1960s—*Frankenstein Conquers the World* (1965) and *Godzilla's Revenge* (1969)—reveal a more pessimistic trend, not only toward world events but his own career; his aspirations for global cooperation at a time of heightened Cold War fears having now been transformed into cynicism and disappointment during the Nuclear Arms Race (in 1968's *Destroy All Monsters*, the first thing Godzilla does after arriving in New York is destroy what was once Honda's great bastion of hope: the United Nations building). Nevertheless he always held-out a grudging hope for the future and never stopped believing in the potential of people; he couldn't, or it would have destroyed him as surely as the first Godzilla destroyed Tokyo.

Many modern audiences expecting the blood, shock, and gore of today's horror films find Honda's mildly disappointing, a reaction which is to be expected in our present age of extremes as Honda's are more subtle than scary and more understated than unearthly. Yet, there is a sense of deadly destiny to them, a repentant sorrow, and an emotional richness as the director was more concerned with what was happening inside of his characters rather than what was changing them on the outside, and in any event, was much too deferential to make movies merely to frighten people.

Eloquent and elegant, Ishiro Honda's horrors are focused treatises on the human condition as well as windows into the director's own desires and demons, and they along with his other fantasy films show a visionary that to some is still overlooked while to others is now over-praised, a director both underappreciated and over-analyzed! But the ultimate testament of Honda's ability to take his viewers onto believable journeys into unmanageable worlds with meaning and feeling can be assessed by a certain simple sound. Each one of his horror films is characterized by a unsettling noise—the "pinging" in *The H-Man*, *The Human Vapor*'s trembling French accordion and the Mushroom People's insanely giddy laughter—yet for Honda, all three resonated with the most treasured sound of all: the beating of the human heart.

6.
SUSPICION:
EPISODE 24: "VOICE IN THE NIGHT"

Broadcast Date: March 24, 1958

Directed by: Arthur Hiller **Teleplay by:** Stirling Silliphant (based on William Hope Hodgson's "The Voice in the Night") **Cast:** Barbara Rush (Eleanor Thomason), James Donald (James Thomason), Patrick Macnee (Captain John Biersdorf), James Coburn (Matt Carson)

Academy Aspect, Black & White, 51 Minutes

SYNOPSIS A ship out at sea in a dark fog hears a voice in the night calling to them from a small life boat. The man makes it known to the captain and the first mate that he doesn't want the spotlight shown on him for fear of his appearance. He begs the ship for food for he and his wife stranded on a nearby island and they send him a crate with food across the waters. Grateful, he tells them his tale. His name is James Thomason, a ship captain. He had taken his new bride, Eleanor, with him on his latest voyage. When their ship was struck by a fierce storm, they found themselves the only survivors. Thomason and his wife find a ship adrift at sea. It meets their needs, but it is covered in a grotesque, black fungus. For fear that it might infect them, they take a lifeboat to a nearby island only to find it completely overrun by the fungus. Soon, the fungus appears on James, who besieges his wife to save herself and leave him but she refuses. Later, as a boat passes in the fog James goes to light a signal fire but Eleanor stops him, showing him that she too now suffers from the fungus. The two agree to never leave the island lest they spread it to the rest of the world.

COMMENTARY In 1907, William Hope Hodgson wrote "The Voice in the Night" which was published in *Blue Book Magazine*. The story begins with the crew of a ship at sea encountering a man in the night (whom the titular voice belongs to) who rows next to them in the fog. The man explains that he and his fiancé are stranded on a nearby island and are in need of some food and supplies. When the crew offers to rescue the man, he refuses the offer nor does he let them see his appearance. He then proceeds to explain how he and his fiancé became stranded on a wretched island overcome with a strange fungus that has mutated their bodies.

Toho fans know that this story was adapted by the studio in 1963 as *Matango* (aka *Attack of the Mushroom People*). Fewer fans are aware that several years before this, Alfred Hitchcock's Shamley Productions adapted it for an episode of their

Screengrab from the episode.

ambitious TV series *Suspicion* (1957-1958). Whereas the film only utilized the aspect of being stranded on an island infested with a bizarre fungus, the TV version is much more faithful to Hodgson's original—though *Matango* is unquestionably better.

Though *Suspicion* was given Hitchock's imprint, he didn't actually direct "Voice in the Night". Instead it was helmed by Arthur Hiller, the future director of such films as 1970's *Love Story*. The story is carried well by actors James Donald (one of the future stars of *The Great Escape*) and Barbara Rush[1] generating plenty of sympathy from the viewers who already know the duo's fate thanks to the story's bookends in the present which reveal both to be barely alive.

The episode begins with a ship at sea sailing for Melbourne when the captain and his first mate hear a voice coming from the darkness. The man calling is Donald, of course, our tragic hero who explains his predicament to the crew (played by none other than Patrick Macnee and James Coburn!).[2] The story shifts back in time and we meet his wife Eleanor (his fiancé in the story), who begs to go with him on his next voyage. The ship scenes don't last long, and the two are shipwrecked hastily. They find their way to a new ship, similar to the one crashed on the island in *Matango* actually, where they first see the strange fungus. When the ship proves unsatisfactory due to the strange black fungus growing everywhere, the two decide to take their chances on a nearby island which they reach via a small rowboat.

The fungus-infected island is actually somewhat grander in size than the one in *Matango*. Specifically, the main set is small, but a matte painting shows the island to have fungus that has grown so huge it can be seen from afar, which is a magnificent optical effect in black and white. Donald describes the island as having "horrible and fantastic mounds which seemed almost to quiver with quiet life…" However, unlike Hodgson's original story and Toho's film there are no actual mushroom people to terrorize the couple on the island.[3] Nor do we ever see Donald and Rush's final forms. Actually, the surviving print is so dark Donald's character might have been briefly glimpsed but it is hard to say. James Coburn's character describes what he sees a "great grey sponge."

Overall, the episode has the feel of an early black and white Hammer production, and on that note, James Donald starred in one Hammer film, *Quartermass and the Pit* (1967). The episode has never been put onto DVD or VHS, and the version on YouTube is so poor that the night scenes are barely viewable, giving one the impression of listening to a radio play.

Chapter Notes

[1] Rush has many esteemed screen credits, but readers of this book will be most interested to know that she was in *It Came from Outer Space* (1953) and *When Worlds Collide* (1951).

[2] This was James Coburn's second acting job, and he did two other episodes for *Alfred Hitchcock Presents* as well. Patrick Macnee of TV's *The Avengers* plays the ship's captain.

[3] Presumably, the budget or TV censorship of the time wouldn't allow. On the note of censorship, Hodgson's "The Voice in the Night" was published in Alfred Hitchcock's 1957 book, *Alfred Hitchcock Presents: Stories They Wouldn't Let Me Do on TV*, before Hodgson's story was adapted for *Suspicion* in 1958.

HODGSON'S "VOICE IN THE NIGHT": MATANGO'S LITERARY FORERUNNER
BY ALLEN A. DEBUS

"I had never imagined such secrets of the sea and the grave (which are one and the same)."—from William Hope Hodgson's 1909 short story, "Out of the Storm."

When the title of Toho's 1963 film, *Matango*, surfaces, one usually notes a subtle reference to author William Hope Hodgson's (1877-1918) short story, "The Voice in the Night" (*Blue Book*, Nov. 1907). This is because *Matango* is said to have been based upon Hodgson's story. But who is Hodgson, and did he actually write a story about bizarre "mushroom people" decades *prior* to Toho's filmic entry?

Yes, essentially Hodgson did, and in doing so, he may have written the first of weird, creepy misshapen human monsters, a tale that, conceptually has withstood the test of time. In reading "The Voice in the Night" (text of which is available online), I was struck as whether it may have been fear or loathing of those affected by leprosy, victims who were forced into isolation on colonies, that inspired his eerie tale. The movie doesn't parallel the story's plot too closely, although the general theme and basis of horror is apparent in both.

This atmospheric 1907 horror story is literally about a "voice in the night" heard by "George," one of several aboard the deck of a ship at sea in the vicinity of an uncharted northern Pacific island. The night is starless and the waves are cloaked in fog. A man (the source of the titular "voice" in the night) in a rowboat hails the ship, accepting food and water for himself *and* fiance'. Although starving and utterly desperate, the man most curiously *refuses* rescue. While taking great pains to avoid physical contact with anyone onboard, this strange, unseen man rows the provisions ("Christian charity") back to his lady who awaits on the island shore. Then he returns later, maintaining proper distance in the water while recounting his sorrowful tale.

Their vessel, the *Albatross*, had sunk several months earlier, a circumstance which ultimately led to their abject doom. After escaping being drowned at sea, after four days on a makeshift raft, drifting through a "strange haze" they chanced upon this nearby island, arriving at a lagoon. Spying the hull of another shipwrecked vessel elicits their thanks (ironically) to God. Disturbingly, however, a "grey, lichenous fungus" is seen enveloping the vessel... "the decks were covered, in great patches, with grey masses, some of them rising into nodules several feet in height..." Nobody answers their calls. Striving to make the ship's confines habitable, they scrape away the curious mounds of fungus, only to see it all grow back in a single day. A chemical disinfectant (carbolic acid) is more effective in removal, but the fungal growth still returns within a week.

So they leave the ship, existing in tents ashore instead, whereupon they make a terrible observation that the "vile fungus" has spread, now growing rampantly, enveloping the island, except for a small white patch of what appeared to be "fine sand" where it inexplicably doesn't grow. Soon, the rot is seen festering upon the skin of the couple, who are quickly running out of food. The desolate man proclaims, "God would do with us what was His will... We had now given up all thought or hope of leaving the island. We had realized that it would be unallowable to go among healthy humans, with the things from which we were suffering."

Facing starvation, his wife becomes the first to eat the forbidden 'fruit'–the grey fungus, and actually likes it! One day, the man encounters an awful manifestation, a grotesque mound of fungus with distorted arms that *moves*. "The head of the thing–a shapeless grey ball..." He realizes this creature is what one of the men aboard the ship wrecked in the lagoon had transformed into! The monster's "vile arm" brushes his face causing him to inadvertently taste the fungus, giving him a "hungerlust," for more. Ultimately, "...punishment was upon us; for, day by day, with monstrous rapidity, the fungoid growth took hold or our poor bodies." Having concluded his ghastly tale, the strange forlorn man in the rowboat dips oars into the sea wishing a heartfelt 'goodbye'. But as he rows further away, the sun's rays penetrate the fog momentarily, briefly illuminating him. Crewman George now sees who or rather *what* he's been conversing with! "I thought of a sponge–a great, grey nodding sponge... the head... the thing went nodding into the night."

So, who was this W.H. Hodgson, a talented writer of the macabre? Before H. P. Lovecraft there was Hodgson (1877-1918). A native Englishman, he went to sea at the tender age of 13 as a cabin boy apprentice, eventually becoming a certified mate. Hodgson, never a tall individual, may have been bullied by those earthy salts at sea. This led to the body building phase of his life, achieving a remarkable physical stature, and eventually opening "W. H. Hodgson's School of Physical Culture" in 1899 devoted to exercise and weight lifting. Some of his earliest publications were on the subject of attaining physical fitness.

But eventually, inspired by fantastic writers such as Sir Arthur Conan Doyle, Edgar Allan Poe, Jules Verne, and H. G. Wells, Hodgson turned his lurid pen to fiction, becoming a prolific author and achieving audience acclaim but not much financial success. Many of Hodgson's tales dealt with occult terror at sea, such as in his "Sargasso Sea" cycle. Some of these weird writings, particularly his 1907 sci-fi/supernatural novel *The House on the Borderland*, are said to have astonished H. P. Lovecraft who had in turn 'discovered' (Lieutenant) Hodgson years after the latter's World War I death at Ypres in April 1918. In particular, this novel also employs the device of a fungal growth affliction. Hodgson's dark works have recently been collected and published by Night Shade Classics. He has quite a following today with fan websites and reissues of *Sargasso: The Journal of William Hope Hodgson Studies*.

Many of Hodgson's Sargasso Sea 'chronicles' (collected in *The Ghost Pirates and Others: The Best of William Hope Hodgson* [2012]), dealt with sailing ships caught in slow currents, sometimes suggestively cloaked in alternate-dimensional mists, while *things* come out of the ocean, onboard, terrifying the crew. His writing is uniformly expert, although following the seaman's lingo can sometimes be a bit difficult. His 1909 novel *The Ghost Pirates* seems to be a precursor to John W. Campbell's 1938 novella "Who Goes There" (later adapted as *The Thing*). *The Ghost Pirates* reads like Stephen King's *The Mist* blended with *Alien,* with horrors taking place on a ship at sea (rather than space), the genre Hodgson excelled in.

(Excerpted from *Mad Scientist* #32, Summer 2017, where this article was originally published in its entirety as "There's a Fungus Among Us: *Matango's* literary forerunner," pp. 38-42. This portion is reprinted with permission of the author and Martin Arlt—editor of *Mad Scientist*.)

7.

WOMAN VAMPIRE

Japanese Title: *Woman Vampire*
Release Date: March 7, 1959

Directed by: Nobuo Nakagawa **Screenplay by:** Katsuyoshi Nakatsu, Shin Nakazawa & Sotoo Tachibana **Music by:** Hisashi Iuchi **Cast:** Shigeru Amachi (Shiro Sofue/Nobutaka Takenaka), Takashi Wada (Tamio Oki), Junko Ikeuchi (Itsuko Matsumura), Yoko Mihara (Miwako Matsumura), Tsutomu Wakui (dwarf), Yuzo Harumi (muscle man), Fujie Satsuki (witch)

Shintohoscope, Black & White, 78 Minutes

SYNOPSIS Twenty years ago, Miwako Matsumura disappeared, leaving behind a husband and an infant daughter. In the story's present, she mysteriously returns on the night of the daughter's birthday, not having aged at all. As the stunned family tries to piece together the mystery of her disappearance, they discover a painting of her exact likeness. The painter, Shiro Sofue, is a vampire that has survived since feudal times who had been keeping Miwako captive because she is a direct descendant of his ancient love. Eventually, Shiro kidnaps Miwako again and returns her to his underground castle in the mountains. A lucky break is had when a thief at the police station reports stumbling into a strange castle high up in the mountains and barely escaping. Miwako's daughter Itsuko, along with her fiancé Tamio and a rescue party, go to investigate. Itsuko and Tamio are separated from the party and Itsuko is captured by Shiro. Tamio finds the castle's secret entrance through a rocky enclave. Tamio confronts Shiro and aid arrives in the form of the police department. After a lengthy struggle, Shiro reverts to his true, aged form and the castle is destroyed. Everyone escapes but Miwako, who Shiro had turned into a statue.

Shigeru Amachi as the film's menacing vampire.

COMMENTARY If Toho's better known Bloodthirsty trilogy of the 1970s was inspired by the Hammer Studios Dracula movies, then Shintoho's *Woman Vampire* is clearly their more Universal Horror-like precursor. Actually, that's not entirely accurate. Truth be told, *Woman Vampire* was influenced as much from *Horror of Dracula*'s successful 1958 Japanese release as the Bloodthirsty trilogy was. What makes *Woman Vampire* seem more Universal-like is mostly its black and white photography and tamer atmosphere (tame, that is, by today's standards. For the time, it was quite racy).

The film's title should clue one in to the fact that it is simple exploitation, because even though Miwako's "woman vampire" is the titular character, she's ironically also the least-developed of the film's leads. As Shintoho was making a practice of giving their horror films sexually lurid titles—for 1950's standards—that is likely the only reason this film was titled *Woman Vampire*. In fact, the original title was to be *Nude Woman Vampire*. However, in the finished film, there is no actual nudity, just a few shots of women in their underwear (Shiro's previous lovers who he turned into statues) which was certainly racy for the time. The film was produced by Mitsugu Okura, who eventually became notorious for producing titillating films that were "fast, cheap, and exciting."[1] This model was

51

first established with his 1957 film *The Military Policeman and the Dismembered Beauty*.

The real star of the film is Shigeru Amachi as the Japanese silver screen's first real vampire. Of course, he is also distinctly Japanese (read: unusual) in that he almost always wears sunglasses with his cape and suit. Oddly, this vampire is bothered more so by moonlight than sunlight, as the moonlight will make him sprout fangs, claws, and lose control of his inhibitions, making it harder to mask his identity.[2] Amachi's vampire is also the recipient of an epic flashback scene not dissimilar to what Francis Ford Coppola would do in *Bram Stoker's Dracula* (1992). The dramatic sequence features excellent period costumes, sets, and even an epic battle with lots of extras— presumably culled from another Shintoho film. At the end of this sequence, a miniature castle even explodes!

Yoko Mihara (left) as Miwako Matsumura.

Amachi's vampire has an assortment of henchmen including a dwarf, what looks like a giant, bald Buddhist monk, and a white-haired witch in his service. Of the three, the dwarf gets the most screen time and the relationship between he and Shiro is not unlike Nick Nack and Scaramanga in *The Man with the Golden Gun* (1974). The other two henchmen don't come into play until the climax when the heroes mount a rescue to the castle. Kisaragi Castle is full of the usual tropes: skeletons chained to the wall, secret passageways, vaporous sulfur pits, and western-style furniture. There is plenty of wrestling and fisticuffs between Tamio, Shiro, and his giant servant. While these scenes are probably riveting for younger children—which this film was in no way intended for—they are nothing but silly for older viewers. Eventually, all the action actually makes the climax become tedious and overlong. In fact, after five minutes of this silliness, one can't help but wonder when Bud Abbott or Lou Costello will come around a corner.

Finally, an accident occurs that causes the roof of the castle to partially cave in, exposing Shiro to direct moonlight. Shiro then suddenly begins to age and takes on the appearance of a decomposing old man—perhaps for no other reason than it was time for the movie to be over. After a few more instances of superfluous fighting, Shiro finally commits suicide and jumps into the sulfur pit. The witch then lights some gunpowder so that the castle can explode and tie up the film's remaining loose ends.

The film was directed by Nobuo Nakagawa, who usually directed period ghost films. In fact, this was said to be his first modern horror film. Nakagawa makes good use of the black and white photography and accompanying shadows—though the film isn't particularly scary for today's modern viewers. Still, the atmosphere is enjoyable for those who enjoy the old Universal horror films in the same way that Hammer aficionados enjoy the Bloodthirsty trilogy.[3]

Chapter Notes

[1] Macias, *Tokyo-Scope*, pp.85
[2] The film's Japanese Wikipedia page implies this aspect was inspired by *The Wolf Man* (1941).
[3] That said, the scene where Shiro visits Miwako in her bedroom is clearly inspired by a similar scene from *Horror of Dracula*.

8.
THE FINAL WAR

Japanese Title: *World War III: 41 Hours of Fear*
Release Date: October 19, 1960

Directed by: Shigeaki Hidaka **Special Effects by:** Shigeaki Hidaka & Shozo Konishi **Screenplay by:** Hisataka Kai & Shigeaki Hidaka (treatment) **Music by:** Ko Ishimatsu **Cast:** Tatsuo Umemiya (Shigero), Yoshiko Mita (Tomoko), Yayoi Furusato, Noribumi Fujishima, Yukiko Nikaido, Michiko Hoshi

Toeiscope, Black & White, 77 Minutes

SYNOPSIS As Cold War tensions mount, a group of high schoolers lead by Shigero flee Japan in a yacht. When the yacht is overtaken by a typhoon, they are rescued by reporter Masaaki, who makes the story front page news. Around the same time, Masaaki begins dating Tomoko, a nurse in Tokyo. Tensions mount when a U.S. air force plane accidentally detonates a nuclear bomb over South Korea, who in turn blames North Korea. This cranks Cold War tensions up to a fever pitch. The U.S. 7th Fleet mobilizes at a base in Japan and soon, a U.S. plane is shot down over the Soviet Union. The Soviet Union warns Japan that all air bases in Japan will be bombed. Masaaki, Shigero, and his family flee to the forest while Tomoko elects to stay behind with a sick child patient in Tokyo. The city is bombed as the evacuees watch from the wilderness. A panicked Masaaki braves Tokyo's radiation to search for Tomoko, whom he finds dead next to her patient. Masaaki himself dies from the radiation exposure soon after.

COMMENTARY Back in 1998, the U.S. box office was astir wondering just which asteroid movie would win out: Michael Bay's *Armageddon* or Mimi Leder's *Deep Impact*. Despite both films having the same subject matter, neither suffered at the box office as a result. Other instances of similar competing films included when Roger Moore's real Bond film *Octopussy* was released the same year as Sean Connery's unofficial return as 007 in *Never Say Never Again* in 1983.[1] Back in 1960 Japan, Toho and Toei both began working on an end of the world movie at almost exactly the same time. Like the aforementioned blockbusters, both films were released relatively close to one another (Toho's film came out in 1961), and both were hits.

It seems that both *The Final War* and *The Last War* were born out of a story published in the *Weekly Shincho*, called "41 Hours of the First World War III" published in the summer of 1960 (*The Final War* was entitled by Toei *World War III: 41 Hours of Fear*). Tomoyuki Tanaka wanted to adapt the project and then learned Toei already beat them to the rights. The media soon reported on the competition between the two studios working on what was essentially the same film. And indeed, Toho's first draft for *The Last War* is incredibly similar to Toei's *The Final War*—right down to Saeko Tamura being a nurse who refuses to leave a sick patient behind! As a result, Toho shut down their version for a time to rework the script[2] and as a result, Toei's version beat Toho's to theaters in October of 1960.

It's tough to say which of the two films is more effective. Though Toho's version is in color and has more effects scenes, Toei's version is actually more grounded. For instance, whereas Toho chose to mask America and Russia in the form of renaming them the Confederation and the Alliance, here the real superpowers are at play. In all likelihood, Toho chose not to name names in an effort to see their film play in U.S. theaters. Ironically, Toei's film beat Toho's film to U.S. theaters by three years; *The Final War* was released in America by Sam Lake Enterprises in 1962 and *The Last War* played in U.S. theaters courtesy of Brenco in 1965.[3] Showing a vindictive streak, Toho tried, though failed, to copyright their film—*Great World War* in Japan—as *The Final War* and *The Last War* in the United States.

Though Toho's film is no picnic, Toei's still manages to be darker and more grim, due both to the ugly portrayals of the evacuating peoples of Tokyo and the black and white photography. During the evacuation, mankind's lesser nature is emphasized and some women are implied to be taken away to be raped. The film's first post-credits scene is even a showcase of graphic real-life photos of starving and injured children, making this a stylistic precursor of sorts to *Prophecies of Nostradamus* (1974)—itself a spiritual remake of Toho's *The Last War*.

In *The Last War*, the story is told through the eyes of one family, while in *The Final War* several different families, each in a different economic stratosphere, are portrayed. This works well for the climax, as we see how different groups handle the devastating tension as they wait for Tokyo to be bombed. The low income family, consisting of a musician and his sick wife, go to a Catholic church. Tomoko, the nurse, sings to her sick child patient. Some of the people in the hills go mad with anxiety waiting for the bomb to drop.

The effects scenes are sparser compared to *The Last War*, but it doesn't detract from the film at all.[4] In fact, it almost makes it seem more realistic than the overly colorful effects of *The Last War*. The destruction of the Diet Building is probably the best shot in the film but unfortunately, it's the only major effects shot representing the destruction of Tokyo (aside from a brief glimpse of Tokyo Tower also being destroyed). Brief but well-done shots of miniatures representing New York, San Francisco, and Moscow State University exploding follow. There are some well-done miniatures of a destroyed Tokyo as well, on par with a similar shot from *Godzilla* (1954). And while *The Last War* ended with a statement that the film was merely a "what if" scenario, *The Final War* has no such closing remarks to brighten it up.[5]

The Final War was supposedly released theatrically in the U.S. by Sam Lake Enterprises in 1962 but it's also possible it went straight to television. In any case, no prints of the U.S. version have been found nor was it ever released to VHS. Today, it is difficult to prove whether or not this actually occurred (though there are people adamant they saw it on television). In his *Apocalypse Then*, Mike Bogues writes:

> Proof that the movie at least showed in the New York City area is a license to exhibit it in New York State dated December 3, 1962 (this information came from the AFI website). Further proof that the movie at least showed in the New York City area is a brief mention in 1964's *Castle of Frankenstein* #4's "Frankenstein Movie Guide": "Widescreen WW3, destruction of world in atomic war. Japanese made." Later, *Castle of Frankenstein* #9 offered this brief review in its "Frankenstein TV Movieguide": "Japanese sf mainly of interest because familiar landmarks get the total destruction treatment."[6]

To further confound matters, many who saw the movie on American television swear the film included edited-in footage of U.F.O.s from Toei's more fantastical *Invasion of the Neptune Men* (1961)! It is entirely possible that *The Final War* was released theatrically more or less the same film, just dubbed into English, while Medallian TV Enterprises created a new version for television viewings with said *Neptune Men* footage edited in to better appeal to the kiddie audience. The film has been just as obscure in Japan. For decades, *World War III: 41 Hours of Fear* was considered a lost movie. Toei eventually discovered a print and began airing it on Japanese television in 2013, though no DVD or Blu-ray release has been forthcoming. Whether it played in U.S. theaters or not, *The Final*

War is almost certainly gone. As far as anyone knows, the last time it aired on television was back in 1974.

Chapter Notes

[1] Which while successful, was soundly thrashed at the box office by *Octopussy*.

[2] There are still many similarities to *The Final War* in Toho's reworked version. This includes a character with an ill, bedridden wife. The ending, where the romantic lead dies of radiation poisoning for his love is also foreshadowed in the climax of *The Last War*.

[3] *The Last War*'s more well-known TV print made its way to broadcast in 1967.

[4] A few real stock shots from archival footage are also used for the bomb.

[5] Contrary to rumors, there is no final scene with humanity's survivors set in Argentina.

[6] Bogue, *Apocalypse Then*, pp. 266.

9.
THE WHALE GOD

Release Date: July 15, 1962

Directed by: Tokuzo Tanaka **Special Effects by:** Chikara Komatsubara, Takesaburo Watanabe & Hiroshi Ishida **Screenplay by:** Kaneto Shindo **Music by:** Akira Ifukube **Cast:** Shintaro Katsu (Kishu), Kojiro Hongo (Shaki), Shiho Fujimura (Ei), Takashi Shimura (Village Elder), Kyoko Enami (Toyo), Koji Fujiyama (Shatsu), Reiko Fujiwara (Okoma), Kichijiro Ueda

Daieiscope, Black & White, 100 Minutes

SYNOPSIS Early in the Meiji era on the coast of Kyushu, every year a huge whale appears that kills dozens of fishermen in its wake. Among those hit the hardest by this "Whale God" is Shaki whose grandfather, father, and older brother have all been killed by the beast. When the village elder offers up his title, his estate, and his daughter Toyo to the man who kills the Whale God, Shaki is the first to volunteer. However, Shaki is soon challenged by vulgar drifter Kishu, who says he will be the one to kill the whale. As winter sets in, the Whale God swims to other waters while the village both dreads and eagerly awaits its return. In the interim, Shaki's girlfriend Ei is raped by a stranger and gives birth to a baby who Shaki decides to raise even though he knows is not his. This insults both the village elder and Toyo, but Shaki doesn't care, his only concern is killing the giant whale. At the onset of the Whale God's return Kishu argues with Shaki he should live on for his family and not risk going after the whale, but Shaki refuses and the two fight. The next day, the village fleet sets out after the whale and Kishu dives into the water prematurely to take a stab at the beast. Kishu is killed when the whale submerges with him for too long and Shaki swims for the whale, climbs atop its head and stabs it until it dies from blood loss. Shaki awakens days later a hero, but his arms and legs are broken and he is dying. For his last wish, he asks to be placed on the beach next to the head of the Whale God. There, Ei reveals to him that Kishu was the father of the child and she beseeches Shaki to forgive his dead rival. As Shaki loses consciousness and slips away into death, he proclaims that he will come back as the next Whale God.

COMMENTARY Though some may think Daiei's 1962 epic *The Whale God* was merely a Japanese version of *Moby Dick*, there is much more to the tale than that. After the huge success that was 1961's *Buddha*, Daiei's planning office in Tokyo wanted to follow up with another epic historical production.[1] To do so, they set their sights on a novel by Koichiro Uji called *The Whale God* published in July of 1961.[2] The book, praised by famed novelist Yasushi Inoue as being full of "wild energy", had won the 46th Akutagawa Award. Daiei then shelled out ¥1,000,000 for the screen rights and within a year had adapted the book into film and released it to theaters in July of 1962.

The film was directed by Tokuzo Tanaka who helmed many of Daiei's period dramas, such as *Infamy*. Stark and moody in black and white, *The Whale God* excels with its palate of blacks, greys and whites—color would have ruined the film. Adding to the feel are the very recognizable works of maestro Akira Ifukube. Many fans will recognize pieces from this film actually predating better known themes he composed for Toho films. One of the trumpet themes is very similar to ones he would use in *Frankenstein Conquers the World* (1965) and *The War of the Gargantuas* (1966). The native dance on the beach even precedes the same year's release, *King Kong vs. Godzilla*.

The film begins with an ambitious pre-credit sequence where the title character appears right away destroying boats and dragging whalers to their death.[3] One of the recently deceased men's sons stands on the sea shores with his wife and his own children, proclaiming that he will avenge his father's death. From there, the title pops up and Ifukube's wonderfully grim music begins to play. Not long after the credits have finished rolling, the man who proclaimed vengeance is now himself dead, drug beneath the depths, and the man's children look to the waves as their grandmother tells them that they will take vengeance next. "The whale who killed your father and grandfather is laughing at you!" she tells the boys, Shatsu and Shaki.

The film quickly jumps ahead once more and we find an adult Shatsu (Koji Fujiyama, Onondera in *Gamera vs. Barugon*) proclaiming it is his time to hunt down the whale, though Shaki (future Gamera and Daimajin sequels lead, Kojiro Hongo) stays home. Just like the rest, in the third consecutive special effects scene in a row, Shatsu and his crew all become victims of the Whale God.

Dead bodies of all the recovered whalers are stretched along the beach for their mourning families. At one point, a delirious old man—one of the lone survivors of previous excursions—comes running onto the beach proclaiming that the Whale God is coming for him. That's when Takashi Shimura, playing the village elder, calls for everyone's attention. Shimura says that since he is now too old to face the whale head on, instead, he will give his daughter Toyo to whomever kills the beast, plus his title as village elder and his estate.[4]

At his mother's urging, Shaki steps forward to be the first to volunteer to kill the whale. "I will leave the Whale God to no other man!" he shouts.[5] The moment Shaki proclaims his intent, into the frame swaggers Shintaro Katsu's character Kishu, who approaches Shimura and brazenly asks if his offer applies to non-villagers. When Shimura acknowledges that he will give his daughter and estate to any man who slays the whale, Kishu boldly proclaims, "I'll be the one to kill the Whale God!" And from there, the true driving force of the film is born as Shaki and Kishu fight to be the one who kills the whale. As winter is coming, that means the whale will swim to other waters and not return until the spring, giving the two leads plenty of time to clash egos.

Stuck in between these two male leads is Shiho Fujimura's (Lady Sayuri in *The Return of Daimajin*) Ei, possibly the film's most sympathetic character. As Shaki's girlfriend, Ei feels threatened when Shaki accepts the village elder's offer to be the first to kill the whale, fearing he is partially doing so to marry Toyo. Shaki reassures her that this is not the case, but also says he will not marry her until the Whale God is dead. Moments after Shaki has left her on the beach, the distraught Ei is assaulted and raped by Kishu.

In stark contrast to Ei, Toyo (Kyoko Enami, Karen in *Gamera vs. Barugon*) on the other hand is totally unsympathetic. Though she doesn't wish to marry Shaki should he kill the whale, she is also insulted when he marries Ei. At the film's end, she even tells Shaki that she doesn't love him when he asks, and says she only wants to marry him because he is the greatest whaler in the village.

As the narrative progresses, it is revealed that Ei is pregnant with Kishu's child. Ei keeps it a secret until Shaki discovers her in labor. Instead of being angry, in an act of selflessness, Shaki tells the village the child is his (he and Ei have never been intimate).[6] Not only that, when Ei offers to tell him who the father is, he declines saying that it doesn't matter and as such is ignorant that the baby belongs to his main competitor. In this sense, the film has a tragic love triangle that manages to up the ante from the one in *Godzilla* (1954).

Before the whale returns to the waters off the village, much of the film is spent wondering just when Shaki will find out who the baby's father is. This is best exemplified after the baby's baptism, where Shaki proudly shows Kishu the child, unaware it is really his child though Kishu certainly does. Before the boats go out the next morning to intercept the Whale God, Kishu tries to dissuade Shaki from going out to kill the whale arguing that he should survive for the sake of his child. And, perhaps, Kishu is wanting what is best for his own child; it is hard to tell. In any case, Shaki is naturally insulted by this request and the two fight to a standstill amidst the crashing waves on the beach. Kishu tells Shaki that tomorrow will decide who will kill the whale.

As the villagers gather on the beach, there's a palpable irony to the fact that the villagers can't help themselves from avenging their loved ones which only results in further lives lost. There is a particularly good scene towards the end where Shaki looks back to his wife and child as if to wonder whether it's all really worth it.

True to his word, when the fleet approaches the Whale God, Kishu jumps out of the boat early and swims to the surfacing whale which he stabs in the side of the head, badly wounding it. Shaki watches enraged, but also puzzles as to why Kishu didn't go for the kill atop the whale's head. When the whale dives beneath the waves with Kishu's body trapped in the tangled ropes attached to the whale's hide, it stays submerged so long that it kills him. Shaki dives into the water and goes after the whale, finally ready to avenge his family. The scene is extremely bloody as Shaki rides atop the head and stabs it unceasingly, blood spurting everywhere until he finally collapses and the whale dies from blood loss. This is not the true climax of the film however; that comes after Shaki awakens days later from his ordeal to find himself so badly injured that he is dying.

His arms and legs broken, Shaki begs his wife and the village elder to take him to the beach to lay by the head of the Whale God as he takes his last breaths. "I'll die with the sunset tomorrow," he says. As Shaki lays dying in his coffin[7] on the beach, his wife confesses to him that Kishu is the real father of their child. Shaki says he knows this because of how Kishu confronted the whale, weakening the beast instead of killing it, letting the honor of killing it befall Shaki instead.

Takashi Shimura then proves true to his word telling Shaki that tomorrow he will be named village elder and will take his daughter as a wife. Shimura also says now that the whale is dead, he has no reason to live. As Shaki fades away he proclaims that he will return one day as the next Whale God. This is followed by a shot of a whale swimming at sea which is likely a metaphor, and the film ends.

Initially, to bring the whale to life was Yonesaburo Tsukiji, who would later do the effects work on the first Gamera film. However, some sort of scheduling conflict arose and he was off the project before the bulk of filming began. Instead, the brunt of the effects work was handled by three men: Chikara Komatsubara, Takesaburo Watanabe, and Hiroshi Ishida. Naturally, with scenes featuring the actors on the full sized prop, Tokuzo Tanaka did the bulk of effects directing though.

The special effects filming took place in Daiei's big pool in Kyoto. Amazingly, Fuminori Ohashi constructed a scale Kujira Gami prop[8] said to be over 30 meters in length for filming which cost around 8 million yen. In addition to this was a smaller 5.5 meter model. Unfortunately, these large scale models suffered from very limited mobility due to their immense weight, and so, most of the filming was done with a small model created by Ryosaku Takayama which was run over rails hidden beneath the water to give the illusion of movement. That said, the full scale model was used for scenes with the actors and the 5.5 meter model was used for diving scenes. Animation was used for the birds that follow the whale in a similar manner used in *Buddha*.

The Whale God was double-billed with *Wanderer of Tragic Love* when it was released in 1962. This wasn't the only film adaptation and in 1971, it was made into a cartoon by Saitama Taka. It was released to VHS in 1984 and DVD in 2006.

Chapter Notes

[1] Among them was the man responsible for Gamera, Daiei president Masaichi Nagata.

[2] It was published in the Bunki Spring/Autumn magazine. The tale was later published in book form by Bungei Spring Equipment Co., Ltd., in 1962.

[3] That the "monster" would appear in the first scene may be a surprise for some, but in truth, this is probably for the best. Had the whale only been talked about, then anticipation for its appearance may have grown so high as to disappoint once it finally appeared for the climax.

[4] Later, it appears his intentions aren't as altruistic as they seem when he makes the comment to his daughter that whoever kills the whale won't make it back with their life intact. And, as it turns out, he is right, though he appears to be willing to give all that he has to Shaki once he completes his task.

[5] This line will later prove to be very important to the entire film, in particular a subplot involving Kushi.

[6] At the same time, Shaki being a surrogate father to the baby isn't totally selfless though, as, at one point, he says that if he dies, the child will avenge him which angers Ei.

[7] The coffin is meant to be a nod to Quequeg's coffin from *Moby Dick*.

[8] The whale's design was based off of a type of baleen whale, the North Pacific Right Whale.

10.
FRANKENSTEIN VS. THE HUMAN VAPOR

Japanese Title: *Furankenshutain tai Gasu Ningen Daiichigo*
(*Frankenstein vs. Gas Human Being No.1*)
Intended Release Date: 1963
First Draft Date: February 20, 1963

Screenplay by: Shinichi Sekizawa **Proposed Cast/Characters:** Mizuno, the Vapor Man (Yoshio Tsuchiya), Goro Maki [reporter], Frankenstein Monster, Fujichiyo [Mizuno's dead lover], Mayumi [Fujichiyo's sister], Michi [Goro's editor], Dr. Gildor [mad scientist]

SYNOPSIS In Hong Kong, the deranged Dr. Gildor has not only revived the Frankenstein Monster, but is also using the Monster to assist him in continuing Dr. Frankenstein's research. Mizuno, the Vapor Man, has tracked Gildor down in hopes that he can resurrect his dead love, Fujichiyo. Gildor agrees, but is killed in an accident on the way to Japan. Without Gildor, Mizuno persuades the Monster to help him recreate Gildor's experiments. Fujichiyo is exhumed from her grave and taken to an observatory Mizuno has purchased. Following the case of the Vapor Man is reporter Goro Maki, who tips the police off to Mizuno's whereabouts. Just as Fujichiyo is revived the police storm Mizuno's lab. The Monster, angry at Mizuno, knocks him unconscious and dissapears. The authorities capture Mizuno and Fujichiyo is put under the care of a doctor. The Monster returns to abduct Fujichiyo just as Mizuno escapes jail. Mizuno and the Monster battle one another in a swamp just as Fujichiyo regains her memory. In a tragic twist, all three sink into quicksand and die as a helpless Goro looks on.

COMMENTARY It was a fateful day that John Beck came to Toho's doorstep with the script for *King Kong vs. Prometheus*. Obviously, it sparked *King Kong vs. Godzilla*, but what most people don't realize is it also begat Toho's efforts with Frankenstein...or so one source says.[1] As usual with these mysterious, unmade films, there are several explanations for this one's inception. Most sources concur that it was Edward Alperson's Brenco Pictures, the U.S. distributor of *The Human Vapor* (1960, 1964 in America), that hoped to see a sequel.[2] Supposedly Alperson approached John Meredith Lucas, a future writer for TV's original *Star Trek,* about writing the sequel. Lucas's idea was to pit the Human Vapor against the Frankenstein Monster.[3] The idea was given to Toho, who had Shinichi Sekizawa flesh out a shooting script which was completed in February of 1963.[4] However, confusion again rears its ugly head into the proceedings as *The Human Vapor* wasn't released in America until 1964. Therefore, one must entertain the possibility that perhaps Brenco liked the film so much they suggested a sequel in advance when they purchased the rights to *The Human Vapor* in late 1962 along with *Gorath.*

Much like 1965's *Frankenstein Conquers the World,* the first visual of the film was to be of a gloomy cemetery at night—in this case, the cemetery of the Frankenstein family in the United Kingdom.[5] In this scene, a group of men uncover a sarcophagus housing the Frankenstein Monster itself. Presumably after this reveal the title credits would have rolled, as the next scene takes place on a jet airliner where Mizuno is a passenger.

Actually, Mizuno's presence is only hinted at, and it's up for debate whether or not we would have seen Yoshio Tsuchiya's face yet in the airliner scene. As it is, Mizuno is introduced via a pile of smoking clothes on an airliner that frightens a stewardess. Later, a fog enters a parked car and then steals it. We are then introduced to the disciple of Dr. Frankenstein, Dr. Gildor, who is described as having the traditional mad scientist look with white unkempt hair and a bony face.[6] The Frankenstein Monster is revealed, partially at least, in this same scene. At first, he merely appears to be an overly large man whose feet we glimpse, but never his face. We are clued in to this being the Monster when the camera is directed to emphasize the stitches on his hands. Soon after, the Monster gets a full-body reveal, and apparently Sekizawa envisioned the classic Universal look for the monster, complete with electrodes coming from his neck.

Mizuno then gets his full reveal when he walks into Dr. Gildor's lab, much like he brazenly walks into the police station in the first film, and asks a favor. Gildor, naturally enraged, sends the Frankenstein Monster to kill him. The Monster clasps his huge hand around Mizuno's throat who merely laughs him off and dissolves into his gaseous form and then begins taunting the doctor. Impressed and frightened by Mizuno's abilities, he agrees to help Mizuno revive his dead lover.[7]

The film's wildest scene occurs on a commercial airliner and will likely come across as incredibly cool or campy depending upon one's tastes. Apparently fearing they will be arrested upon landing, Mizuno, Dr. Gildor, and the Monster (hidden in a huge crate in the baggage hull) plan to escape the plane in midair over Suruga Bay.

Mizuno breaks into the baggage hull to tell the monster it is time to break free of his crate, which he does. Mizuno then begins to take on his gas form to hide the Monster, which makes some passengers think a tear gas attack is happening. The Monster then appears in the main passenger cabin and rips off the escape hatch in midair! One of the captains begins shooting at them and hits Dr. Gildor, mortally wounding him. Mizuno and the Frankenstein Monster then jump out of the plane wearing parachutes! A parachuting Frankenstein Monster—an image one either loves or hates.[8]

As one can tell, despite the similar design, this script serves up a very different interpretation of the Frankenstein Monster. In a fresh twist, this Frankenstein is fairly well-spoken—for the Frankenstein Monster at least. He has numerous lines of full dialogue. One of the first of Mizuno and the Monster's exchanges occurs in another bizarre scene that has the duo riding together in a station wagon. Mizuno asks the Monster if he can help him bring Fujichiyo back to life even though the Monster is no Dr. Frankenstein. But, as already stated, bizarre as it is, it's an interesting twist on the Frankenstein mythology to even imply that the Monster is smart enough to help recreate his creator's experiments. The true extent of the Monster's intelligence becomes clear when he and Mizuno dig up Fujichiyo's body in the cemetery, and the Monster expresses concerns about how badly burned the body might be. Mizuno then informs him that he used a special preservation chemical on her body when she was buried. It is also written that only Fujichiyo's hands would be shown in this scene.

As in the original film, a good deal of this picture again revolves around a reporter trying to figure out the identity of Fujichiyo and why she is important to Mizuno. The reporter character is none other than Goro Maki, and was perhaps a precursor to the same-named ambitious reporter character in *Son of Godzilla* (1967) written by Sekizawa.[9] Overall, Goro mostly serves as a regular avatar for the audience in a film populated with far out characters. Along for the ride with Goro is his female editor, Michi. Goro's editor being a woman would've been innovative for the time period, particularly in patriarchal Japan. Another minor character in the film is Fujichiyo's sister, Mayumi, who notices her sister's grave has been disturbed. It is Mayumi that confirms the events of the script take place three years after the events of the first film—meaning Fujichiyo has been buried for three years!

Fujichiyo's face isn't revealed until one of the lab scenes and it is burned enough that Mizuno looks away in pain when he sees her.[10] Remarkably, the Monster has been able to advise him on everything he needs to recreate Dr. Gildor's experiment. It would even seem the Monster is the one to stitch up Fujichiyo's face, for when Mizuno sees his handiwork he becomes so enraged he strangles the Monster who tells him the scars can heal in time. Clearly in this story, the Monster is the one we are supposed to be rooting for as Mizuno is rather manipulative and abusive towards him. Actually, Mizuno is so one track-minded and predictable in this script he loses any charm he managed to build up in the previous picture. In the last film, though misguided, Mizuno was still able to muster a little audience sympathy. In this script, the minute the Monster does something to disappoint him, Mizuno immediately attacks him on several occasions.

Mizuno's abilities don't take a backseat to the Frankenstein Monster at all and the Vapor Man uses his powers in several interesting scenes. One of the better ones has Mizuno attacking the transport of a blood bank to get new blood for Fujichiyo (in his rage upon seeing the Monster's handiwork on Fujichiyo's face, he accidentally spilt the beakers that contained the correct blood for his beloved). Mizuno tries to escape with the blood in his jeep but is pursued by the police. To escape, Mizuno turns into his gaseous form, levitates the blood, and floats out the jeep sending it careening into an oncoming train.

The script naturally features the perennial Frankenstein lab scene where a lightning storm brings to life a corpse—in this case Fujichiyo. This scene serves as an exciting precursor to the climax. In it, the police arrive at Mizuno's lab (a converted observatory he purchased) just as Fujichiyo is coming back to life. In a bit of a cheat, just as she begins to breathe, Fujichiyo's breathing stops and she immediately dies again. Mizuno shoots the Monster in the chest in his rage, and it drips with black blood. The Monster informs Mizuno that only God can kill him. Then, another freak lightning bolt revives Fujichiyo, who is too overwhelmed with flip-flopping between life and death to recognize Mizuno. As gunfire from the police continues, Mizuno and the Monster, carrying Fujichiyo, escape out the back door. In a surprise move, the crafty Monster grabs a syringe on his way out and stabs Mizuno in the neck with it. The chemical compound within it will not allow him to transform into his gas form. The Monster picks up Fujichiyo and walks out into the lightning storm, and at one point the lightning strikes the electrodes protruding from his neck in what would have made a fantastic visual (possibly inspired by the opening of Universal's *The Ghost of Frankenstein*). The Monster eventually sets Fujichiyo down as the police shout at him and he walks off a cliff. The screen would have faded out and the next few scenes would have built to the real conclusion.

The focus of this portion of the script tries to answer the question of whether or not Fujichiyo's soul has returned to her body. Though interesting, had actress Kaoru Yachigusa reprised her role, she really wouldn't have had much to do. Fujichiyo mostly lays around unresponsive until she finally gets up and begins to dance to the radio. Not long after, the Monster breaks into the room where she is being held and absconds with her. As it is, the Monster sees her as a kindred spirit having been revived from the dead like him. Presumably, he believes that she wants to return to an eternal slumber with him under an old, dead tree in a swamp that infatuates the Monster throughout the script. Indeed, the Monster takes Fujichiyo to the tree in the swamp where he is confronted by the Vapor Man and the two do battle.[11]

Tokusatsu fans who like to point out that Shinichi Sekizawa often ended his monster battles with the kaiju falling into the ocean will probably not be surprised to learn that Mizuno, Frankenstein's Monster, and Fujichiyo all sink to their deaths in a quicksand-infested swamp. Actually, Universal ended both *House of Frankenstein* and *The Mummy's Ghost* (both 1944) with the Monster and Kharis the Mummy, respectively, sinking into quicksand. That said, there is a good moment where Fujichiyo and Mizuno touch hands at the last moment before they die.

The film was announced by Toho in May of 1963 for production and then never materialized. Interestingly, the book *Godzilla Toho Special Effects Movies* (2014) suggests that the production of *Matango* somehow killed *Frankenstein vs. the Human Vapor*. There could be several reasons for this, one of which was *Matango*'s failure at the box office. The lack of enthusiasm may have soured Toho on future mutant films, and one will notice there were no more films about human-sized monsters again until 1970's *Vampire Doll*.

Overall, it's better this script wasn't adapted for several reasons. It undermines the ending of the original film, which was a classic Ishiro Honda tragedy. Here in hindsight, Mizuno spends a great deal of time trying to revive Fujichiyo who only regains her consciousness moments before she dies along with Mizuno and the picture ends—basically an inferior repeat of the last film. The other reason fans are fortunate that this wasn't made is because if it was, Toho likely would never have come upon the idea of a giant version of the Frankenstein Monster.

Chapter Notes

[1] This is implied in *Toho Tokusatsu Unpublished Works*, but other Japanese books make no mention of this.

[2] Brenco also distributed Toho's *Gorath* and *The Last War* in the U.S.

[3] Oddly enough, that same year Jerry Sohl (another future *Star Trek* writer) pitched Toho *Frankenstein vs. the Giant Devilfish*. So, apparently, there was some strange connection between the future writers of *Star Trek* and Toho in 1963 concerning Frankenstein. Hopefully one day a clearer picture of events can be pieced together, but for now it may just have to be labeled as coincidence.

[4] It's somewhat odd the job was given to Sekizawa considering Takeshi Kimura wrote *The Human Vapor*. Furthermore, Sekizawa's script is so gloomy it could pass for Kimura's work.

[5] Traditionally Victor Frankenstein was from Switzerland, but Sekizawa chose to place him in Britain in this script.

[6] Though it's never explicitly stated, it was presumably his men who open Frankenstein's grave in the first scene. Furthermore, some English sources state that Gildor is a descendant of Dr. Frankenstein, though this author didn't get that impression from the script.

[7] As always, the broken translation makes certain things hard to ascertain 100%, but this author thinks Mizuno is fully aware that Fujichiyo detonated the explosion in the theater. Mizuno though, took it as an act of love, so that they could die together—or at least this is how I interpreted the "broken English dialogue" that one gets with these translations.

[8] Since Mizuno can effectively fly, it may have been less silly to have him do so while the monster simply jumps into the water rather than both wearing parachutes.

[9] Ironically, this name would in turn be used by another reporter character in *The Return of Godzilla* (1984). The mysterious unseen character in *Shin-Godzilla* (2016) whose adrift pleasure yacht that sets up the story belongs to one Goro Maki. So in essence, the name became a strange favorite of Toho writers, and in fact, this aborted script was the first use of it.

[10] Another possibility is that this was to hide that the original Fujichiyo, Kaoru Yachigusa, likely wouldn't be back.

[11] The choreography is fairly limited, and mostly has Mizuno shooting the monster with a gun and also trying to strangle him in his gas form.

11.
THE JAPANESE APACHE

Intended Release Date: unknown, presumably 1965
First Draft Date: 1964

Screenplay by: Nobuo Yamada **Proposed Director:** Kihachi Okamoto **Proposed Cast/Characters:** Kuroda Fukuichi [weapons expert], Jiro Futago [leader of Japanese Apache tribe], Yamada Tansu [political criminal], Urakami [reporter]

SYNOPSIS In an alternative universe version of Post-war Japan, the nation is fully militarized with air, land and sea units. Under this new regime, all Japanese citizens are forced to be hard workers. Being unemployed is a capital offense and violators are banished from society to a barren wasteland in the vicinity of Osaka Prefecture. This fate is considered worse than the death penalty—which has been abolished. Kuroda Fukuichi, who has not found employment quickly enough after having been fired, is banished to this wasteland. Living in this wasteland is a group of survivors, called the Japanese Apache, that have survived and evolved due to eating iron and copper. Kuroda and another exiled man, Yamada, are taken in by the tribe and their leader, Jiro Futago. Kuroda becomes a part of the tribe, and uses his knowledge of weaponry to help the Japanese Apaches lead a revolt against the tyrannical government.

COMMENTARY If you initially saw this title in the table of contents and assumed it to be some sort of strange, Japanese western, you know that assumption to be incorrect; it is actually a rather unique tale of dystopian Japan.[1] It was also based upon the first novel ever published by the legendary Sakyo Komatsu, who would not long after begin writing *Submersion of Japan*.

Published by Kobunsha Kappa Novels, the book sold an impressive 50,000 copies in 1964 and Toho quickly optioned the book for a film. Komatsu was not hired to adapt his own story though, and that job went instead to Nobuo Yamada who primarily wrote dramas for Nikkatsu in the late 1950s. The proposed director was to be Kihachi Okamoto, who was by this time an accomplished director who would in the future helm *Japan's Longest Day* (1967) and *Blue Christmas* (1978) among many others. Though these two players make sense behind the scenes, the proposed cast most certainly did not. Believe it or not, the Crazy Cats were the actors slated to star in *The Japanese Apache*! The Crazy Cats[2] were a jazz band established in 1955 that eventually went on to star in a series of films for Toho beginning in 1962 and ending in 1971. As most of these films were comedies, it would seem safe to presume that this was to be a comedic adaptation or a legitimate spoof of Komatsu's novel.

That the Crazy Cats would star in this *Mad Max*-like future wasteland tale seems strange to say the least. But then again, the Japanese Apaches themselves are incredibly strange. Komatsu describes them as a group of scrap iron scavengers that have taken to eating copper and iron! As such, their skin is hard, metallic and copper in color. With their physiology changed due to years of ingesting the metal, they are now stronger and faster than normal humans. Their clothing is described as being similar to Native Americans and they even refer to old cars and motorcycles as livestock! This tribe is democratic, and vote rather than ruling by a dictator, though they do have a chief.

Komatsu's dystopian, labor force-obsessed Japan is also fascinating. It would seem that in this new society that to be unemployed is the greatest sin one can commit. This is also the reason why the protagonist is banished—he hasn't found another job within the allotted time after being fired. This new Japan also possesses a mighty military complete with atomic weapons at its disposal.

Not much is known of the scrapped film adaptation because Komatsu neglects to mention it in his autobiography. From the best that this author can gather, the proposed director Okamoto thought Komatsu's story was too dark. Okamoto even asked another sci-fi novelist, Hirai Kazumasa, to draft a lighter and more fantastical version of the story. Kazumasa was too busy and declined the offer.[3] There was only one draft written by Nobuo Yamada and it is unclear if this was a treatment, a script or a simple story proposal.

The project's cancellation didn't sour Komatsu on Toho though. In an interview with *Science Fiction Studies*, he stated:

"When the publishing house Hayakawa Shobo started *SF Magazine* in 1959, they held a contest, the Hayakawa Science Fiction Competition. I sent in the story "Pacem in Terris," and that was the beginning. The sponsor who provided the prize money was the Toho movie studio, which produced *Gojira* [1954]. The condition was that Toho would retain the movie rights to the winning story. That first year of the contest, I received an Honorable Mention and 5000 yen. The second year I shared the prize with Hanmura Ryo, who later won the Naoki Prize. We each got 30,000 yen from Toho, and I felt so obligated [laughs] that in 1973 when we were discussing a film version of *Japan Sinks*, I gave them the movie rights with almost no conditions. I think they paid 1.5 million yen.[4]

And, though *The Japanese Apache* never was adapted into a film, it did become a radio play in 1972.

Chapter Notes

[1] This author's synopsis is based on the novel, not the screenplay which this author has never seen.

[2] The group comprised of Kei Tani, Hitoshi Ueki, Hiroshi Inuzuka, Senri Sakurai, Shin Yasuda, and Etaro Ishibashi. Many of the Crazy Cats films featured actors familiar to the Godzilla series, even Yumi and Emi Ito, Mothra's fairies. Hiroshi Inuzuka was also one of the male leads in *Daigoro vs. Goliath* (1972).

[3] Later, Kazumasa's manga, *Wolf Guy*, would be adapted into *Horror of the Wolf* by Toho in 1973.

[4] www.depauw.edu/sfs/backissues/88/komatsu%20interview.htm

12.
INTER ICE AGE IV

Intended Release Date: 1966
First Draft Date: September 7, 1965

Screenplay by: Kobo Abe **Producer:** Tomoyuki Tanaka **Proposed Director:** Hiromichi Horikawa **Proposed SPFX Director:** Eiji Tsuburaya **Proposed Cast/Characters:** Professor Katsumi [inventor], Tanomogi [Katsumi's assistant], Wada [lab worker], Dr. Yamamoto [head of Aquan lab], Tomoyasu [bureaucrat], Mrs. Katsumi [Professor Katsumi's wife]

SYNOPSIS To compete with the world's first super computer, "Moscow-1" in Russia, Japanese scientist Dr. Katsumi creates the "KEIGI-1". The new machine can do everything that the one in Moscow can and more, including replicating people's brainwaves and thought patterns. When Katsumi is forbidden by the government to predict the political future he decides instead to predict the future of a single stranger he sees on the street. Together he and his assistant, Tanomogi, shadow the man and are shocked when the man is later murdered. Katsumi hooks the corpse up to the machine and learns there is more to the murder than meets the eye. Katsumi and Tanomogi learn the man was killed to keep secret the experiments of an organization that specializes in turning land based organisms into aquatic life—including humans. To his horror, Katsumi's own unborn son is taken to become one of the new underwater humans called Aquans. To his shock, this has all been orchestrated by KEIGI-1 itself along with Tanomogi. As KEIGI-1 has Katsumi's thought patterns, Tanomogi and the other conspirators consider the machine to be the true version of Katsumi, and thus take the machine's orders over the real doctor's! As the machine has looked into the future and predicted a new ice age, it deems the Aquans the best choice for mankind's survival. When the real Katsumi refuses to go along with this plan, the machine orders him to be terminated.

COMMENTARY Kobo Abe's *Inter Ice Age 4* has been described by some as the first full-length Japanese science fiction novel. It was published July 5, 1959 by Kodansha. Before that, in March of 1958, it was serialized in *Sekai Magazine*.[1] Abe's first movie adaptation was *Pitfall* (1962) which was followed by *The Woman in the Dunes* (1964) which was very well received. Having found great success in the field of fantastical films, in 1965, Toho secured the screen rights to *Inter Ice Age 4*. The screenplay was written at a condominium in Shiraki Ranch at Sengaki Falls by Abe himself. The film's proposed director was to be Hiromichi Horikawa, second unit director on such Kurosawa classics as *Seven Samurai* (1954) and *Throne of Blood* (1957).[2] Horikawa was quoted as saying, "I was obsessed with making this work into a movie."[3] What exactly killed *Inter Ice Age 4* is unknown, as Toho was experiencing smooth sailing for the most part in 1965. It is presumable that perhaps the needed effects work and copious underwater filming is what led to the film's cancellation.

Many of the book's more fantastic scenes focus on underwater farms where livestock like cows and pigs have been genetically modified to have gills. Along with them are the Aquans, a group of humans created from "aborted" fetuses that the scientists manipulate into having gills. However, the Aquans are certainly not grotesque gill-men, but appear to be normal humans with gills. Their only other strange feature is that they never blink being underwater.

Though this author has never seen the script, he has read the English translation of the novel done by Dale Saunders. It was published in 1970 by the publisher Alfred Knopf out of New York. Since author Abe wrote the movie script it is presumable it follows the novel fairly closely. Though one can't say how the novel would have translated on screen, it makes for an intriguing read that keeps the reader guessing. For instance, when Katsumi begins following a random stranger to test out his predictive machine on and it leads to a conspiracy involving gilled-humans it seems like too much of a coincidence. Or rather, from a narrative standpoint it seems odd that a story seemingly about a super computer would take a turn into Gill Man territory. As it turns out, the coincidence is no coincidence at all, and Katsumi was very subtly lead by his assistant Tanomogi into following the "stranger". As the story progresses, we learn that Tanomogi actually murdered the man[4] on Katsumi's own instructions!

Over the course of the story, Katsumi receives mysterious, threatening phone calls at his home warning him not to delve too deeply into the conspiracy. Eventually it becomes evident that the voice is remarkably Katsumi's own! This isn't a voice from the future though, but a voice that can predict the future belonging to the machine. As it turns out, Tanomogi input the professor's thought patterns into the machine creating a mechanical clone of his brain. The machine is referred to as a smarter, more ideal version of

Katsumi, and has been orchestrating all the events in the story since it came online. Ironically, Katsumi's own staff begins to follow the order of the machine over his own, considering the machine a better, more perfected version of Katsumi's own mind! When the machine predicts that Katsumi will not go along with the Aquan plot, it suggests that they kill him and they have no trouble obliging. However, they do at least try to make Katsumi see the future so that he may change his mind.

The climax of the book has Katsumi watching a simulated prediction of the future. This is where Eiji Tsuburaya would have excelled, as it features the sinking of Japan and the rest of the world under the rising oceans. One scene in the book has a tidal wave decimating parts of Japan while beneath the waves, the Aquans go peacefully about their day—not even noting the turmoil above them. The book delves so deeply into the future that eventually the Aquans, initially slaves of sorts, transition into the true rulers of the earth. Eventually, normal human society disappears altogether. The final sequence has Katsumi watching a simulation of a young Aquan man who longs to visit the surface—even if it costs him his life. The young Aquan manages to make his way to a small island where he crawls ashore and soon dies. The small island is soon engulfed by the sea, and the film ends as Katsumi seems to view the dead Aquan as a kindred spirit in that both of them refuse to accept the future. Katsumi sits in wait for his killer, listening to his footsteps just outside the door, and the novel ends. Perhaps this was Abe's way of showing that the future isn't certain, and we the reader will never know Katsumi's fate even though all signs point to him being murdered.

The bleak future shock script would have been ahead of its time for cinemas in 1966 and would have predated *Planet of the Apes* (1968) as one of the great sci-fi shockers. Tsuburaya would have also had his hands full if the script was adapted faithfully from the book. For instance, there is a lengthy scene where the doctors tour the testing facility and are introduced to underwater cows, dogs and pigs among other creatures. There are also two overgrown fly larvae kept in a cage. While Tsuburaya always excelled at creating made-up kaiju, sometimes his recreations of real life animals were lacking.[5] Here Tsuburaya would have had to create gilled pigs and cows. Had these sequences been created poorly it would have greatly undermined the story's serious tone. And, as stated earlier, perhaps it was these effects concerns that cancelled the production, though no official reason has ever been stated.

Chapter Notes

[1] The novel was reportedly longer, and more detailed, than the magazine serialization.

[2] Horikawa also served as director on 25 films between 1955 and 1989, though none of them are particularly well known outside of Japan.

[3] *Shincho Japanese Literature Album* #51, (Shinchosha, 1994) pp. 48-49

[4] The dead man is a character in of himself in the novel when he gets hooked up to the computer. You see, the computer doesn't just read his mind, but reanimates his brain in such a way that the man believes himself to still be alive after his attack. In fact, Katsumi has to dupe him into thinking he has bandages over his eyes (explaining why he can't see) and is recovering in the hospital to get a calm, coherent answer from him.

[5] The horse in *Frankenstein Conquers the World* (1965) and the lion in *Latitude Zero* (1969) as examples, though the lion was more the fault of the American producers screwing Toho out of budget money.

13.
"PROJECT X"

Intended Release Date: Unknown
First Draft Date: mid-to-late 1960's

Screenplay by: Unknown **Proposed Cast/Characters:** Col. Jack Cunningham, Maj. David D. Nelson [U.S. Air Force], Maj. Kelly Connors [U.S. Army], Maj. Cooper [Navy], Capt. Susan Steuilla [space physiologist], Dr. Beacham [rocket scientist], Burke [reporter]

SYNOPSIS In the year 197X, NASA launches a new space program under the Andromeda Program. The purpose of the Andromeda ship's mission is to study the moon and claim it as a territory of the earth. The ship will be manned by five U.S. astronauts. The Soviets beat the U.S. into space but their ship is struck by a freak meteorite, stranding them in space. The U.S. decides to answer Russia's call for help and launches the Andromeda prematurely to rescue the cosmonauts. Trouble arises when the Andromeda doesn't have enough fuel to escape the moon's gravitational pull. The Russians then reveal that they left a spacecraft on the moon's surface back in 1969 which can be used to repair Andromeda. The plan works, and all the astronauts return to earth.

COMMENTARY Among the most mysterious projects listed in *Toho Tokusatsu Unpublished Works* is this one, known only as "Project X"—essentially unnamed and undated. All that remains is its treatment, which is believed to have been written sometime the late 1960's by the compilers of *Unpublished Works*.[1]

The treatment is made even odder in that all the main characters are American, and the film is likewise mostly set in America and outer space. Considering the story's theme of global brotherhood, it would seem likely that Ishiro Honda was involved in some capacity or perhaps this script was a heretofore unknown co-production between Toho and Henry G. Saperstein's United Productions of America. It could have been written by an American like Reuben Bercovitch and then translated into Japanese, though this is just conjecture.

Set in the future of the 1970s, the story is essentially like a more fantastic precursor to *Apollo 13* (the real event had not yet taken place either when this script was written) as it involves a spacecraft stranded in space. Specifically, a small meteor strikes a Russian spacecraft stranding the cosmonauts in space. To make matters more dramatic the cosmonauts are stranded outside of their ship, floating in space.

Script notes give some backstory, stating that in 1967 the U.S. President decreed that all astronauts would be deemed "representatives of the human race" and that in the case of an emergency they shall be given as much aid as is possible. The first part of the treatment largely explains the process of the Andromeda program, describing the mission in great detail. As Saperstein often said he despised how many of Toho's thrillers would open with a press conference, this could be a good sign that this script was written by the Japanese.[2]

As for the main characters, Jack Cunningham is the typical stoic military male lead common in 1960s B-movies and would have been perfect for Rhodes Reason. Major Nelson of the Air Force is described as a perfect physical specimen, while naturally Major Cooper from the Navy is an adept diver. The other main character is the lone female astronaut, Susan, who acts as the Andromeda's doctor.

There is one brief Japanese character in the script and Japan is notably the only other nation to help out in the crisis, sending a rocket full of fuel and oxygen to Andromeda. The climax is interesting in that Andromeda itself becomes stranded in space while rescuing the cosmonauts. The Russians then reveal they have a space craft that was abandoned on the moon in 1969, and that it is capable of breaking through the moon's gravitational pull. Naturally, there is something lost in translation here but essentially the old Russian ship plays a part in getting everyone back to earth. As a story that aimed for realism above fantasy, it is presumable it was cancelled due to the challenge of filming a big-budget space film with an all-American cast.

Chapter Notes

[1] One small clue at least exists in the form that it was written after President Kennedy's death as it is referred to in the treatment.

[2] Saperstein apparently changed the beginning of *Invasion of Astro-Monster* so that the film would begin with the rocket already in space.

14.
THE FLYING BATTLESHIP

Intended Release Date: 1967
Draft Dates: unknown, 1966 (treatment); October 3, 1966 (first draft script)

Screenplay by: Shinichi Sekizawa & Kazuyoshi Wada (story) **Producer:** Tomoyuki Tanaka **Proposed Director:** Ishiro Honda **Proposed SPFX Director:** Eiji Tsuburaya **Proposed Music Composer:** Akira Ifukube **Proposed Cast/Characters:** Goro Yamoto [reporter], Anne [photographer], Kanami Todo [Captain of Super Noah], Jack [aerospace investigator], the Black Conductor [head of NOO], Dr. Nobuyuki [botanist], Masaru [child of Nobuyuki], Emiko [child of Nobuyuki] **Proposed Monsters:** Giant Plant [treatment only]

SYNOPSIS A new technical marvel, the Super Noah, launches for outer space but soon disappears. At the same time, the World Population conference is threatened with a hydrogen bomb by the terrorist organization NOO, and in the Amazon, the famous botanist Dr. Nobuyuki goes missing. Investigating both mysteries is reporter Goro Yamoto and his photographer, Anne. Goro deduces that the Super Noah is the product of Dr. Kanji Todo, and tracks down his daughter Kanami. Goro's suspicions are proven true when Dr. Nobuyuki's children are kidnapped by NOO operatives and Kanami springs into action to save them. With the children rescued, Kanami takes Goro and Jack, an aeronautical investigator, to her dead father's secret base beneath Kurobe Dam where the Super Noah is kept. A NOO warship attacks Tokyo and the flying battleship springs into action to defend Japan. When NOO's ship retreats, Kanami flies the Super Noah to the Amazon to rescue Dr. Nobuyuki. However, this is all part of NOO's plan and the Super Noah is captured. At the last moment, Kanami and her crew are rescued by Jack, but in all the chaos, the head NOO operatives get away. Dr. Nobuyuki reveals that NOO has a satellite in space capable of burning the earth by harnessing the sun's rays. The heroes launch a rocket at the satellite and it is destroyed along with the NOO operatives.

COMMENTARY Of all the lost projects in this book *The Flying Battleship* probably had the highest chances of success had it been completed. Not only that, the concept also evolved into the Tsuburaya TV series *Mighty Jack*. Often touted as a quasi-sequel to *Atragon*, *The Flying Battleship* is really more of a remake/retelling of *Atragon* (much like 1977's *The War in Space*).[1] Actually, the best way to sum up the script would be to say that it is essentially *Atragon* crossed with a James Bond movie.

Centering on reporters, photographers, and kidnapped scientists, *The Flying Battleship* is classic Shinichi Sekizawa. It is also very close to *Atragon*, which featured similar characters—albeit with quite a twist. In *Atragon*, a central character is Makoto, the daughter of Captain Jinguji, the creator of Atragon. Here, a central character is once again the daughter of the titular warship's inventor, Dr. Kanji Todo. Only in this case, Todo is dead and his daughter Kanami is the captain of the Super Noah.

Needless to say, the character is quite progressive for 1966 Japan. The next year, Sekizawa (or more, perhaps, female co-writer Kazue Shiba) would debut one of his most progressive female characters ever with *Son of Godzilla's* jungle girl Saeko who not only holds her own among the male characters but often physically outdoes them. Actually, Beverly Maeda would seem to be the perfect choice for Kanami had this script been filmed.

Kanami is quite the character, introduced during Dr. Noboyuki's farewell at Haneda Airport where she catches Goro's eye. In a later scene, she is revealed to be the wild driver of a motorcycle when she takes off her helmet and flips her hair. Considering this film was written in 1966 at the height of the Bond craze, Sekizawa may have been inspired by *Thunderball* (1965) which featured villainess Fiona Volpe, who rides a motorcycle and is just as deadly as the men.

Goro Yamoto is another typical Sekizawa reporter character who is notorious for tailing the other characters in the script. There is a running gag that always features Goro eating a snack of some sort. In one scene, Goro is discovered hiding in the trunk of Kanami's car eating a sandwich. Less prominent in the action is Goro's photographer, Anne. There are also two child characters, Masaru and Emiko, who tag along for the end battle!

Similar to Robert Dunham's gaijin diamond G-man from *Space Monster Dogora* is the character of Jack, an American aerospace investigator. For all anyone knows, perhaps Dunham would have played Jack, as the role is sizeable but not quite large enough to warrant another Nick Adams or Rhodes Reason. Like Kommei and Jackson in *Space Monster Dogora*, Goro shares an antagonistic relationship with the mysterious Jack, whom he often tails in an attempt to figure out just who he is. At the picture's end, Jack leads a ground-based mission into the Amazon and ends up rescuing the characters after the Super Noah is forced to land by NOO when Kanami is taken hostage. Oddly enough, Jack is absent from the first treatment. It's also worth theorizing that Sekizawa and Tsuburaya liked the name Jack so much that perhaps it influenced the TV series title, *Mighty Jack*.

The main villain[2] is described like an orchestra conductor, and if you assume this is just to illustrate that he dresses nicely, you would be wrong. The Black Conductor, as he is called, not only holds a baton but also says things like, "My future symphony is already close to completion, preparation for the curtain call of the century is soon to commence." His plan for a weaponized satellite[3] pre-dated Ernst Stavro Blofeld's similar idea in *Diamonds Are Forever* (1971). The satellite would act as a giant magnifying glass, using the sun's rays to scorch the earth and burn away the surface. This is also why the NOO organization has kidnapped famous botanist Dr. Nobuyuki, whom they hope to use to reform the earth.

Speaking of the botanist, the first treatment had a monstrous plant in it. However, it is hard to determine whether the plant simply battles Goro and Kanami outside of the Super Noah, or if it battles the Super Noah itself at some point. Likewise, no description is given of the monster (called Dow in the translation). This same "dragon plant" is mentioned as a legend in the full script, and is the reason for Dr. Nobuyuki's trip to the Amazon. However, it is never seen in the script! There is a brief instance where the Black Conductor threatens to feed Dr. Noboyuki's children to "Dow", but the plant monster is never actually seen. Presumably something was lost in translation or Sekizawa would have done away with the plant monster entirely in the second draft, which was never written. Interestingly, monster plants also figured into an early draft of *Latitude Zero* which many sources say had a few bits in it inspired by *The Flying Battleship*.

The second battle between the two warships in the Amazon is very reminiscent of the final battle between the Alpha and the Black Shark in *Latitude Zero*. In one scene, the Super Noah emits magnetic silver flakes that attach themselves to the NOO warship, which then crashes into a wall like the Black Shark in *Latitude Zero*. Though Ted Sherdeman wrote the *Latitude Zero* script, Sekizawa also contributed and it would seem to be too much of a coincidence that he didn't incorporate the idea from *The Flying Battleship*.

As to the final climactic battle, it is mostly land-based. This is because Kanami leaves the ship with some of her men to infiltrate the NOO base and is then captured. The Black Conductor projects Kanami's image into the air signaling to the Super Noah that their captain is captured and so Goro convinces the ship's operatives to land. All hope seems lost when the ship lands and NOO operatives attach explosives to it but from there, Jack shows up to save everyone and a typical James Bond-esque gun battle ensues.

The last moments of the script involve the Black Conductor and his men escaping into space in their own battleship to the satellite that will destroy the world. From there, it becomes unclear as to how exactly the heroes destroy the satellite. This is because many times the script simply refers to the Super Noah as "battleship", which is also the same term that it uses for the NOO warship. It would seem that the heroes launch a rocket at the satellite which destroys it, but it is also possible that they launch the Super Noah into space, sans crew, on a suicide mission and it collides with the satellite. In either case, the satellite goes boom and the world is saved, and the script immediately ends.

Though derivative of *Atragon*, judging by the script's scope it very well likely would have eclipsed it. And had the film been released in 1967 as hoped, it could have capitalized on the Bond craze, which was at a fever-pitch in Japan that year due to the release of the Japan-centric *You Only Live Twice* (which was partially shot at Toho studios). As to this scripts' more Bondian elements, the NOO base looks like a primitive village with huts on the surface, but underground it is a modern Bond villain lair. There is also a wonderful, Bond-style boat chase through the Uraga Straight involving gunfire and smoke pellets which this author unfortunately can't fully comprehend, but it looks to be quite exciting.

In another tip of the hat to 007 and Q-Branch, Kanami's car has several special gadgets installed. Specifically, it blows a sleeping gas into the backseat that makes Goro and Jack unconscious as Kanami drives them to her hidden base. The treatment reveals right away that the base is near Kurobe Dam when the car drives into a doorway hidden within a huge tree. The script has an element of surprise though, as we see the events through Goro's perspective and don't initially know where the base is located. The script describes Goro and Jack staring at the Super Noah as it sits on what the men assume is the sea floor behind a "wall of water."[4] At first, the men ask if the base is at the bottom of the Pacific Ocean to which Kanami responds, "I'll leave that up to your imagination." Only when the ship surfaces is it revealed to Goro and the audience that they were under Kurobe Dam the whole time. The launch scene is much like *Atragon*'s and occurs as Tokyo is under attack by the NOO warship. During this scene, Kanami also reveals that the ship is powered not by nuclear energy, but by centrifugal force.

One of the film's most ambitious and exciting scenes surely would have been the battle between the NOO warship and the Super Noah over Tokyo Bay, as part of it is set inside a thunder cloud. This idea brings to mind the climax of *Star Trek II: The Wrath of Khan* set in the Mutara Nebula; the two battleships enter the thundercloud and the Super Noah is rocked by lightning strikes as the characters fight for balance in the control room. At the same time, the battle is somewhat hard to follow on paper, as previously mentioned, both ships are often referred to as "battleship" with no clear differentiation. Another of Sekizawa's marvelous ideas had the Super Noah shooting out two self-propelled aerial turrets that emit lasers and are let loose on the NOO battleship.

The designer of the Super Noah on paper was the talented Shigeru Komatsuzaki, who had also designed—uncredited—the super weapons from *The Mysterians* (1957), *Battle in Outer Space* (1959), and *Atragon.* His design is similar to a classic bomber plane combined with a battleship, thus making it a precursor to the famous *Space Battleship Yamato* (1974). Toru Narita also did some design work on the uncompleted film, specifically for the NOO warship. This design was later used for the Ultrahawk No. 1 on *Ultraseven* which came to life shortly after the decision was made to cancel the film in favor of producing *Latitude Zero*.

The Flying Battleship wasn't just the product of Shinichi Sekizawa, but was actually dreamed up by Kazuyoshi Wada, who was primarily a director. Among the films he worked on were the *Crazy Cats* series and other comedies.[5] Initially, this film was scheduled to film in 1967 as was *ESPY* (1974). However, 1967 (Toho's 35th anniversary year) was far too crowded for Toho (they were additionally producing *King Kong Escapes* and *Son of Godzilla*) and so the film was possibly bumped to 1968.[6] From there, it's possible *Latitude Zero's* production was the death knell for this film, and the *Toho Special Effects Movie Complete Works* implies that this is the case.

Not wanting to lose the project entirely, Eiji Tsuburaya transplanted the concept over to Tsuburaya Productions for television. Shinichi Sekizawa wrote scripts for this series, which evolved into *Mighty Jack*. Fundamentally, it is the same as *The Flying Battleship*, with a group of spies that battle an organization called Q bent on global conquest.[7] They didn't battle aliens and monsters as was the case in nearly every other tokusatsu TV series on the airwaves at the time. The series started airing on April 6, 1968 on Fuji TV. The first 13 episodes were serious and had an hour running time but received poor ratings. This caused Fuji TV to request an overhaul of the concept, and therefore the second half of the series featured monsters and ran only 30 minutes. This more comical version of the series even included a cameo guest role from by Koji Moritsugu, that spoofed his role as Dan Moroboshi from

Ultraseven. This version of the series lasted 26 episodes, had better ratings and ran until December 28, 1968.

Mighty Jack was never dubbed into English for American markets, but did finally come to America from Sandy Frank in the form of a faux made-for-video movie that was broadcast on TV in 1986. Taking the first and the sixth episodes of the series, Frank edited them together into this new iteration. Naturally, it is disjointed and feels like what it is, watching two random episodes of a TV series back-to-back. It was also featured on *Mystery Science Theater 3000* (having previously been used back when it aired on public-access KTMA).

Chapter Notes

[1] In the initial treatment, the enemy organization's name is spelled MOO in English in the script, so though it isn't Mu the name is pronounced the same. In the script it was changed to NOO.

[2] Hideyo Amamoto, who appears as a hero in *Mighty Jack*, would have been an inspired choice to play the Black Conductor.

[3] The same year that *The Flying Battleship* was slated for production in 1967, *ESPY* was written by Ei Ogawa which had the villain's lair located within a satellite.

[4] If this is to imply a glass wall or some sort of water force-field is unknown.

[5] Wada is the director of a true lost film, *Escape* (1972) which was completed but shelved by Toho due to similarities to a real life incident and so was never released.

[6] Toho Kingdom also states that this film may have been a planned co-production with UPA and Henry G. Saperstein.

[7] The first episode even focusses on the efforts to rescue a kidnapped man from Q.

15.
VENUS FLYTRAP

Alternate Titles: *Body of the Prey, Revenge of Dr. X,*
The Devil Garden
Release Date: April 16, 1968

Directed by: Norman Earl Thomson **Screenplay by:** Norman Earl
Thomson (based upon a story by Ed Wood Jr.) **Cast:** James Craig
(Dr. Bragan), Atsuko Rome (Noriko Hanamura), James Yagi (Dr.
Paul Nakamura) **Suit Performers:** Insectivorous ("Garr Goyle")

1.85 : 1, Color, 94 Minutes

SYNOPSIS Dr. Bragan is a frustrated NASA scientist who has just
endured yet another failed rocket launch at Cape Canaveral. A
Japanese colleague, Dr. Nakamura, suggests that Bragan go on a
vacation to Japan. Nakamura assures him that his cousin will show
him around. Bragan agrees to the trip, stating that he will rekindle
his first love: botany. In Japan, Bragan is shocked to learn
Nakamura's cousin is a beautiful woman named Noriko. Bragan and
Noriko fall in love as Bragan embarks on a wild experiment to
conjoin a Venus flytrap from America with a carnivorous, marine
plant native to Japan: the Venus vesiculosa. Bragan brings the
human-sized monstrosity to life with lightning. The creature
becomes dangerous and runs afoul of a local village. Bragan lures it
to the top of an active volcano, and he and the creature tumble into
the lava together.

COMMENTARY *Venus Flytrap* is among the most rare birds of lost
tokusatsu films. I say that not because it's hard to find, quite the
opposite really, but because many fans don't even know that it
exists! What is known of the nebulous production is that the genesis
of the story came from none other than Ed Wood, the famous B-
movie filmmaker behind *Plan 9 from Outer Space* (1959). The proof
is in one of Wood's resumes, dated 1970, which reads "The Venus
Flytrap (Japan)."

Now, you may ask, why isn't Wood's name on the opening credits?
Well, that's because the opening credits are missing, and any video
release one sees of the film will have new credits—more on that later.

To return to Wood, he may have written the film as far back as 1959 for Atomic Pictures. The simple story concept was inspired by Frankenstein, only involving a plant man, more or less.

Somehow Wood's story idea ended up in the hands of one Norman Earl Thomson in 1967. Thomson was an entertainment supervisor for American military bases in Japan. As you'll no doubt remember, 1967 was the year of the Great Monster Boom. According to Robert James Kiss's excellent article, "Shut Your Venus Flytrap" (*MAT* #8), Thomson was drinking with a military friend one night when an idea hit him. Amidst the libations, the two men supposed that they could make a Japanese monster movie themselves. Soon they had somehow secured a budget of $75,000 and had acquired Ed Wood's old story, which they retrofitted to focus on Japan. Thomson asked his actor friend and Clark Gable lookalike James Craig to headline the film. By October of 1967, shooting commenced and the project was done filming in only two weeks!

It is believed that the film screened theatrically only once. It premiered at a screening for U.S. servicemen and was torn to shreds—figuratively—by the lone critical reviewer who compared it to an inept remake of *Frankenstein*. The film, which never secured a major distributor, disappeared until the advent of VHS in the 1980s. Regal Video released the film in 1985 as *The Revenge of Dr. X*. The entire package was misleading. Firstly, the box art made the film out to be a slasher flick. Secondly, the back cover text was for the wrong movie: *Mad Doctor of Blood Island* (1968) and promised an American adventurer and a female reporter becoming entangled with a "half-man half-beast" in the jungles. Worse still, the opening credits for that film were for some reason grafted onto the beginning of *Venus Flytrap*! With that in mind, perhaps now you can understand why this counts as a "lost film" of sorts with a history that convoluted.

As for the film itself, it's not very good. Just imagine a movie on a par with the new Caucasian scenes for *Half Human* (1958) and *Varan, the Unbelievable* (1961) and no superior, original Japanese footage to bump it up. On that note, it even sports James Yagi, of the American version of *King Kong vs. Godzilla* (1962/1963), as a significant character. *Venus Flytrap* also succumbs to the typical condescending *Varan, the Unbelievable*-type romance between Bragan and Noriko, whom he berates as though he's a drunk Richard Boone in *The Last Dinosaur*!

Fuzzy screengrab of the goofy Insectivorous.

There's also a lengthy scuba-diving sequence reminiscent of *Space Amoeba* (1970), only sans giant monsters. It's also notable for containing nudity in the form of topless Japanese divers. The breasts aren't glimpsed fleetingly either; they are onscreen in numerous shots for lengthy periods of time (presumably, this was shot with the U.S. servicemen in mind as opposed to general audiences). This is odd because this film isn't what you would consider an exploitation movie. There's not even any real gore to speak of when the monster enters the picture. And speaking of that, the creature doesn't appear until two-thirds into the movie at the one hour mark.

The "birth" scene is directly inspired by *Frankenstein* (1931) and has the monster brought to life in a colorful, detailed laboratory full of beakers and various mystery machines. It's actually rather comical as Bragan even has a hunchbacked Japanese assistant as a stand-in for Igor. It gets worse, and by that, I mean more comical, as Dr. Bragan yells, "Your father will be the lightning!" over and over again.

Actually, there is another scene preceding this where the line is used. It occurs when the doctor checks on his plant creation on a dark and stormy night, which predates a similar scene from *Godzilla vs. Biollante* (1989). He tells his tiny flytrap that "you'll become the most powerful thing in this universe!" He then utters the Frankenstein line, telling the plant that the soil may be its mother, but that lightning will become its father. As for other similarities to Universal Horror films, the villagers go out looking for the creature with torches drawn during the climax.

As for the monster design, the incredibly silly creature has Venus flytraps for hands and feet and looks like a throwaway villain from the *Power Rangers,* if anything. In other words, this is not a monster capable of carrying a feature film.

If you like bad movies, *Venus Flytrap* is worth watching online for free; otherwise, take my word for it and don't waste your time with it.

16.
ADAM OF THE STARS

Intended Release Date: 1970
Draft Dates: December 9, 1968 (first draft script); December 10, 1969 (second draft script)

Screenplay by: James Miki **Producers:** Tomoyuki Tanaka & Fumio Tanaka **Proposed Director:** Hideo Onchi **Proposed Cast/Characters:** Adam, Eve

SYNOPSIS A group of scientists in conjunction with the space agencies of the world make contingency plans for the survival of the human race. In their "Species Migration" plan, humans would be launched into space to find new planets to colonize. As an all-out nuclear war consumes the globe, two people (designated as the "new Adam and Eve") are shot into space just as the world endures its "last day". In their photon rocket the duo land on the mysterious Planet R-1. However, things end in an unexpected manner.

COMMENTARY *Adam of the Stars* started life as the winner in the 18th New Film Scenario Competition by novice writer James Miki. The director, Hideo Onchi, was quite eager to make this project with Toho, which was supposedly submitted to Tomoyuki Tanaka by Onchi himself. Toho had hoped this ambitious production could be another U.S./Japan co-production though it's unknown if UPA was ever approached or if it would've been another company entirely. In 1969, Toho had an unfortunate production with Don Sharpe when making *Latitude Zero*. Sharpe unexpectedly dropped out of production, leaving Toho to foot the bill for the high profile actors such as Joseph Cotten. The movie bombed at the box office and Toho failed to recoup their investment.[1] Having been the second time[2] such a thing had happened, this soured Toho on any future co-productions with Americans any time soon.

Even after the hardships of *Latitude Zero*, and with American co-producers or not, Toho still had ideas to shoot the movie with an eye for release in 1970. Though at this point bedridden from illness brought about by overwork, Eiji Tsuburaya was still scheduled to handle the effects work (his condition would not improve and he died in late January of 1970). As things progressed, the title changed

89

from *Adam of the Stars* to *Myth of Man and Woman*—the title of the second draft script. Coincidentally, the second draft was submitted almost a year to the day later on December 10, 1969.

Had it been produced, *Myth of Man and Woman* would have also served as a technical update of sorts of 1961's *The Last War*, in which the cities of the world are destroyed with nuclear weapons.[3] In this case, however, the entire earth itself was apparently set to explode as the photon rocket leaves earth. In an era where downbeat thrillers like *Planet of the Apes* (1968) were just becoming popular, this would have been a timely tale for Toho.

One of the writers for the Japanese website cyberkids1954 says they heard Teruyoshi Nakano speak on *Myth of Man and Woman* at an event in Kyoto on April 29, 2016. According to Nakano, it was he, not Tsuburaya who would have been the main special effects director. However, perhaps the film was still planned after Tsuburaya's death, and this is what Nakano meant.

Ten years after the film's cancellation, it was adapted into a manga by Hirano Hitoshi and published by Shogakkan on July 20, 1979. Reportedly the manga was 100 pages long.

Chapter Notes

[1] Supposedly this lead to the cancellation of a Filmation animated Godzilla TV series in order to produce *All Monsters Attack* to make a quick buck at the box office at the end of 1969.
[2] The first was when John Beck made Toho foot the bill for the rights to King Kong on *King Kong vs. Godzilla* at the last minute.
[3] It's also likely this film may have used stock footage from that film had it been produced.

17.
THE INVISIBLE SWORDSMAN

Release Date: March 21, 1970

Directed by: Yoshiyuki Kuroda **Screenplay by:** Tetsuro Yoshida
Special Effects by: Yoshiyuki Kuroda **Music by:** Takeo Watanabe
Cast: Osamu Sakai (Yusuke Sanshiro), Yasushi Yokoyama
(Marukichi), Kiyoshi Nishikawa (Kikichi), Oka Hachiro, Yoko Atsuta,
Kiyoshi Nishikawa, Yoshi Yokoyama

Daieiscope, Eastmancolor, 78 Minutes

SYNOPSIS Yusuke Sanshiro is a novice swordsman in a small dojo.
When his father is killed by a group of sinister tattooed men, he
receives aid from the most mysterious of sources: a yokai. As it turns
out, the villainous men also disturbed the local yokai shrine. The
yokai instructs Sanshiro where to find a mystical plant that when
mixed with a special seaweed can turn him invisible for a short
period of time. Sanshiro collects the needed ingredients and begins
tracking his father's killers. He learns the head of the nefarious
group is Geno Suzuki, the head of a rival dojo. In the middle of their
duel, Sanshiro's invisibility serum (which also gives him increased
confidence) wears off and he must face Suzuki as a normal man.
Sanshiro manages to defeat Suzuki and avenges his father.

COMMENTARY Daiei is known in the west primarily for their
Gamera and Daimajin films. However, predominantly, Daiei's
output throughout the 1950s and 1960s were jidai geki (historical
drama) epics. In the same manner of American and Italian studios
that cranked out numerous western pictures, Daiei accomplished
this task by constantly reusing their period sets. Several of their
jidai geki had supernatural elements to them, the most famous
being the yokai (a sort of Japanese protective ghost or spirit) trilogy
of the late 1960s. The first of the trilogy, *100 Ghost Stories*, was
released on a double bill with *Gamera vs. Viras* (1968) and the last
one, *Along with Ghosts*, was on a double bill with *Gamera vs. Guiron*
(1969). It was apparent by that time that Daiei was losing steam
with the series as the last film has nary any yokai action compared

to the preceding two films, which more or less uses the yokai as its main characters.

In 1970, Daiei knew they wanted to pair the new Gamera movie for that Spring Break with another fantasy jidai geki film.[1] Though it's possible they considered another yokai film, they instead took inspiration from 1960's *Invisible Tengu*,[2] which featured an invisible Samurai. Perhaps not coincidentally, the new film was written by *Invisible Tengu*'s writer Tetsuro Yoshida and scored by that same film's composer, Takeo Watanabe. Yoshida also wrote all three of the yokai films and *The Invisible Swordsman* was directed Yoshiyuki Kuroda, the Kyoto division of Daiei's resident special effects artist. Kuroda did the effects for all three Daimajin and yokai films, directed all of *Spook Warfare*, and co-directed *Along with Ghosts*. Couple this with the fact that *The Invisible Swordsman* is heavy on magic, involves the disturbance of a yokai shrine[3] and a major yokai character, one could almost consider it the unofficial fourth yokai film, or if not a close relative or spin-off of sorts.[4]

Unlike the original, adult-oriented *Invisible Tengu* (1960), this film is more lighthearted and aimed at children to double bill more peacefully with *Gamera vs. Jiger*.[5] The film lets you know this right away through its upbeat opening theme sung by a chorus of children and the comical first fight set within in a dojo. Many of the film's later invisibility scenes are also played for laughs and work well in this regard. A good example is Sanshiro eating noodles while invisible in front of two of the film's supporting comedy actors.[6]

Tetsuro Yoshida, the film's writer, is also to be commended for addressing the nudity issue that can sometimes plague a film regarding invisibility. Typically for the invisible person to be rendered as such, they must also take off all of their clothing. Whereas most writers of a children's film might simply ignore logic, here Yoshida writes in a scene where Sanshiro accidentally spills some of the potion on his clothes, causing them to disappear along with him.

Sanshiro's first invisibility transformation scene isn't nearly as impressive as Eiji Tsuburaya's effects from his two Invisible Man films years earlier. Here, Sanshiro's hands disappear first and one can tell the actor is merely hiding his hands behind his sleeves as he looks at them in disbelief. However, the film does one-up its predecessors in that it occasionally shows the audience Sanshiro in an alternate "invisible plane" along with the friendly yokai that aids him. The effect was nothing new, however, and was simply a reprise of Kuroda's technique from the yokai trilogy to make the spooks look ghostly and semi-transparent.

For effects work where Sanshiro levitates objects, mostly wireworks were used but there are a few scenes where it is apparent that a man in an all-black costume against a black background is picking up various objects and moving them around as in *Invisible Avenger* (1954). At other times, to avoid both wireworks and optical printing, Sanshiro's sword is merely held out of view of the camera as it pokes at the various villains.

Much of the climax where the invisible Sanshiro takes on the evil dojo students and their master is played for laughs with plenty of slapstick maneuvers. At first, the dojo students don't even know that Sanshiro is among them as they keep having mysterious accidents during practice. In an amusing moment, Sanshiro picks up some wooden sandals and begins beating the men with them! Eventually, the fight kicks into high gear and spills outside the dojo where Sanshiro drops a bell on one of the men's heads and rather than kill them, it drives them into the ground. In a scene that is both comical and suspenseful, the men manage to throw a sheet over Sanshiro which they then pin in place and stab their swords through over and over again as Sanshiro somehow evades them.

Despite the comical scenes, the film does have its serious moments. The murder of Sanshiro's father naturally is the most dramatic. This leads to an atmospheric scene where Sanshiro calls to his dead father over a bridge. He is then mystically transported to what this author assumes is the Japanese equivalent of the land of the dead. The set is incredibly well done and atmospheric, with a certain *Clash of the Titans* (1981) vibe to it. A ferryman even shows up to take Sanshiro's father away to the land of the dead. The film is actually bookended by another scene on the same set, where the villain is taken away by the same ferryman after Sanshiro defeats him. Before this, the final duel between Sanshiro and the villain is also played straight, as Sanshiro loses the invisibility serum and must fight him on equal footing.

The Invisible Swordsman was released as part of a special double bill for Expo 70 with *Gamera vs. Jiger*. *Swordsman* not only ended up being Yoshida's final screenplay, but would end up being one of the last of Daiei's period fantasy effects films as well.[7] And, despite being the most distinct Japanese take on the Invisible Man mythos, sadly both of Daiei's jidai geki invisible man films are relatively unknown in the U.S.

Chapter Notes

1 Before this though, Daiei did toy with a female-centric invisible person film called *Transparent Beauties*.

2 A tengu is a type of Yokai.

3 A popular plot device in the yokai trilogy.

4 The film's Japanese wikipedia page states that several Japanese fans argue whether this film should be considered as a yokai film. Regardless, another contender for an unofficial fourth yokai film is *Sakuya: Slayer of Demons* (2000) which briefly features many of the yokai from the three Daiei films.

5 Though it should be noted, *100 Ghost Stories*, which was paired with *Gamera vs. Viras*, was a straight, adult-oriented horror movie.

6 The accompanying Daiei DVD booklet states that the comedic actors adlibbed most of their lines and gags on set and some of the ideas were not in the screenplay.

7 The last would be Kimiyoshi Yasuda's horror film, *Horror of an Ugly Woman/The Massuer's Curse* in June of 1970.

FEAR OF THE GHOST HOUSE: THE BLOODSUCKING DOLL (AKA VAMPIRE DOLL, 1970) In 1969, at the wrap party for his feature film debut, *Resurrection of the Beast*, director Michio Yamamoto (who had been an assistant director since the 1950s on films such as *Throne of Blood*) mentioned wanting to do an Alfred Hitchcock-style thriller. Yamamoto recalled to Stuart Galbraith IV in *Monsters Are Attacking Tokyo* that, "I started talking with someone and told them I'd like to make a film that would really make audiences scream. The producer was listening to that conversation, and three days later I was given the assignment."[1] The producer Yamamoto speaks of is Fumio Tanaka, who had handpicked Yamamoto to direct *Resurrection of the Beast*, an action thriller, after being impressed with his work as a television director. However, though Yamamoto was talking about wanting to make a psychological thriller, for some reason, in Tanaka's mind this translated to a vampire movie.

"I wanted to make stuff like Hitchcock's *The Birds*. The producer, Fumio Tanaka, misunderstood; he thought I wanted to make monster movies. He liked Dracula a lot," Yamamoto told Galbraith.[2] As it was, Hammer's Dracula films had been incredibly popular in Japan from the start with 1958's *Horror of Dracula*.[3] Japan tepidly dipped its foot into the vampire game with efforts such as Shintoho's *Woman Vampire* in 1959, but most of the time, their vampire movies were of a most unusual variety, such as 1956's *Vampire Moth* and 1968's *Goke, Body Snatcher from Hell*.

Tanaka quickly sent Yamamoto horror novels and comics to review with instructions to do a vampire film. Initially, Yamamoto refused Tanaka's offer, disliking the idea, but Tanaka persisted and eventually Yamamoto met him in the middle by adapting a story by Edgar Allen Poe, though he refused to put Dracula into the mix. The Poe story was *The Facts in the Case of M. Valdemar*, which involved hypnotism to reanimate the dead. As such, the film would feature a vampire who was hypnotized at the moment of death by her father.

The backbone of the plot, about a sister searching for her missing brother, was apparently taken from a TV movie (or episode) called *Love Trap* previously directed by Yamamoto during his television days in the 1960s. So technically he contributed to the story along with writer Ei Ogawa (who had also written *Resurrection of the Beast*). Relatively new writer Hiroshi Nagano (not to be confused with the future Ultraman star who had yet to be born) also wrote with Ogawa on *The Vampire Doll.*

Before production commenced, Fumio Tanaka borrowed a print of *Goke, Body Snatcher from Hell* from Shochiku to screen for the crew. Reportedly all involved were confused that the usual light, fun output of Toho was going to produce such a gloomy horror film. Yamamoto also doubted that the Japanese would embrace a Japanese-made Western-style vampire movie. "I told [Tanaka] that it's not a good idea to bring Dracula to Japan—you just can't beat Terence Fisher."[4] Nonetheless, to prepare for the film, Yamamoto watched *Horror of Dracula* (1958),[5] *The Fearless Vampire Killers* (1967), and *Rosemary's Baby* (1968).

Ei Ogawa and Hiroshi Nagano wrote their first draft by May 4th and the film would end up being released exactly two months later. The developmental process for the film came about so quickly that apparently it resulted in the script's short length, and also the fact that very little changed from draft to draft which is unusual. The story concerns a young woman, Keiko (Kayo Matsuo, the suffering wife in *Deathquake*), who goes in search of her missing brother, last seen at the estate of his dead fiancé Yuko (Yukiko Kobayashi of *Destroy All Monsters* fame). When she and a friend, Hiroshi (Akira Nakao), arrive at the Western-style estate, they find it to be inhabited only by Yuko's somber mother and mute groundskeeper. Keiko and Hiroshi are soon menaced by a ghostly young woman until they finally realize it is the dead Yuko, hypnotized when she was at the point of death by her father. The story ends with Yuko killing the doctor responsible for her hypnosis (Jun Usami) by stabbing him in the neck—in fact the film's only bloody moment.

Though a vampire film, when filming commenced Yamamoto's main stylistic goal was still a psychological thriller filled with sudden scare tactics.[6] The influence of Alfred Hitchcock is still there too, notably *Psycho*, as the plot concerns a couple looking for a missing sibling. There is also a shot not dissimilar to Norman Bates' mother in the chair when Keiko finally finds her brother's dead body sitting in a chair.

Riichiro Manabe, soon to be notorious for his odd themes composed for *Godzilla vs. Hedorah* (1971) and *Godzilla vs. Megalon* (1973), was chosen to score the film. When David Milner asked Fumio Tanaka who made the decision he replied, "I think Mr. Yamamoto did. He and Mr. Manabe were friends. However, it's possible that the decision was made by the people who were working in Toho's music division at the time."[7]

As for the film's titular character, Yukiko Kobayashi (who became seriously ill in 1974 and retired from acting) was reportedly very enthusiastic about her role. To set her apart from previous screen

vampires, she was given reflective, gold contact lenses[8]—
Yamamoto's idea, and an ingenious one at that which sets the films
apart from Hammer's entries into the vampire mythos. That said,
the film isn't terribly well written. It is paced decently enough but
the climax, which consists of a very lengthy piece of exposition, is
poorly done and comes across as being a bit too last minute in its
execution.

Keiko is played by 28-year-old Kayo Matsuo, who had been acting
since the late 1950s and was best known for *Outlaw: Gangster VIP*
(1968). The male lead is none other than Akira Nakao, later to be
famous to tokusatsu fans for playing General Aso in the Heisei
Godzilla series. As for the rest of the cast, reportedly several of them
came from the recently disbanded Nikkatsu, who had done away
with their old studio system and was now making pinku eiga (porn
films). Likewise, Toho would soon disband their own studio system
and many studio-contracted actors and employees would leave the
studio after filming *Space Amoeba* released one month after
Bloodsucking Doll.

Possibly to appease Yamamoto, who never warmed to the idea of
a vampire film, he was allowed to shoot a psychological thriller back-
to-back with this film on the same sets. In fact, *Terror in the Streets*
was double billed with this film upon its July 4, 1970 release (it was
written by Ogawa and produced with the same behind the scenes
crew). The double bill, released during Japan's summer ghost
season, proved to be a hit, thanks to a largely female audience that
embraced *The Vampire Doll*. In fact, it was such a success that at
the August meeting of the Toho National Branch, the Toho president
stated that he wanted to see more such films released in the future.[9]

THE BLOODSUCKING EYES (AKA LAKE OF DRACULA, 1971)

Though Yamamoto wiggled out of Dracula the first time around, for
the follow-up, Tanaka insisted that a Japanese version of the
Christopher Lee Dracula be cast. "He still wanted to shoot a horror
film about Dracula," Yamamoto told Stuart Galbraith.[10] The first
draft script was entitled *Phantom Vampire* and Tanaka had Masumi
Okada (Dr. Jules Mason from *Latitude Zero*) in mind for the vampire
role but a scheduling conflict prevented this.[11]

Yamamoto then suggested Shin Kishida (currently appearing in
Return of Ultraman) whom he had worked with on the TV series
Tokyo Combat in 1968. "Shin Kishida was a good friend of mine, and
his face always reminded me of Dracula!" Yamamoto told
Galbraith.[12] Initially, the Toho brass disagreed with this decision, as
Kishida was not tall enough to play the vampire. However,
Yamamoto won out and Kishida was given lifts. Kishida liked them
so well he made them a permanent part of his wardrobe.

Once again, Yamamoto had an uncredited hand in the story. The previous year, Yamamoto had hopes of doing a film adaptation of Kazuo Okuma's "Rupo Spirit Ward" which was serialized in the *Asahi Shimbun Evening Society* in 1970. The film never came to fruition but ideas from this story, namely that no one believes lead character Akiko's story, carried over into *Bloodsucking Eyes*. And like *The Vampire Doll*, the script was adapted as written with very few changes during the writing process and filming itself.

Again set in modern day Japan, the story concerns a young woman, Akiko, haunted by a terrifying childhood memory that her friends and family think is just a dream. The terrifying vision concerned a man with blazing eyes—a man who has recently returned to Akiko's hometown. Soon her friends (including her sister Natsuko) are vampirized one by one as she and her fiancé Dr. Saeki confront the vampires. The duo eventually track down the perpetrator of the vampiric curse to an old gothic house. There, they find the corpse of old man whose notebook reveals he and his family are the descendants of Dracula. When the vampire returns, he and Saeki begin to struggle while Natsuko terrorizes Akiko. Dracula's descendant is killed when he is impaled on a stair post.

Though never called Dracula,[13] as stated above, Kishida's character is indeed supposed to be a descendant of the Count. And like the female vampire in the last film, Kishida's vampire has the same reflective gold-tinted eyes.[14] Kishida and Yamamoto discussed his character not as a mindless monster, but as a tragic individual who can't survive without blood. How well this plays out on screen is debatable, but Kishida's performance in this film is better than the somewhat cartoonish portrayal in the third film (or the bizarre Norwegian voice given to him in Toho's international English dub).

Though this film is arguably an improvement over the last, it too suffers from a rushed climax with a heavy helping of exposition. It is also somewhat confusing, as the old man's corpse has been dead for some time, yet momentarily returns to life to trip his son onto the stair post, despite not being a vampire! The climax is clearly inspired from Hammer's *Dracula Has Risen from the Grave* (1968), where Dracula falls over the edge of his castle's battlements and is impaled on a giant cross in the climax. In this film, Saeki and Kishida's vampire wrestle endlessly atop a staircase until Kishida's heretofore dead father intervenes and causes his son to fall, impaled by a stair post from behind. From here, the film transitions into a near shot-for-shot remake of Christopher Lee's death from *Horror of Dracula* that begins with a glimpse of Kishida's deflating hand, and then switches to him clawing at his face. Though Teruyoshi Nakano's version is bloodier and gooier, it is nonetheless inferior.

Unlike the rushed first film, *Bloodsucking Eyes* was actually completed in February of 1971, and held off for the summer ghost season for release.[15] As was done with the previous film, Yamamoto was allowed to film a companion thriller without a vampire, in this case *Rainy Night*. Unlike the other film, it wasn't filmed simultaneously, but was shot in April after *Bloodsucking Eyes* had wrapped. The two films were double-billed together and proved to be another hit.

THE BLOODSUCKING ROSE (AKA EVIL OF DRACULA, 1974)

Immediately after *Bloodsucking Eyes*, Fumio Tanaka pushed for another entry in the series but Yamamoto was reluctant to do another. As Toho disbanded their old studio system, Tanaka failed to transfer over to the newly created Toho Eizo, the division of Toho that handled special effects films.[16] Instead, Tanaka and Yamamoto both went to Toho's television division, and so the third vampire film was put on hold.[17]

Then, in 1973, after the huge success of various horror films in America, a fire was lit under Toho to produce another horror film of their own. Remembering the success of the previous two vampire movies, this lead to the revival of the Bloodsucking series—and likely the aborted *Human Torch* script as well. But, like Hammer's own vampire films which would go extinct with the following year's *Legend of the 7 Golden Vampires*, Toho's final vampire film had worn out its welcome with audiences. Vampires were out, and more visceral horror films (like *The Exorcist*) were in—a fact lost on Toho and Hammer both.

Unlike the previous two films, the developmental process on this film was somewhat more complex. Whereas usually the early draft scripts greatly resembled the finished product, apparently Ei Ogawa turned in a draft that was quite different from the eventually-produced film, initially called *The Bloodsucking Claw*.[18] No details are known of this proto-draft, but most Toho books consider it different enough to sometimes identify it as a lost project along with the likes of *Mothra vs. Bagan*. Whatever it may have entailed, eventually the title *Bloodsucking Rose* was chosen, and the film would feature a white rose that supernaturally turns red as the vampires feed.

Though it has its moments, the trilogy capper is quite possibly the weakest link in the trilogy. As Stuart Galbraith puts it in *Monsters Are Attacking Tokyo*, "Yamamoto didn't want to make it and his lack of enthusiasm shows in this lackluster production." Even Riichiro Manabe's score seems to be lacking compared to the last two films. While his compositions in the last two films were appropriately strange, some of the ones here can't even be called compositions and amount more to strange noises! Even the film's star, Toshio Kurosawa, apparently refused to ever watch the film.[19]

The film's storyline involves Kurosawa as a new teacher, Shiraki, arriving at a secluded all-girls' school. He is surprised to learn the news that he will soon succeed the school's eccentric principal, the vampiric Kishida.[20] Strange occurrences plague the school, with girls becoming pale and anemic until finally it is learned the current principal and his "dead" wife, both vampires, are to blame. Also in the mix is Katsuhiko Sasaki (Goro in *Godzilla vs. Megalon*) as a Renfield-type character who falls under Kishida's spell.

Though lackluster in some respects, fans of Hammer horror will find this entry the most interesting of all, as it is undoubtedly the most Hammer-esque of the three. It would seem that Yamamoto, who as stated earlier really didn't care anymore, fully gave in to Tanaka's wish to go full Christopher Lee. Whereas he had some dignity in the previous film, here Kishida's new vampire character is an almost cartoonish caricature of Lee's portrayal, hissing and baring his fangs on multiple occasions. He also finally wears a red lined cloak. Better done are the more subtle touches, such as his walk down the staircase which is basically identical to the scene where Dracula first meets Jonathan Harker in *Horror of Dracula*. Hammer's Karnstein trilogy had also come around to influence the series as the film's other major setting is an all-girls school dormitory inspired by *Lust for a Vampire* (1971) where see-through nightgowns and breasts abound.[21] The film's ending is at least artfully done and features the best climax of the three. Unlike the previous two films, the mystery of the vampire is solved at a better pace rather than being regulated to a last-minute info dump as in the prior films. In the scene, Kishida is impaled by a fireplace poker and enters his death throes.[22] He and his vampire wife both crawl to one another across the floor in the midst of decomposing until finally their skeletal hands touch.

When released in the summer of 1974, audiences were indifferent to *Bloodsucking Rose*, and as such the Bloodthirsty trilogy would stay at that. Had the film been a hit, in all likelihood the series would have continued. It's even possible that the film's failure gave Toho cold feet regarding *The Human Torch* which was written that same year.

As it turned out, *Bloodsucking Rose* would be director Yamamoto's final feature film, and after this he would work only in television, which he did all the way up to 1999 with the *School Ghost Story Spring Special*.[23] As for producer Fumio Tanaka, he would go on as a major producer for Toho up until the mid-1980s. Riichiro Manabe continued to score films throughout the 1970s, but more or less retired after 1980's *Taiyo no ko teda no fua*.

Shin Kishida would sadly pass away in the early 1980s when his two entries into the Bloodthirsty trilogy were airing on U.S. television.[24] One of the last people to see him was none other than a favorite Toho villain, Goro Mutsumi (the evil alien commanders in *Godzilla vs. Mechagodzilla, Terror of Mechagodzilla,* and *The War in Space*). Mutsumi and Kishida, good friends, were hospitalized at the same time. Mutsumi was released early but would often go back to visit Kishida who tragically passed away not long after. According to Mutsumi, he was one of the last people to talk to him before he died on December 28, 1982.

Before then, however, Kishida slipped on the vampire's fangs one last time, spoofing his horror movie persona in Nobuhiko Obayashi's 1979 comedy, *Kosuke Kindaichi's Adventure*. As to Shin Kishida's vampiric legacy, in his home country, the Japanese consider Kishida to be the second greatest screen vampire ever... after Christopher Lee.

Section Notes

[1] Galbraith, *Monsters Are Attacking Tokyo*, pp.112-113
[2] Ibid.
[3] Hammer even went so far as to film extra gory footage just for their Japanese releases, where censorship standards were lower.
[4] Galbraith, *Monsters Are Attacking Tokyo*, pp.112-113
[5] Female vampires seemed to be on Yamamoto's mind from the beginning. In particular, Yamamoto was influenced by the scene where a vampirized Lucy tries to kiss her brother-in-law and is driven away by a crucifix. Apparently writer Hiroshi Nagano jumped in his seat at this scene when the cross burns her forehead, and Yamamoto took note.
[6] This is most apparent when an inanimate mannequin in a coffin somehow jumps out. As the mannequin is literally a decoy for Yuko's body—the "Vampire Doll" of the title—there is no logical reason for it to jump out of the coffin. However, much like Italian horror films, Japanese films favor style over logic.
[7] http://www.davmil.org/www.kaijuconversations.com/tanak.htm
[8] Kobayashi has said that when wearing these contact lenses, she had absolutely no visibility, just like her European progenitor Christopher Lee's blood-red contacts.
[9] This could have also inspired the release of *Horror of the Wolf* in 1973.
[10] Galbraith, *Monsters Are Attacking Tokyo*, pp.112-113
[11] Ironically, Okada would play the vampire in Toei's 1979 release, *Vampire Dracula Comes to Kobe*. It was directed by Hajime Sato.
[12] Galbraith, *Monsters Are Attacking Tokyo*, pp.112-113
[13] The character is called "the man who resembles a shadow".

¹⁴ Which strangely would not reappear in the sequel. Perhaps the contacts got thrown away?

¹⁵ A practice not uncommon for Toho. *Destroy All Monsters* had been completed in May of 1968, but held off until August.

¹⁶ This division of Toho would naturally produce the 1970s-era Godzilla films (*Godzilla vs. Hedorah* excluded) along with megahits like *Submersion of Japan*. It was disbanded in early 1978 when Tomoyuki Tanaka went from being the president of Toho Eizo to the president of Toho in general. It was more or less replaced later in 1978 by Toho Eiga.

¹⁷ During this time, Yamamoto adapted more teleplays by Ei Ogawa. One production even starred Shin Kishida, so the Bloodthirsty team was still together even though the series was on hiatus.

¹⁸ Though it translates as "claw", perhaps it means "thorn" which would make more sense and tie in with the eventual rose title.

¹⁹ Kurosawa agreed to appear only because he had worked before with Yamamoto, who asked him to star in the film.

²⁰ He was not playing the same character as in the last film, however.

²¹ *Bloodsucking Rose* was actually the first entry of the trilogy to contain nudity, which was also prevalent in the previous year's *Horror of the Wolf*, also by Toho.

²² Originally as he died, Kishida's character's face was supposed to revert back to the form of the original Anglo priest who cut off the other principal's face.

²³ Specifically, Yamamoto directed the fourth episode, which was produced by Fumio Tanaka. This author gets the impression that Tanaka brought Yamamoto onto the project, and that portions of the episode might be an homage to the Bloodthirsty trilogy.

²⁴ The two films aired as *The Lake of Dracula* and *Evil of Dracula*, see Appendix IV for more details.

18.
HORROR OF THE WOLF

Japanese Title: *Crest of the Wolf*
Release Date: September 1, 1973

Directed by: Masashi Matsumoto **Special Effects by:** Teruyoshi Nakano **Screenplay by:** Jun Fukuda, Kazumasa Hirai, Shiro Ishimori & Masashi Matsumoto **Music by:** Riichiro Manabe **Cast:** Taro Shigaki (Akira Inugami, Wolf Guy), Yusaku Matsuda (Do Haguro), Michiko Honda (Kiko Kimura), Koji Kawamura (Takeo Haguro), Masao Imanishi (Principal), Toshio Kurosawa (Akira Jin)

Tohoscope, Fujicolor, 83 Minutes

SYNOPSIS In the snowy wilds of Alaska, young werewolf boy Akira Inugami lives happily with his family until they are brutally gunned down by the Tomei Society. Years later, Inugami attends high school in Japan where he falls in love with his teacher, Kiko Kimura. The son of the Tomei Society boss, Do Haguro, has eyes for Kiko also. Haguro leads his violent gang against Inugami and kidnaps Kiko. Inugami goes to rescue her and kills Haguro in a duel to the death. Badly wounded, he then takes on the yakuza thugs employed by the Tomei Society before he and Kiko are rescued by a detective friend, Akira Jin. As they drive a bloodied Inugami to safety, his fate is uncertain.

COMMENTARY Most fans are aware of Toho's takes on Frankenstein and Dracula, but fewer are aware of Toho's movie on lycanthropy, 1973's *Horror of the Wolf*. Actually, those hoping that this film is similar to Toho's Bloodthirsty trilogy may be disappointed, as it's not really a gothic horror or werewolf film. The film was based upon the horror novel *Wolf Guy*, about a high school student[1] who is a werewolf written in 1969 by Kazumasa Hirai.[2] *Wolf Guy* was then more popularly adapted into a manga for *Bokura Magazine* in 1970. Toho acquired film rights in the early 1970s right around the time that the great studio shakeup was going on. As a result, it seemed that Toho Vision and Toho Movies, both separate divisions of Toho Co. Ltd., vied to produce the film. As Toho Vision (or Toho Eizo) typically produced the company's effects films, it became something of a co-production between the two divisions. Three drafts of the script were written, and according to *Toho Complete Works*, very few changes were made from one draft to the next. The only major difference was initially Inugami had more dialogue about his dead mother but in the finished film, his feelings are illustrated through the numerous flashbacks to her death. Likewise, Do was supposed to have an intense hatred of his father that was apparently glossed over in the finished product.

This author has yet to find a subtitled version of *Horror of the Wolf*, but it looks like it would be a semi-hard film to follow even with subtitles. Much of the film is spent jumping around between montages of Inugami and the other characters being brutally beaten by the evil high school gang lead by Do Haguro.[3] But the visuals, cinematography, and overall direction are so stimulating, this isn't necessarily a problem. The film is striking right from the start as we watch a group of wolves (technically just German Shepherds) run through a snowy wasteland in Alaska (in fact Akitsuka Mountain in Aizu) to a well-done song by Jiro Sugita. The happy moment is soon over when a helicopter dramatically flies overhead and shoots down the toddler Inugami's mother and blows up the family cabin. Inugami howls in grief in his human form against a giant moon backdrop (an image prevalent throughout the entire film) and the story jumps to then present day Japan.

As with the Bloodthirsty trilogy, this film utilizes Teruyoshi Nakano's notorious blood spurting technique copiously (more on that later), and is also scored by Riichiro Manabe. Manabe's score is very similar to the one he composed for *Godzilla vs. Megalon*,[4] and *Godzilla vs. Hedorah* from two years earlier. But like the Bloodthirsty trilogy, Manabe's odd music works much better in this film than it does his two Godzilla offerings.

As for Nakano's werewolf effects, for his Wolf Guy form, actor Shigaki merely wears a mask, albeit a well-constructed one made with real Siberian wolf fur.[5] However, though well-constructed the mask looks more like a Japanese theater mask, or something from Daiei's yokai films and lacks any sense of realism. More effective than anything else are the eyes, which glow blue in the dark. For his full wolf form, a German Shepard was used and for close up shots a hand puppet with light up eyes was used. Like the mask, if one takes a good long look at it, it's not terribly realistic. But then again, Japanese special effects don't aim for realism and furthermore, the film itself is surreal. The gang members polish their samurai swords in the middle of class and throw knives at Inugami like normal kids would throw spitballs. Inugami also lives in an office building and whenever Kiko goes to visit him there, they are magically transported to a beautiful green field where they bound about in happiness.[6]

Inugami only transforms into his wolf form twice, once at his home with Kiko and lastly during the climax where he must rescue Kiko who has been brutally beaten and raped. The editing (by Isao Takeda) at least makes the climax rather than breaks it—a hard feat considering the limited ability of both the wolf puppet and the German Shepard itself. This climax also points out a rather large plot hole: we are reminded time and time again that Inugami's wolf family was slaughtered with machine gun spray. But Inugami himself seems invincible, as he survives multiple gunshots and deep sword cuts gushing Nakano's fake blood all the while. Actually, he gets impaled on Do's sword while in his human form. At that moment he finally reveals his wolf form to Do, grabs him, and then impales him on the same sword, killing him. It is after this that a group of yakuza thugs come onto the scene and a weakened Inugami goes full werewolf on them via the German Shephard double.

The reason the film was never released in the U.S. can probably be attributed to the content of its climax. As it is, there is too much nudity and gore during crucial story moments which, if cut out, would make the film incoherent. Plus, with a scant 83-minute run time, there wouldn't have been a great deal left of the film when it was cut. In fact, this film is even bloodier than the Bloodthirsty trilogy, and that includes the entry produced after this film in 1974. Actually, with its yakuza villain and abundant, exploitive nudity and gore, this seems more like something that rival studio Toei would have produced rather than Toho.[7]

Toho completests, as well as those who love seventies era cinematography and directorial touches, will still find this film worth a watch.

Chapter Notes

1 Supposedly the high school age for the character came about due to the recent popularity of Spider-Man.

2 Hirai is perhaps best known as the co-creator of the manga superhero *8-Man* with artist Jiro Kuwata.

3 This was the debut film of Yusaku Matsuda as Do. He would later go on to star as the villain in Ridley Scott's *Black Rain* (1989).

4 Speaking of *Godzilla vs. Megalon*, the actor who played the Seatopian agent—Kotaro Tomita—also has a minor role in this film.

5 Supposedly each strand of fur was interwoven into the mask.

6 Reportedly this scene was not in the shooting script and was a directorial decision.

7 Speaking of Toei, in 1975 Toei produced what some call an unofficial sequel to this film called *Wolf Guy*. Whether it's intended to be in continuity with *Horror of the Wolf* is debatable, but it is based upon the same *Wolf Guy* manga characters, only grown up. Sonny Chiba played Akira Inugami this time around and as is to be expected with a mid-1970s Toei film is incredibly violent. Chiba never does turn into a wolf though and basically just has super strength and healing powers. Unlike *Horror of the Wolf*, it has been released to Blu-ray in the U.S.

19.
THE HUMAN TORCH

Intended Release Date: 1974
First Draft Date: January 31, 1974

Screenplay by: Masahiro Makoto **Producers:** Tomoyuki Tanaka & Fumio Tanaka **Proposed Director:** Jun Fukuda **Proposed Cast/Characters:** Chihiro Kurokawa [photographer, eldest daughter], Masahiko Sugiyama [Ryuko Kurokawa's fiancé], Takeshi Kurokawa [head of Kurokawa family], Mizutani [Kurokawa family servant], Takizawa [Kurokawa family secretary], Yuko Kurokawa [third oldest daughter], Junko Kurokawa [youngest daughter], Ryuko Kurokawa [second oldest daughter], Yoshiko Kurokawa [Takeshi's second wife], Genosuke [Kurokawa family servant], Maki [family doctor]

SYNOPSIS Chihiro, the eldest of her wealthy father's four daughters, returns home for her sister Ryuko's wedding. The union will join her wealthy coal family with that of Masahiko Sugiyama, heir to another wealthy coal family. On her wedding night, Ryuko is killed in a mysterious accident. Chihiro and Sugiyama both believe there is foul play involved and begin an investigation into her death. Soon the Kurokawa mansion is beset by fiery accidents that take the lives of Chihiro's half-sister, Yuko, and step-mother, Yoshiko. During the accidents a flame-bodied human is sighted within the mansion. The flame human turns out to be Chihiro's hidden half-brother, Mizutani, the family servant who shares the same mother with her. Mizutani doesn't wish to harm Chihiro, but will still kill her only remaining half-sister, Junko, just to punish their father, Takeshi Kurokawa, who had his first wife murdered while she was pregnant with Mizutani. Sugiyama, Chihiro, and Junko, escape the house as it bursts into flames killing Takeshi.

COMMENTARY In the late 1950s and early 1960s, Toho had three major sci-fi genres they dabbled in. There were giant monster films like *Rodan* (1956) and *Mothra* (1961), there were space-based sci-fi spectacles like *The Mysterians* (1957) and *Gorath* (1962), and then there were Toho's mutant human films like *Invisible Avenger* (1954), *The Secret of the Telegian* (1960), and *Matango* (1963). Supposedly

107

it was the failure of *Matango* that soured Toho on any further mutant films. However, in the early 1970s, movies like *The H-Man* (1958) were garnering high ratings when airing on television. Tomoyuki Tanaka noticed this and in June of 1973 announced plans for a new slate of "Strange Human Sci-Fi Series". Immediately, plans were thrown around for a new invisible man and also a "plant man", which apparently never got past the story pitch stage.

The first of the "Strange Human Sci-Fi Series" to be developed was *The Human Torch*. Its first treatment was rather different from the script and revolved around Toyo Industries, a developer of scientific drugs. In addition to a mysterious flame human, the story centered around family politics within the company, with two brothers vying for control of their father's legacy. Also present in this treatment is a scene where a dead body is consumed by flames within a casket and disappears—a scene that would make its way into the script. The main story elements from the treatment would carry over into the script but with some differences. This new story revolved around family politics and siblings vying for control of their father's company but in this case, it is four sisters rather than two brothers. And, instead of an urban drug company, it is a coal company located in a rural area that is the focus of the power struggle.

The story would have begun with a fairly lengthy pre-credits sequence and the first shot would have been of a lonely train traveling through some spooky woods. On board is a beautiful young woman, Chihiro, a photographer and potential heiress to a huge coal empire. She gets off in a rundown rural area in the forest of Japan where her family has a large coal mine and an estate. There to pick her up is her family's manservant Mizutani, unbeknownst to her the mysterious flame human (and her half-brother) which will torment her family over the course of the story.

Chihiro arrives at her family's luxurious mansion for her sister's wedding and, like many films of the era, information and exposition is divulged to the audience through some of Chihiro's inner monologues as she is reunited with various family members. Among the more prominent characters are Chihiro's father, Takeshi, who remarried long ago after Chihiro's mother died. Chihiro also has a step mother, Yoshiko, and three half-sisters: Ryuko, Yoko, and Junko. Ryuko is set to marry a large coal magnate, Sugiyama, effectively joining two coal empires together. The wedding features a scene that had played out in many a horror film before it. In it, a drunken older family member barges in on the ceremony, shouting about the Kurokawa family being under a curse due to the actions of the family patriarch, Takeshi. A rush of wind hits the shutters and lightning strikes outside. That night, a candle in Ryuko's room mysteriously manages to burn through a rope that tethers an ornamental dragon to the ceiling. The rope breaks, and the dragon falls from the ceiling, killing Ryuko. This cues the opening credits, set to appear onscreen in a fiery manner, which continue to roll over the girl's funeral procession in the woods.

This sets off the main mystery of the film, with a painting by the deceased Ryuko playing a key role in the investigation. Actually, many elements of the story are reminiscent of *Night of Dark Shadows* (1971) which involved supernatural happenings at a spooky estate and mysterious oil paintings. Also, unlike Toho's mutant human films of the 50s/60s, this mutant human is the result of the supernatural rather than science gone awry. This makes sense, as in the late 1950s science was all the rage but by 1973, occult horror films (kicked off by *The Exorcist*'s monumental success) were very popular. In this story, the flame human is speculated to be related to an old legend based upon coal workers, whose bodies became so saturated with the material that they could catch fire themselves. Even though the story is based in the supernatural, there is still one scene set in a laboratory that features scientific testing and exposition typical of Toho films. In it, Sugiyama demonstrates how with the right chemicals, a small fire can be generated on the skin without actually burning.

The story does a good job of keeping you guessing who the flame human is. Sister Yoko would seem to be a prime candidate at first, as she is presented with no sympathetic qualities whatsoever. In fact, she is so jealous of Chihiro that she tries to kill her at one point. When the family doctor mentions she has schizophrenia this would seem to be a clear indicator that she will be the culprit. Then, imagine the surprise when Yuko ends up dead herself due to a gas leak. Another candidate is Shunsuke Kurokawa, the crazy old uncle who interrupts the wedding and seems to know more than he lets on. That the flame human turns out to be Mizutani is quite a surprise, as is the fact that he is Chihiro's secret half-brother! The only time that Mizutani drops a hint that he may be the flame human is when he tells Chihiro that she should leave back to Tokyo—and unbeknownst to us he is really trying to protect her. Actually, one could begin to think Mizutani has a romantic attraction to Chihiro, which is cleverly misleading on the part of the writer.

Though meant to relaunch Toho's mutant human films, in reality *The Human Torch* had more in common with the Bloodthirsty trilogy—three vampire films directed by Michio Yamamoto and written by Ei Ogawa that began with *The Vampire Doll* in 1970. It's presumable Toho had ideas of reusing some of the sets from the Bloodthirsty trilogy set to conclude that same year with *The Bloodsucking Rose*. In any case, the Kurokawa family mansion is described as looking like a medieval castle on the inside, with high ceilings, pillars, and red carpet. The flame human's origin story is better handled than those in the Bloodthirsty trilogy, which often came across as lazy, last minute exposition. Here, it is revealed that Chihiro's mother became pregnant—presumably by another man— and Takeshi lit her on fire![1] When the family servant, Genosuke, is sent to clean up her remains, he is astonished to find a baby boy amongst the ashes! He then takes the boy and raises it as one of the household servants.

Though it's uncertain how the flame human would have been brought to life, the story seems to be plotted rather conservatively. Actually, the script is made up of only 86 scenes, whereas usually Toho fantasy scripts were made up of at least well over 100 scenes. The main effects sequences naturally all involve the flame human, and the most memorable probably would have been when the flame human envelops a casket in flames and incinerates the dead body inside during Yoko's wake! Another visually stimulating scene had the flame human materializing out of a fire place to terrorize Yoshiko. Just when we think the flame human will kill the sympathetic Junko, a trap has been set for him that freezes him. Presumed dead, Mizutani is buried in a makeshift grave. But just as Chihiro, Junko, and Sugiyama are about to escape, the "dead" Mizutani's hand rises out of the ground during a thunderstorm. The ending is simplistic and reminiscent of many Hammer horror films where the house/castle burns down with the monster inside. Actually, it's quite similar to the climax of the same year's eventually-produced *ESPY*, which ended with a mansion burning down.

Though written by Masahiro Kakefuda, it is thought that the intended director, Jun Fukuda, had a hand in the story process due to themes present in the story that were also prevalent in episodes of *Strange Campaign*[2] written by Fukuda. The stories for the series involved political struggles amongst family members within large companies. In any case, writer Kakefuda would eventually become known for writing the *Sister Streetfighter* films for Toei, in addition to Toei's trucker movies directed by Norofumi Suzuki. Before this, Kakefuda had written the infamous horror/exploitation film *Horror of the Malformed Men* (1969) among many other screenplays. According to the book *Toho Special Effects Movie Complete Works*, Kakefuda was also offered the chance to work on a Godzilla film at some point but declined.

Just why *The Human Torch* script was passed over is unknown because it was very well-written and seemed doable from a financial standpoint. It's possible that the failure of the gothic flavored *The Bloodsucking Rose*, released in July of 1974, soured Toho on similar films in the future. Others simply speculate the film got lost in the shuffle, as Jun Fukuda was busy in 1974 directing two major films: *Godzilla vs. Mechagodzilla* and *ESPY*—a film that may have replaced *The Human Torch* in the Toho lineup.[3] In any case, it's a shame the film was never made and whether or not it relaunched a new era of Toho mutant films will remain a mystery.

Chapter Notes

[1] Due to translation issues, this author was never able to discern who Mizutani's father was, or if the pregnancy was the result of an affair or rape.

[2] A 1968–1969 Tsuburaya Productions TV series.

[3] *ESPY*'s Japanese Wikipedia page says that *Invisible Man vs. the Human Torch* was delayed due to the production of *ESPY*. As the first draft for that film is listed as being from 1975, more likely it was the original *Human Torch* that was delayed due to the production of *ESPY*.

20.
THE DEVELOPMENT OF
ESPY

Alternate Titles: *E.S.P./Spy* (U.S.)
Release Date: December 28, 1974

Directed by: Jun Fukuda **Special Effects by:** Teruyoshi Nakano
Screenplay by: Ei Ogawa **Music by:** Masaaki Hirao **Cast:** Hiroshi
Fujioka (Yoshio Tamura), Kaoru Yumi (Maria Harada), Masao
Kusakari (Jiro Miki), Tomisaburo Wakayama (Ulrov), Katsumasa
Uchida (Goro Tatsumi), Yuzo Kayama (Houjo), Goro Mutsumi
(Teraoka), Eiji Okada (Salabad), Andrew Hughes (ESPY International
Manager)

Cinemascope, Eastmancolor, 94 Minutes

SYNOPSIS Yoshio Tamura and Maria Harada are two of the top
members of ESPY, a secret government agency comprised of psychic
spies. To stop an assassination attempt on the Baltonian Prime
Minister by the evil Counter-ESPY organization ran by Ulrov, they
recruit the help of psychic race car driver Jiro Miki. It is Ulrov's hope
that the assassination will incite World War III, and to deal with the
agents of ESPY, he sends psychic assassin Goro Tatsumi to take
care of them. After defeating Goro and thwarting the assassination
via Yoshio's new ability to teleport, together the trio track Ulrov to
his castle where he is defeated once and for all.

COMMENTARY The end of 1974 marked another Sakyo Komatsu-
induced New Year's hit for Toho. Though it's easy to presume that
after the astronomical success of *Submersion of Japan* Tomoyuki
Tanaka immediately set out to find another Komatsu property to
adapt, this isn't entirely the case. To be precise, Sakyo Komatsu's
Esupai (or a spy with ESP) was a manga first serialized in *Weekly
Manga Sunday* back in 1964, and the film rights were acquired by
Toho and announced for production in February of 1966 with
intentions to release the film in 1967. It was planned to be produced
along with *The Flying Battleship* in 1967 with Jun Fukuda directing
a script written by Ei Ogawa. And, with the Japanese-themed James

Bond film *You Only Live Twice* slated for release that same year, 1967 seemed a prime time to produce *ESPY*.

The first problem with the 1967 *ESPY* emerged when the proposed film's hopeful starlet, Akiko Wakabayashi (Aki, the ill-fated Bond girl in *You Only Live Twice*), was leaving Toho at the time.[1] The other proposed actors for *ESPY* had been Tatsuya Mihashi (1970's *Tora! Tora! Tora!* and "Phil Moscowitz" in Woody Allen's *What's Up Tiger Lily?*), Makoto Sato (Uchida in *The H-Man*), and Mie Hama (Madame Piranha in *King Kong Escapes* and Kissy Suzuki in *You Only Live Twice*). In addition to the casting woes with Wakabayashi, the Toho crew soon found themselves preoccupied with prepping *Latitude Zero*, which turned into a disaster of sorts from start to finish. *ESPY*, it would seem, was lost in the shuffle until 1973 when Komatsu's *Submersion of Japan* turned into the biggest Japanese hit of the decade. However, that wasn't the only reason why interest in the film was rekindled. A visit to Japan by famed psychic Uri Geller in 1974 also struck a fire under Toho to dust off the mothballs from Ogawa's *ESPY* script.

Producer Fumio Tanaka shed some light on this process when asked about *ESPY* by David Milner in 1995:

David Milner: When was the script for *ESPY* written?

Fumio Tanaka: The screenplay was based on a novel by Sakyo Komatsu. Toho purchased rights to the novel shortly after its publication, which was in the mid-1960s, and then commissioned a script. It was forgotten about until [*Submersion of Japan*], which was based on another of Mr. Komatsu's novels, was released. The great success of that movie made Toho's executives want to base another film on one of Mr. Komatsu's novels. There was a great deal of interest in E.S.P. in the early 1970s. That also prompted Toho to produce *ESPY* when it did. I remember that the pages of the screenplay were already beginning to turn yellow when I read it.[2]

Initially Toei's Masahiro Kakefuda (having just written *The Human Torch* for Toho) wrote another version of the script in 1974, but it was overhauled by the original writer, Ei Ogawa, before shooting.[3] Producer Fumio Tanaka said to Guy Tucker that budgetary constraints forced some changes to be made. "For example, the hideout of the villain originally was going to be a satellite in orbit instead of a mansion in the mountains." In fact, this satellite remains on the release poster! Apparently, in the original 1967 script the villain, Ulrov, was an alien that lived in a satellite, which Yoshio would teleport himself to for the climax.[4]

On top of this, some of the character names were changed from the manga. For instance, Maria Tosti from the manga became Maria Harada. Added into the film version was a character that didn't even appear in the manga (or the 1967 script), Jiro Miki—a race car driver (initially just a college student rather than a racer)—and ESP International's newest recruit just discovering his abilities. Ulrov's alien aspect was done away with completely to become an ESP-enhanced human bent on avenging the death of his father. Furthermore, in one draft, Ulrov was called Linz (who claimed to have the abilities of Buddha) and hailed from Armenia. The Prime Minister in Ulrov's crosshairs was not from the fictional Baltonia but China. The final draft was close to the finished film and the only notable scene cut was Ulrov executing one of his operatives, Judy, inside his western-style estate. This makes sense, as in the finished film Judy mysteriously disappears. Another cut scene would have featured actress Linda Blair. While promoting *The Exorcist* in Japan in July of 1974, Toho reached out to her with an offer to appear in the film. Blair was interested, but her agent advised her against it.[5]

Though director Jun Fukuda was planning to film *The Human Torch* around this time, that project was shelved—forever as it turned out—in favor of the *ESPY* revival. After directing three straight Godzilla movies, Jun Fukuda seemed skeptical of the project initially, though *ESPY* was given a higher budget than his Godzilla features. Despite being an ambitious production, filming lasted only one month.

With his background in action, notably the two James Bond-inspired *100 Shot, 100 Killed* films of the late sixties, Fukuda was the perfect director for *ESPY*. Like a Bond film, *ESPY* begins with pre-title scene wherein Katsumasa Uchida (later Murakoshi in *Terror of Mechagodzilla*) assassinates four men in a swiftly-moving train in Switzerland. And like the Bond films, on-location filming was done in Istanbul, the Swiss Alps, and Paris by assistant director Kenjiro Omori.[6] Ulrov even has a Blofeld-like lair in a huge, western style gothic mansion.

Said mansion is decked out with an assortment of medieval booby traps that cause the heroes much trouble during the climax. As Ulrov uses telekinesis to throw spears and chandeliers at the heroes—and in particular, nearly murders Maria—Tamura finally sets Ulrov on fire using the fireplace, burning him to a crisp. Nakano's mansion miniature then explodes fantastically as the heroes escape. Apparently the house was meant to merely burn, but too much gunpowder was used and so the miniature exploded into nothing. Actually, the fiery climax is enough to make one wonder if some prep work had already commenced for *The Human Torch*, either the set or the pyrotechnic effects themselves. If nothing else, this ending could have been lifted from the aforementioned script, written by Masahiro Kakefuda who also did a draft of this film.[7] In *The Human Torch*, the script ends with a western-style estate much like this one burning to the ground.

The special effects department certainly had their hands full with this film. There are many composite shots demonstrating the agents' ESP abilities similar to shots of cyborg girl Katsura Mafune's eyes in *Terror of Mechagodzilla* (1975). Apparently, creating these scenes were very "trial and error" for the effects department. There is one scene involving miniatures set on a jumbo airliner, which looks good enough when it is flying at normal speed but becomes clunky when it accelerates too fast and almost crashes into some rocky mountains. Other than the constraints of the time though, the scene is exciting overall as Tamura must fly the jet through the mountains when the pilots (one of whom is *Godzilla vs. Megalon's* Robert Dunham) become hypnotized by a magnetic storm created by Counter-ESPY.

Most of Nakano's effects work is constrained to blood and gore, though. Several men are dramatically blown apart by massive shotgun blasts midway through the film in an action scene set in Switzerland. The climax naturally features some interesting effects shots as well. As the Prime Minister of Baltonia gives his speech, Ulrov makes the audience hallucinate that the building is collapsing in an earthquake.[8] Meanwhile, Tamura is locked in a car about to explode but once he senses that his friends are in danger, suddenly succeeds in teleporting out of the car (an ability he'd been trying to accomplish through the film) as it explodes and delivers a flying body slam to Goro, saving the day. Apparently a variety of unspecified effects techniques were experimented with until one of them proved satisfactory for this scene.

The film's most notorious scene takes place in Istanbul's red light district where Maria is psychically forced to strip for the patrons with a captured Tamura forced to watch. Believe it or not, the erotic dance scene was from the original manga and not cooked up for the film version. When one of Ulrov's goons attempts to kiss her, Tamura psychically rips his tongue out! Naturally, this scene was removed from the American version as is the bloody beating Tamura receives on Ulrov's's yacht directly after. In true Bond fashion, when Tamura refuses to join Counter-ESPY, he is shackled to several cannon balls and thrown overboard. As he sinks to the depths, he is saved by fellow agents of ESPY who take him to a nearby submarine.

As Toho's New Year's release for 1974, the film is a quality production through and through. Returning from *Submersion of Japan* is Hiroshi Fujioka, and from *Great Prophecies of Nostradamus* Kaoru Yumi.[9] From the two Mechagodzilla films are Goro Mutsumi and Katsumasa Uchida. As for Masao Kusakari (Jiro Miki), he was a popular TV star at the time. As stated earlier, Fukuda's direction is spectacular and Masaaki Hirao's score matches it well, making for a very enjoyable 70s-era action film.

Though the film was a resounding success as the second-highest grossing Japanese film of that year (after *Great Prophecies of Nostradamus*, bringing in ¥827,896,000), author Sakyo Komatsu was somewhat displeased with the effort.[10] Unfortunately, no sequels were ever produced, nor has there ever been a remake.

Chapter Notes

[1] When Wakabayashi's contract with Toho lapsed she chose not to renew and production was shut down indefinitely.

[2] www.davmil.org/www.kaijuconversations.com/tanak.htm

[3] There was hope Komatsu would author the script but he did not.

[4] This aspect was cut by Tomoyuki Tanaka himself. However, there's a throwaway line at the end that perhaps Ulrov was possessed by some evil power, maybe one "not of this earth" that makes no sense in the finished film.

[5] *The Japanese Fantasy Film Journal* #11.

[6] In watching the film this is apparent, as the actors are only seen in close-ups during on-location scenes. There were also many recreations in Japan, such as Yatsugatake Takahara in Nagano Prefecture which stood in for Switzerland.

[7] As stated earlier, the original script for *ESPY* from 1967 had Ulrov living in a satellite in space. It was likely Kakefuda in his 1974 rewrite of Ogawa's script that added in the mansion.

[8] The scene was filmed using Toho stages 8 and 9, apparently two of their bigger studio buildings.

[9] Reportedly Komatsu wanted Yumi in *Submersion of Japan*, so her casting in this film was per his wishes.

[10] In *Science Fiction Studies* #88, Komatsu remarked that, "...the rights to [buy] *ESPY* were half a million yen [for Toho]. But it earned 2 billion!" (laughs)

21.
INVISIBLE MAN VS. THE HUMAN TORCH

Intended Release Date: 1976
Draft Dates: May 5, 1975 (first draft script); October 24, 1975
(second draft script)

Screenplay by: Masahiro Kakefuda & Jun Fukuda (second draft only) **Producers:** Tomoyuki Tanaka & Fumio Tanaka **Proposed Director:** Jun Fukuda **Proposed Cast/Characters:** Shiro Saijo [detective/ invisible man], Koichi Shimada [research engineer/flame human], Taeko [Shimada's wife], Yoshiro Iwakura [President of Iwakura Co., Ltd.], Kajiura [Iwakura's assistant], Tsukisaka [Club owner], Tachibana [Club manager], Anesaki [gangster boss], Marumi [gangster boss], Sachiko Kagawa [Anesaki's employee], Teranishi [Saijo's partner]

SYNOPSIS When chasing down a group of bank robbers into a chemical plant, Detective Shiro Saijo falls into a radioactive cyclotron. When Saijo awakens from his accident, he discovers that he has the ability to turn himself invisible. Soon after, Saijo's best friend from high school, Koichi Shimada, has died in a fiery car crash. Saijo investigates the accident and discovers Shimada was killed by the mob. Soon, the mobsters are killed off one by one by a mysterious flame human. At the scene of one of the killings, Saijo finds an old lighter of Shimada's and takes it to Shimada's wife, Taeko, who confirms that it is his. Saijo stakes out a gangster club and manages to confirm Shimada is the flame human in question. As Shimada gets into a getaway car with an accomplice, Saijo shoots the driver in the arm. Later, Saijo is shocked to see Taeko with an injured arm. Saijo learns Taeko not only knew Shimada was alive, but was working with him to kill Shimada's boss, Iwakura, who is also Taeko's uncle. As it turns out, Iwakura burned Shimada's father alive years ago and also killed Taeko's father. Saijo begs the couple to let him arrest Iwakura, but they refuse and go after him themselves. Iwakura has developed a new flame gun that can harm the seemingly indestructible Shimada. However, when Iwakura fires the gun at Shimada, his wife Taeko takes the blow. Saijo shows up in the chaos and also saves Shimada's life, but soon the duo again

117

begin to fight. After Iwakura has been killed, Saijo fears Shimada's bloodlust will lead him to kill others and so shoots Shimada with the special flame gun, effectively killing him.

COMMENTARY Despite deciding not to produce *The Human Torch* in 1974, the very next year, Jun Fukuda was busy prepping another mutant human film, *Invisible Man vs. the Human Torch*. Actually, according to Fukuda in an interview with David Milner of *Cult Movies*, it would seem the film began developing long before 1975, and may have been some sort of quasi-sequel to 1960's *The Secret of the Telegian*:

> **David Milner:** Why wasn't the sequel to *The Secret of the Telegian, Transparent Man Against Flame Man*, [what Milner calls *Invisible Man vs. the Human Torch*] produced?
> **Jun Fukuda:** The script wasn't accepted. The film wasn't as successful as Toho had hoped it would be. That's why the sequel wasn't produced.
> **DM:** In what year was the sequel written?
> **JF:** It was written four or five years after *The Secret of the Telegian* was released.
> **DM:** Do you remember anything about the plot?
> **JF:** I just remember that the transparent man was pitted against a flame man.

Taking Fukuda's word to heart, this would mean that this script was written in 1964 or 1965. If this is true, it's possible *The Human Torch* was written in 1974 as a way to precede the 1975 version of *Invisible Man vs. the Human Torch*. Or, as was often the case with directors, Fukuda had simply gotten his dates mixed up. However, others simply consider *Invisible Man vs. the Human Torch* to be a second draft of *The Human Torch*. If so, this likely implies that Tomoyuki Tanaka felt the Mutant Human series would be of more interest if two mutants battled one another.

It's hard to say if *Invisible Man vs. the Human Torch* is better than *The Human Torch*, because both certainly have their merits. Overall, *Invisible Man vs. the Human Torch* is essentially a dark, gritty Yakuza film with sci-fi elements. The first such scene occurs when Saijo discovers his newfound powers when he wakes up bandaged in the hospital. As he begins to take off the bandages, he is horrified to see his hand is gone. As he takes off more bandages he can no longer see his body in the mirror. A nurse walks in to see an empty pile of bandages on the floor and runs off to get help. In the interim, Saijo rematerializes (likely naked) and in walks the hospital staff to scold him for being out of bed.

However, as the script progresses there are numerous gritty deaths thanks to the flame human. The flame human's first scene occurs in a boiler room, where he materializes and strangles a gangster with his flaming hands. Saijo finds the man's charred body. Later, as more mob men fear for their lives, Shimada appears with blazing eyes, and bullets have no effect upon him. This scene playing out in a club is likely a nod to *The H-Man* or *The Secret of the Telegian*. As the flame human runs away, the script describes him as casting a huge, monstrous shadow on an alley wall. In another scene, it would seem that the flame human causes a gas main to explode and in the process, one of the gangster's limbs is blown off.[1]

That the "dead" Shimada is the flame human is hinted at throughout the script, but this isn't confirmed until a little over halfway through. The biggest hint is planted in a scene where a lighter with Shimada's initials are found at a crime scene where the flame human was sighted. Saijo takes the lighter to Taeko who confirms she bought the lighter for Shimada on a trip to Sweden. Shimada's origin is somewhat hard to figure out, though perhaps this author merely missed something in translation. As far as I can tell, the only mention of how Shimada transformed himself was through a strange machine in his basement, which is seen once and mentioned a few times. The only explanation for this is that Shimada was an engineer for Iwakura Co., Ltd. However, our introduction to Shimada in the story is through a newspaper article explaining his death. We never see him working in a lab for Iwakura Company or know what he really does. Perhaps these issues would have been addressed in the next drafts had the scripts progressed.

The biggest problem with the whole script may well be the origins of the two mutant humans which are never adequately explained enough. In Saijo's case, the fact that he fell into a cyclotron seems to be enough information for the audience as to why he is invisible.[2] Furthermore, it is Saijo's prescription drugs for his injury that cause him to disappear and he is unable to turn invisible without them. There isn't even a single scene of Saijo consulting a scientist friend to explain his transformation. However, this is only a minor quibble compared to the lack of emphasis on Shimada's origin. The story might have been better to make Shimada's flame powers supernatural and tie them in with his father's horrific death. At one point, Shimada has a line about having "already died once" and "having been to hell"—whether these lines were meant to be metaphorical or literal is unknown.

That being said, there are some carryovers from the 1974 *Human Torch* script in regards to the origins of the flame human. In that script, there is talk of men who worked in the coal mines for so long that their skin became saturated with coal to the point that their skin became flammable.[3] This same theory is postulated in this script and a similar scientific exposition scene takes place. Here, Ota, a lab tech, shows Saijo how one can light their skin on fire with the right chemicals and not get burned.

As for the invisible man, there are naturally several well done scenes that showcase his powers. There is a suspenseful scene where Saijo is bound and tied to a chair. On the floor before him are the scattered contents of his jacket pocket. He spies his medicine from the hospital, which he has not been taking for fear of disappearing again. As he hears footsteps fast approaching, Saijo rocks his chair onto the ground and laps up one of the pills with his tongue. He disappears right before the men open the door. The invisible Saijo, who has managed to wiggle free of the ropes, then proceeds to beat the frightened goons. One of the coolest scenes has Saijo approaching the gangsters in classic invisible man garb: a trench coat and bandages, which he slowly peels off one by one until he is invisible. He keeps smoking his cigarette however, which he puts out on one of the thug's faces (why he was wearing the trench coat and bandages, other than to make a cool visual entrance for the audience, really makes no sense).

Overall, the script is full of 70s tropes that nostalgia buffs would love. There are the overly dramatic happy flashbacks to Shimada and Saijo playing football together (and presumably running and laughing in slow motion). There are colorful gangster characters, such as Tsukisaka, owner of the "Oriental Club," who has a glass eye. The action scenes also have a style and flare to them that are distinctly 1970s. There is a well-described scene where Saijo spots an attacker approaching from behind through his reflection in a glass bottle. And like any good crime noir film, there are twists galore. For instance, though it's no big surprise that Shimada is the flame human, it is a big surprise that his grieving wife was in on the secret all along.

A crucial scene plays out in the third act between Taeko and Saijo. It occurs right after Shimada and Saijo have been fighting and Shimada escapes by jumping into the water and swimming away. Taeko pulls up in her car next to Saijo, who proceeds to tell her that he thinks Shimada only married her to get close to her uncle, Iwakura, to kill him. Taeko then surprises Saijo by telling him that she knows this because she also wants to kill her uncle as he had killed her father. Saijo warns her that he overheard Iwakura saying he has invented a new gun that can kill Shimada so he must arrest Iwakura to save Shimada's life. Taeko argues against this and says, "If a man lives for nothing other than revenge, if you take that from him, he will be left with nothing." Saijo won't relent and says he is going to arrest Iwakura. Taeko then slips a pistol from her overcoat and shoots Saijo in the arm before she disappears into the fog.

In another surprise twist, just when we think Taeko has killed Iwakura sleeping in his bed, a whip strikes the gun from out of her hand. Iwakura steps from out of the shadows, saying he suspected her of trying to kill him all along. This brings the onset of the climax which has Shimada walking into a trap to rescue Takeo at Iwakura's mansion. In a scene that surely would have been wonderfully directed by Fukuda, Shimada walks into an underground entrance to the mansion with his eyes blazing in the dark. He then proceeds to kill Iwakura's guards, but Iwakura is able to wound Shimada with the special fire gun. Taeko jumps in front of Shimada just as Iwakura is about to deliver a death blow to his chest and dies on the spot. Cut to outside the mansion, where footprints can be seen in the sand one by one and we know that Saijo is entering the scene. A guard dog attacks the invisible Saijo who dispatches him easily and makes his way downstairs where he saves Shimada from Iwakura. However, staying true to the title, the duo don't join forces but rather begin to fight one another again! It seems Saijo is as dead set on arresting Iwakura as Shimada is on killing him. Shimada backs Iwakura into an electrical transformer and fries him. Strangely, instead of letting his old friend go, now that he has sated his revenge, Saijo tries to arrest Shimada.

The climax, due to the shoddy translation, is hard to decipher. On the one hand, it would seem to make Saijo a rather stiff, unlikeable character, determined to arrest his friend who only wanted to avenge a tragedy. So perhaps something was lost in translation? In any case, Saijo is forced to shoot Shimada with the special fire gun when Shimada seems to threaten Saijo's fellow policemen who arrive on the scene. Shimada burns into nothing, and the last shot was to be of a depressed Saijo walking into the sunrise.

However, the ending described in the above paragraph is apparently the one from the first draft script. The book *Toho Special Effects Movie Complete Works* says that Jun Fukuda revised the story in the second draft which did away with the special fire gun and had Shimada and Saijo team up to take down the villain.[4]

Toho actually had ideas of producing the film as the 1970s wore on but the difficulties with *Nessie* apparently lead to the film's official cancellation. Before that, the film was announced in the 1976 Toho lineup with this tagline: "Strange human series first bulletin! Wrapping the whole body with a flame of grudge one after another brutal revenge! A detective who became a transparent human in a cyclotron follows!"

The final nail in the film's coffin likely occurred when Toho begat plans to revive Godzilla in 1978. There are also theories that the hard-boiled film was considered to anchor a Champion Matsuri Festival until it was decided the film was too adult in nature.

Chapter Notes

[1] As always though, take that with a grain of salt translation issues being what they are.

[2] The cyclotron isn't described very well, but the script describes Saijo falling down "to the bottom of an endless pure white abyss" and then the titles would begin to roll.

[3] That's not to say Shimada is said to be descended from coal miners, just that the legend of coal miners whose skin became flammable was repeated here.

[4] *Toho Tokusatsu Unpublished Works* only prints out the first draft unfortunately. This author has never seen the second draft revised by Fukuda.

THE DISASTER FILMS OF TOHO STUDIOS

THE LAST WAR (1961) *The Last War's* development is a complicated one, and in fact, precedes a similar developmental process that would happen with 1973's *Submersion of Japan*. As it happened, Tomoyuki Tanaka took note of a story entitled "41 Hours of the First World War III" that had appeared in the *Weekly Shincho* and wished to adapt it into a film. The only problem was Toei Studios beat him to the punch in grabbing up the film rights. It would seem that a script was written before this was known, because the first draft of *The Last War* is remarkably similar to Toei's *The Final War* (for these similarities see *The Final War* pages 54-57). Specifically, the script was written July 29, 1960, by Shinobu Hashimoto and Toshio Yasumi, and the film was approved for production at the Toho National Branch Chairperson's Board of Directors' meeting on August 8th. Only a few days earlier Toei had also had their shareholders meeting on the 6th where they announced production of their film, *The Final War*. The Mainichi Newspaper heard about the dueling projects and soon reported on the brewing competition between the two studios.

Toho called in several experts to help consult on the second draft of the script, including Nori University professor Keijiro Irie, a prominent authority on international law as well as Toshio Shinzo, a member of the New Interview Study Team and an expert on the military. The second draft was completed on August 11th, only three days after Toho announced the film for production. However, this draft was incredibly similar to Toei's, which claimed to have the blessing of the original author. Due to the similarities, Tanaka quit trying to beat Toei's release and had Yasumi and Hashimoto do a rewrite on the script to shake any similarities that could lead to legal action.

Another problem arose in the form of the original director, Hironobu Horikawa. The director had been invited to join the project via an urgent telegram from Toho while he was returning to his hometown of Kyoto. However, Horikawa balked at the number of effects sequences and Toho considered the effects scenes to be very important in lieu of *Mothra's* recent success. In fact, *Mothra* opened on July 31st of that year, right around the time that planning for *The Last War* was occurring. As such, Shue Matsubayashi was brought in as the new director.[1]

On September 2nd, Toshio Yasumi and Shinobu Hashimoto turned in a third draft script, which Toho President Iwao Mori feared was still too close to Toei's version and decided to stop production on September 7th. However, the project wasn't considered dead just yet. Yasumi, this time without Hashimoto, turned in a fourth draft script at an unknown date in 1961 as well as a fifth draft script. The sixth and final draft was turned in by Takeshi Kimura on June 26th so that production could finally commence. Though Toei's film had by this time been released more than 6 months ago, Toho had an edge in that their film would not only feature more effects scenes than Toei's, but also be filmed in color.

Eiji Tsuburaya's climax, where the entire world is consumed by nuclear war, is famous for its destruction of famous cities and landmarks, namely miniatures of Moscow, New York, Tokyo, London, and Paris.[2] To film these scenes, the miniatures—made of cake, a technique re-used for the destruction of the White House in *Independence Day*—were actually positioned upside down and then blown to bits with compressed air rather than gunpowder.[3] Being upside down, the debris naturally blew downwards, or rather upwards, on screen thanks to camera trickery. In all, Toho spent $830,000 on the miniature sets.

Amidst all the exploding landmarks, the film's strongest visual may actually be shots of charred bodies, whose ashy remains blow away in the wind—powerful and explicit imagery for 1961 (and strongly invoking memories of Hiroshima and Nagasaki). The film grossed ¥284,000,000 when released to Japanese theaters. In America, the film was released to theaters in 1965 through Brenco. The more well-known television version, cut down to only 79 minutes, made its way to television in 1967.[4]

GORATH (1962) Movies about giant asteroids have been a staple of disaster movies for many years and ironically, one of the pioneers of this genre was Toho itself. Even more ironic, perhaps, is that Toho's asteroid was itself monstrous compared to other celluloid asteroids. In fact, it wasn't a true asteroid at all, but a runaway planet![5]

It would seem that *Gorath* was influenced by *The Last War's* downbeat disaster motif and *Mothra's* fantasy elements. The initial idea was that of Jojiro Okami, who also did the story concepts for *The Mysterians* (1957), *Battle in Outer Space* (1959), and *Space Monster Dogora* (1964). Okami's original story pitch was entitled *Great Earth Modification*, after the effort to modify earth's orbit. Likewise the giant asteroid was originally named Lagos until Toho decided to rename it, discovering it was the name of a city in Nigeria. In the end, rather than moving the earth, the Japanese elite escape earth as the planet is destroyed.

124

Supposedly, Okami may have pitched the idea as far back as 1959, as *Toho Special Effects Movie Complete Works* says the developmental process of this film was three years! As was done with *The Mysterians* previously and *Atragon* the next year, Tomoyuki Tanaka insisted a monster be added to the film to spice up the picture. Takeshi Kimura initially added in a run-of-the-mill dinosaur until Ishiro Honda, reluctant to include monsters of any sort in the film, argued a dinosaur was too derivative of Godzilla and so the walrus Magma was created. If Tanaka had hoped the monster would boost the international appeal, it ironically ended up being cut out of the American version from Brenco entirely.

In an attempt to give the picture some scientific accuracy, Ishiro Honda and assistant director Koji Kajita went to the University of Tokyo's Faculty of Science to the Astronomy division. There, they consulted with various experts about how a star of Gorath's size would affect other celestial bodies and if it was remotely possible to alter the earth's orbit. The scientists, specifically Genichiro Hori, felt that moving the earth's orbit was theoretically possible, but did argue that if the moon was sucked into Gorath's orbit the Earth would be sucked in with it.[6] In order to make the earth modification plan seem more realistic, the story was set in the future of 1979 and 1980 (Christmas and New Year's occur in the story), 17 years from 1962.

The cast for the film was top-notch, including established actors such as Ryo Ikebe (*Battle in Outer Space*), Takashi Shimura (*Godzilla*), and Yumi Shirakawa (*Rodan*) along with "new faces" Akira Kubo and Kumi Mizuno who would go on to become big stars at Toho. Kenji Sahara, a favorite of Honda's, was almost cut out of the film and recast when he broke his leg during shooting, but Honda insisted no one else but Sahara play the role. Shooting lasted nearly a whole year at 300 days, 100 of which were allotted just for the special effects. Overall, the budget was said to be ¥380 million.

The giant pulsating Gorath star was made of acrylic with electric lights that caused it to generate with an angry, orange color. The earth modification scene was one of the more difficult ones to shoot and took Tsuburaya and his crew nearly three weeks according to Teruyoshi Nakano. The huge Antarctica set—where much of the ice was made of Styrofoam—was built inside Toho's Studio No. 8 which covered about 1,652 square meters. The polar rockets were huge and were fueled by a great deal of propane. Due to wind concerns, this sequence had to be filmed on an indoor set which made the studio very hot. Giant walrus Magma[7] was one of the poorer monster costumes created by Tsuburaya's effects department. Magma was inhabited by both Haruo Nakajima and Katsumi Tezuka in different shots.

The props from *Gorath* all had a great deal of longitude. The JX-1 and JX-2 spacecraft models created for this film would appear in several other productions including *Invasion of Astro-Monster* (1965), and even the TV series *Star Wolf* (1978). The space station prop reappeared in *Invasion of Astro-Monster* also. Magma was recycled as the new monster Todora in *Ultra Q* (1966) and almost returned as itself for *Destroy All Monsters* (1968) but didn't make the final roster. Remarkably, the Gorath prop survived for many years and was even used in Koichi Kawakita's *Super Star God* series of the 2000s!

Though it was a big hit, Toho's runaway success with *King Kong vs. Godzilla* later in 1962 would encourage the studio to focus most of their efforts on more giant monster movies, and less so on sci-fi epics like *Gorath*. The film would end up being Toho's last true disaster film for over ten years.

SUBMERSION OF JAPAN (1973) In 1964, novelist Sakyo Komatsu began work on his epic novel *Submersion of Japan*, which was finally completed and published on March 20, 1973 by Kobunsha Kappa in two volumes. The first print run was a smash success selling over 3 million copies, raking in ¥120,000,000. As always, there are alternating accounts of when and where Toho acquired the film rights to the book. One account states that Tomoyuki Tanaka had optioned it for film even before it was published, but the book *Japan Sinks 1973 Complete Documentation* would make it seem Tanaka read it the very day it was published and called Komatsu on the phone that evening! In an interview with *Science Fiction Studies*, Sakyo Komatsu explained that he felt a great deal of gratitude towards Toho for their kind treatment of him in the early 1960s when he was first starting out. "I felt so obligated that in 1973 when we were discussing a film version of *Japan Sinks*, I gave them the movie rights with almost no conditions. I think they paid 1.5 million yen."[8] Actually, before this, Toho's competitor Daiei almost produced the film first. In 1971, word of Komatsu's as yet unpublished novel reached the ears of someone at Daiei who proposed it to Masaichi Nagata, who announced production on *The Sinking of the Japanese Archipelago* without formally securing the rights from Komatsu![9] However, Daiei soon went bankrupt and the issue was moot.

Toho's intent to produce the film was announced in newspapers on May 24th with an expected start date in September. The plan at the time was to complete filming by January and have the film out in March of 1974. Also, one of the proposed directors was none other than Akira Kurosawa himself. At some point, Toho decided to make the film a New Year's release for that December instead, and also increased the film's budget in the process—the equivalent of $3

126

million, then a nearly unheard of cost for a Japanese feature! On June 18th, Shiro Moritani was announced as the chosen director and casting also began with popular *Kamen Rider* star Hiroshi Fujioka cast as Onodera. Despite author Komatsu's wishes to have Kaoru Yumi cast as Reiko, Ayumi Ishida got the part instead. Renowned actor Tetsuro Tamba (best known in the west for his role as Tiger Tanaka in *You Only Live Twice*) was cast as the Prime Minister Yamamoto. Author Komatsu would even cameo in an early scene between Onodera and Yoshimura, and Haruo Nakajima, recently retired from playing Godzilla, has a cameo as the Prime Minister's chauffeur.

Behind the scenes, the film featured a great deal of future talent that would one day go on to work on the Heisei and Millennium Godzilla movies. Assisting Teruyoshi Nakano with special effects was Koichi Kawakita (the Heisei Godzilla series special effects director) and Eiichi Asada (special effects director on the last two Millennium Godzilla films). As assistant director was Koji Hashimoto, who would himself helm a Komatsu disaster film of his own, *Sayonara Jupiter*, after Moritani's passing.

To give their film adaptation as much realism as possible, several authorities actually consulted on the film, among them geophysics expert Professor Hitoshi Takeuchi, seismic engineering professor Yorihiko Osaki, oceanography expert Professor Noriyuki Nasu, and volcanologist Akira Suwa, director of the Meteorological and Earthquake Research Institute. The film went through four script drafts in all. Second unit shooting began as early as late July/early August, and production officially began on September 1, 1973, not coincidentally, the 50th anniversary of the Great Kanto Earthquake.

Shooting was fairly brisk at only four months, especially considering Toho hoped to have the film out by December 22nd. Nakano began shooting the effects scenes on September 3rd with the early sequences set underwater regarding the sinking island and the miniature of the Wadatsumi submersible. As it turned out, this film would be considered by many to be his crowning achievement in special effects. Reportedly, the methods Nakano used to create the oil refinery explosion would actually be illegal under today's fire codes for film shooting! Reporters were invited to the set on September 22nd for the eruption of Mt. Fuji and also for the Tokyo earthquake scene on November 9th. The effects shooting was completed by December 3rd, and the principal photography on December 11th—only 11 days from when Toho originally intended to release the film. The release date was pushed back to December 29th and editing—by Japanese Oscar-winner Michiko Ikeda—began immediately after shooting wrapped. A test screening was held on the 22nd (the original release date) and the film successfully met its pushed back December 29th release date.

The film was a huge hit drawing in 8.8 million admissions making for a profit of ¥1.6 billion and was the most successful Japanese movie of the 1970s. As such, it became the highest grossing Toho film until the record was later broken by *Godzilla vs. Mothra* in 1992. Author Stuart Galbraith summarized it best in his book *Japanese Science Fiction, Fantasy and Horror Films* where he states, "It dramatized one of the most innate fears among Japanese citizens: the disastrous annihilation, natural or otherwise, of their vulnerable nation."[10] Nakano even won an award at the Asia Film Festival for his effects. After this, disaster films were Toho's go-to genre for big hits.

In America, Roger Corman's New World Pictures took note of *Submersion of Japan*'s potential as a disaster film in America and snatched it up.[11] Like *Godzilla, King of the Monsters!* and *Varan the Unbelievable* before it, new footage of an American star was added in to make the film more marketable in the U.S. Following this, Sakyo Komatsu's novel was translated into English and published in America as *Japan Sinks* in 1975 by the Michael Gallagher Company. But, like the movie, it actually cut about 1/3rd of the original's material.

GREAT PROPHECIES OF NOSTRADAMUS (1974) Either hot off the success of *Submersion of Japan*, or perhaps just anticipating it, Toho intended to copy the formula for the next year's blockbuster. In this case, Tomoyuki Tanaka optioned the rights to another hit disaster book, Tsutomu "Ben" Goto's *Great Prophecies of Nostradamus*, published in November of 1973 by Shodensha. Toho had optioned the book by that December[12] which newspapers reported on and in January, it was officially announced by Toho.

To work on the film, both as a heavily involved assistant director and script writer, Tomoyuki Tanaka[13] turned to what some may consider an unlikely source: Yoshimitsu Banno, writer/director of the controversial *Godzilla vs. Hedorah* (1971). Though many sources would have one believe Tanaka loathed Banno, this wasn't necessarily the case. Actually, Tanaka felt Banno had his place, it just wasn't on the Godzilla series. In fact, *Hedorah*'s ecological horror themes are most likely what lead Tanaka to entrust Banno with adapting Goto's book—which was not a novel—to film.[14] As the book didn't have a traditional plot, the script for 1961's *The Last War* was used as a jumping off point. And indeed, elements of that film are easy to spot in the form of the main characters: a patriarch with a sick wife, his daughter, and her fiancé. Experts on abnormal weather, food ecology, ultra-scientific phenomena and plant

128

sociology were brought in to help consult. An early scene wherein children that drink from a polluted zinc mine develop strange *X-Men*-style abilities were based on the real-life Minamata Disaster.[15] Remarkably only two drafts rather than the usual four were written. As for differences, it seems Toho always had cold feet regarding the cannibalistic natives. The scene was in the first script, but was actually removed from the second and final shooting script! When it came time to actually shoot, the scene was reinstated. Also, the prime minister's speech was twice as long in the first script.

The final draft, which director Toshio Masuda slightly contributed to, was turned in April 30, 1974 and shooting began on May 11th with Yoshimitsu Banno heading up location shooting in New Guinea, Teruyoshi Nakano on effects, and Masuda with the main cast. The production suffered a major accident early on during filming of a scene where Tokyo oil refineries go up in an inferno because of volcanic eruptions (only a brief shot of the sequence is in the finished film as a result). The accident occurred in Studio #7 when Nakano's explosions got so out of hand that it destroyed the entire soundstage they were using, as well as the old Mogera suit from *The Mysterians* that was in storage there. By the time the Seijo Fire Department arrived, the studio had already burned down.[16] The crew took advantage of the ruined building though, and shot footage of it as a wrecked location for the finished film! This accident occurred early on May 13th, only two days after filming began. Still, Nakano was able to finish the picture June 30th and have a test screening ready by July 24th.

As had been done with *Submersion of Japan*, a TV adaptation of the film was planned to follow via Fuji TV. Among the proposed directors for episodes were none other than Ishiro Honda and Jun Fukuda. This was first proposed in March and the TV pilot was written by May. Allegedly, some 16mm cameras for filming showed up on the effects studio at one point. If any footage was ever shot is unknown, but for certain the project was eventually canned— perhaps due to controversy around the finished film's content.

The film was released August 3rd and grossed ¥883,000,000 making it the highest-grossing Japanese film of 1974. This isn't surprising considering that audiences were hungry for another big disaster film after the success of *Submersion of Japan*. The fantastic film is full of visuals such as bizarre storms, a disastrous car pileup in Tokyo, massive flooding, and forest fires caused by a hole in the ozone layer. The film climaxes with a global nuclear assault[17] ending with two mutated humans wrestling in a post-apocalyptic wasteland. And this is where the trouble started; the post-apocalyptic mutants (known as Soft-Bodied Humans in Japan), designed by Toru Narita, were deemed by some to be offensive to Hiroshima survivors.

A Bomb Sufferers Organizations Council and the No Nukes Group from Osaka Prefecture went to the Eirin Board (the Japanese equivalent of the MPAA) and demanded Toho stop screening the film. One week after release, Toho ran newspaper ads apologizing for the content of the film. They pulled the movie and recut it down to 90 minutes to remove the offensive footage.[18] For international markets, however, the offensive scenes still remained and the film was retitled *Prophecies of Nostradamus (Catastrophe 1999)*, though this version still ran at 90 minutes.

1980 was the last time that the uncut version was legally screened when it was broadcast as TV Asahi's "Holiday Special" at 7:00 PM on November 3rd. *Prophecies of Nostradamus (Catastrophe 1999)* played in New York and Los Angeles theaters in 1978 (where it was reviewed by the Los Angeles Times as well as an unidentified New York newspaper). In 1981, it was released to American TV by United Productions of America as the heavily recut *The Last Days of Planet Earth* and in 1995 this version was released to VHS by Paramount Home Video. This is the only licensed home video release in America, and the film has never been released in Japan in any format (the recut 90 minute Japanese version is occasionally screened in revivals, though). The movie has been released in Europe (chiefly Denmark, Germany, Italy, and France) on VHS in varying editions.

Yoshimitsu Banno told Damon Foster in an interview that, "This is a movie that's essentially banned in Japan. As I understand it, that came about because some protest groups, just after the movie was released, rallied against it because they didn't agree with the portrayal of nuclear war survivors as mutants. So Toho put a self-imposed ban on it and will not have anything to do with it anymore."

CONFLAGRATION (1975) Naturally, after two back-to-back disaster films (or "panic films" as they came to be known in Japan), Toho had desires of filming a third. Had there not been a great controversy regarding *Great Prophecies of Nostradamus*, Toho's big summer disaster film would have likely been *Great Prophecies of Nostradamus II: Fear of the Great Devil* (see Appendix I). Instead, Toho's next disaster film would end up being far more grounded in reality than either *Great Prophecies of Nostradamus* or *Submersion of Japan* had been. The new film would be based around an oil tanker disaster, a concept based on both a real event and a novel. The aforementioned event was an oil tanker disaster that occurred in Tokyo Bay in November of 1974 when an oil tanker and a cargo ship collided. The novel, *Critical Explosion*—which the film follows— was by Koji Tanaka, a prolific Japanese writer who was just starting his career. As with the two previous disaster films, Osamu Tanaka produced alongside Tomoyuki Tanaka.

The effects portion of the film, *Conflagration* (*Tokyo Bay Burns* in its native Japan), was limited compared to the preceding disaster films. The oil tanker miniature was quite large at 7.2 meters and was designed by Yasuyuki Inoue of the art department. Teruyoshi Nakano's explosion scenes were so good that they seamlessly blended in as stock footage in no less than three Godzilla movies: *Godzilla vs. King Ghidorah* (1991), *Godzilla Against Mechagodzilla* (2002) and *Godzilla: Final Wars* (2004).

Naturally, location shooting was done with the cast on a real tanker owned by Mitsui OSK Lines, Ltd. However, for safety's sake, filming was done on days when the ship was loaded with ore rather than flammable liquids. Returning from *Submersion of Japan* was Hiroshi Fujioka and from that film as well as *Great Prophecies of Nostradamus* was reigning disaster movie champ Tetsuro Tamba, who also went to Toei for their "panic film", *The Bullet Train*, that same year.

Unfortunately, *Conflagration* is one of those films that struggles with "having its cake and eating it too" because the concept revolves around stopping a terrorist attack on Tokyo Bay. On one hand, if the destruction isn't prevented, then the protagonists of the film have failed. On the other, if the destruction of Tokyo Bay isn't shown then the audience will be very, very disappointed. To accomplish this task, the destruction of Tokyo Bay is shown as a simulation in the minds of the characters as well as a sequence where a film crew (headed by an actor who looks suspiciously like Teruyoshi Nakano) try to trick the terrorists with a miniature explosion of the Kiyama Oil Fields, which was more or less the main money shot of the film.

Toho was set to follow *Conflagration* with the "second bullet"[19] of their disaster series called *The Great Evacuation*, also based upon a novel by Koji Tanaka, which was never produced (see Appendix I).

DEATHQUAKE (1980) For reasons unknown to this author, after 1975's *Conflagration*, Toho opted not to produce anymore disaster films in the 1970s. However, in 1979 something inspired the studio to get back in the game with something along the lines of 1973's megahit *Submersion of Japan* and it is likely the 1978 Miyagi Prefecture offshore earthquake that inspired production. Whatever the reason, earthquakes were certainly on the mind of Tomoyuki Tanaka in 1979, because in April, he co-produced an earthquake TV movie with Nippon TV called *Great Tokyo Earthquake Magnitude 8.1*. The high budget (for a TV movie) film starred Sonny Chiba and featured effects by Koichi Kawakita.

At the same that time the TV movie was being shot, Tanaka was also developing an earthquake feature film based upon the novel *Dai Jishin/Great Earthquake* by Jiro Koitabashi, Shigeki Manabe, and Hitoshi Chiba. The story is given further pedigree though writer Kaneto Shindo, a playwright and film director born in 1912. Due to his age, Shindo was old enough to witness the great Kanto earthquake of 1923, and that could have well been part of this story's inspiration. In fact, the main character is the grandson of the man who predicted the Kanto earthquake. The draft went through few changes with the first act concerning predicting the earthquake, act two sees the quake happen, and act three deals with the main characters surviving the aftermath. The only differences concerned the development of the main characters, a geologist, his wife, his mistress, and a reporter.

So, does *Deathquake* top *Submersion of Japan's* Tokyo earthquake scene? That's a somewhat hard question answer. Though entertaining, much of the earthquake scenes are actually made up of stock-footage and B-Roll footage (or outtakes) from *Submersion of Japan*, notably a large highway bridge that collapses. The standout new scene is undoubtedly when a jumbo jet attempts land during the earthquake. That said, Nakano's two main centerpieces—and challenges—were the scenes involving the protagonists trapped in two different locations. The first, Tomiko's apartment building, was based on a real building in Sangenjaya and reproduced with a 1/25th scale and 1/12th scale miniature built, plus a full-sized apartment room that was rocked back and forth by hydraulics.

The biggest expense was the climactic subway scene set in Akasaka-Mitsuke. Reportedly, it cost 20 million yen to obtain the full-sized subway cars submerged for filming and another 10 million yen to film the scene making for 30 million yen total. Rumors persist that a bit of guerilla filmmaking (filming without proper authority or clearances) was done at Akasaka-Mitsuke, though this has never been confirmed. 10 tons of water was also used in the scene.

Supposedly, this film may have caused the Earthquake Resistance Building Standard laws to be tightened the following year. At the Lalaport Tokyo Bay earthquake museum, footage of this film was shown as an exhibit. This also has what some may consider the dubious distinction of being the first Toho special effects film to end with a pop song, *Amethyst Sunray* by Shibata Hatsumi.

SAYONARA JUPITER (1984) The development of Toho's final Showa era disaster film is a curious one which, as always, seems to have conflicting accounts about its development. The most common account states that the film's genesis lies in 1977 when Tomoyuki Tanaka saw *Star Wars* at a screening in Hawaii. Tanaka returned to

Japan and requested hit-maker Sakyo Komatsu to write a *Star Wars*-inspired film.[20] Komatsu ignored the *Star Wars* idea, and assembled a team of writers that began meeting in September of that year. From these meetings supposedly sprang *Battle of the Galactic Empire* (see page 180). An alternative to this tale says that Komatsu was already thinking about a space-based sci-fi film in 1976 before Tanaka ever saw *Star Wars*. This comes from *Toho Special Effects Movie Complete Works* and the book states it was planned to be an animated TV movie or series.

Whatever the case, Komatsu took too long for Tanaka's liking and he commissioned an outer space remake of *Atragon* instead from Shuichi Nagahara.[21] This film became the rather rushed *The War in Space*, and Komatsu continued working on his idea separately. In fact, Komatsu hoped to take it to Hollywood rather than Toho and made sure that his second draft contained space battles similar to *Star Wars*. However, Komatsu eventually realized he didn't wish to compete with *Star Wars*, and so cut the space battles and created a more introspective story.

Komatsu took his idea to Hollywood, pitching it to as many studio executives as he could. One of the execs was none other than Alan Ladd, who had greenlit *Star Wars* but did not greenlight Komatsu's idea. However, not all the studios rejected Komatsu's idea. One agreed to produce the film but Komatsu would not be allowed to contribute from that point forward and so the author refused. Komatsu, who had hoped his film could star Orson Wells, instead went back to Japan and turned the story into a novel serialized in May of 1980 in *Weekly Sankei*. In 1981, Komatsu even created his own small film company, IO, to get the movie off of the ground. From his novel, he not only created the third draft but also storyboards and a possible shooting schedule. Komatsu even hired designers for concept drawings and physical models of which he shot test footage. Sadly, Toho told him his third draft script was unfilmable on a technical level. This didn't mean Toho rejected the script, however, and in June of 1982, Toho made their plans official to make Komatsu's film on a more limited scale.

In choosing a director, originally *Submersion of Japan's* Shiro Moritani was the main contender. However, Moritani became ill soon after he was chosen and so his second unit director on that film, Koji Hashimoto, was chosen instead.[22] *House* director Nobuhiko Obayashi was also considered as director at one point but was rejected due to being "too difficult to control." Komatsu handed over the script to director Koji Hashimoto who drastically cut the script, combining characters and compressing the story in order to shorten the lengthy running time. The final version of the story was completed in March of 1983.

The original ¥1.8 billion budget was slashed significantly to only 1/3rd of the original budget but was still considerably large for the time. Filming began in April of 1983 with Koichi Kawakita in charge of the special effects. Hashimoto began shooting with actors that May. In a rare instance of an author directing the motion picture adaptation of their book, Komatsu was allowed to co-direct with Hashimoto. Actually, Komatsu even helped to set-up miniatures in some shots! In terms of effects, it was a groundbreaking production and involved the first use of computer generated imagery in a Japanese film as well as motion camera control.

The production had finished shooting in October of 1983 and then began the long post-production process. In the end, the film had cost ¥600,000,000, but that cost ballooned to around ¥1 billion by the time of post-production and promotion costs. Toho had faith in the film due to the success of Komatsu's past adaptations. However, due to the huge budget, the film's grosses were not enough to make the massive production worthwhile and was considered a failure at the box office.

Critically the film was a dud, with Komatsu's own fans sometimes hitting it hardest. One wrote that, "Komatsu revealed that his talent is limited to novels." Even Koichi Kawakita said in an interview that he preferred the edited-down version of the film that aired on Japanese TV that cut out all sequences on earth. Kawakita said to David Milner of the TV version that, "I prefer the edited version. I share Sakyo Komatsu's concerns about the environment, but I feel that the scenes which take place at the Jupiter Foundation are not necessary."

Despite its big budget appeal, *Sayonara Jupiter* never secured a U.S. release of any sort until it was issued to a special edition DVD by Discotek in 2007. Toho's international version (*Bye-Bye Jupiter*) did manage to make it to several other countries, though.

Section Notes

---

[1] Why Ishiro Honda, a noted pacifist and experienced director of tokusatsu films, wasn't brought in was likely due to Honda already being busy on *The Man in Red*, a yakuza film.

[2] This footage was reused many times, first on TV for the series finale of *Ultraseven*. It was later used in 1974's *Great Prophecies of Nostradamus* to portray nuclear annihilation and later even aliens attacked the world via this footage for 1977's *The War in Space*. Stock footage of Tokyo in lava was used as late as 1995 in several teaser trailers for *Godzilla vs. Destroyah*.

[3] Filming of the miniature flaming charcoal balls was filmed at a steel factory in Chiba prefecture.

[4] It is unknown if the theatrical version was the same length as the TV version as sources vary on the runtimes.

[5] Or "star" as used in the Japanese language.

[6] Speaking of the moon's destruction, some fans speculate that because the moon is never glimpsed in *The War in Space* (1977) that it could be a sequel to *Gorath*. Also, the space station from *Gorath* is glimpsed in *The War in Space*.

[7] Whose tusks made by Ryozo Murase so impressed Eiji Tsuburaya that he thought they were real ivory, when in fact they were just poly resin.

[8] *Science Fiction Studies* #88 , Volume 29, Part 3, November 2002
https://www.depauw.edu/sfs/backissues/88/komatsu%20interview.htm)

[9] Komatsu ironically stated in an interview with *Science Fiction Studies* that, "When I wrote *Japan Sinks*, I had no expectation that it would become a movie."

[10] Galbraith, *Japanese Science Fiction, Fantasy and Horror Films* pp. 214

[11] They also released a subtitled print of the Japanese version in select theaters before it was yanked for one of two rumored reasons: a conflict with Toho International or the MPAA over the film's rating—it had none.

[12] Since *Submersion of Japan* was released December 29th, it was most likely before Toho even knew for sure the film would be a hit.

[13] Tanaka has a cameo at the first meeting scene with the prime minister.

[14] From the best this author can tell, Goto's book seemed to be a hypothetical scenario about what would happen to Japan if Nostradamus's predictions were to actually happen.

[15] People didn't develop remarkable abilities, but they were severely affected or died as a result of drinking water polluted with mercury by a nearby factory.

[16] Nakano earned his nickname "Mr. Explosion" the hard way.

[17] Ironically made up of both new footage and stock shots from *The Last War,* which this film's story was partly inspired by.

[18] And other bits here and there such as the sequence where Jun Hamamura's character wails about his deformed grandson.

[19] Back in those days entries in a series were called bullets. For instance, a poster identified *Terror of Mechagodzilla* as the "second bullet of the Mechagodzilla series".

[20] The main reason Tanaka knew he could beat *Star Wars* to Japan was due to the fact that 20th Century Fox had such little faith in the film they didn't bother trying to book it in Japan. When they did, all Japanese theaters were booked until the summer of 1978.

[21] The first draft of *Sayonara Jupiter* wasn't done until August of 1978.

[22] Some sources would have you believe Moritani died before production, but he passed away on December 2, 1984 after the film's release.

22.
AFTER JAPAN SINKS

Developmental Period: 1974-1978

Producers: Tomoyuki Tanaka & Osamu Tanaka **Proposed Director:** Shiro Moritani **Proposed SPFX Director:** Teruyoshi Nakano

SYNOPSIS The surviving Japanese who fled the continent before it sank try to reconnect with other survivors and integrate into a brave new world.

COMMENTARY Plans for a sequel to 1973's biggest hit movie (actually, the most successful Japanese film of the 1970s), began right away in 1974. In early spring, a small speed poster appeared in Toho theaters advertising *Continuation: Sinking of Japan* stating, "Are the Japanese who lost their homeland obliterated from world history?" Likewise, *Famous Monsters of Filmland* in America also reported on *After Japan Sinks*. Toho had initially hoped this to be their big 1975 summer release, but Sakyo Komatsu had no concrete ideas at this time, and Toho wanted his vision.

Then came another trade ad for the film in 1976 by Toho. This time the catchphrase read, "30 million Japanese who lost their homeland! Ethnic energy that explodes in persecution, to Europe, to the United States, to Australia!" The Toho lineup for 1978 again announced the film touting, "30 million Japanese people scattered from the sinking archipelago to the world! In persecution conflict, they were organized and a nation without a land was born!" This would almost seem to imply the Japanese try to gain another landmass to call home. In any case, this was sadly the last anyone heard of a sequel to Toho's 1973 *Submersion of Japan*. In the late 1970s, Toho had been embroiled in an ill-fated co-production with Hammer called *Nessie*, which killed/delayed a number of other Toho films. This, in addition to the 1978 Godzilla Revival meeting, likely lead to the abandonment of the *Submersion of Japan* sequel.

How does one follow up a movie called *Submersion of Japan* with a sequel when at the end of the first film, Japan had mostly sank? As one can see from the taglines in the previous paragraph, the film would have focused more so on the survival of the Japanese people over more natural disasters.[1] However, the ending of the first film doesn't actually show the entire continent disappear into the ocean, and perhaps the sequel would have begun with that very scene?

While the details of the aborted film sequel are scarce (it's possible no treatment of any kind was ever written), Sakyo Komatsu finally wrote a sequel to his novel in 2006.[2] At the time 75 years old, Komatsu teamed with younger writer Tani Koshu to pen it. Titled *Japan Sinks, Part II* and published by Shogakukan, Komatsu envisioned the sequel focusing on the effects that the sinking of Japan had on the rest of the world. In this new story, volcanic ash from the eruptions would have plunged the world into a colder climate which causes a food shortage. In an interview, Komatsu specifically mentioned these two ideas being "global cooling" and "the end of the Japanese people".

In the finished book, the story picks up 25 years after Japan has sunk. With forty million Japanese dead from the sinking, the population now sits at 80 million people scattered across the world. The Japanese have settled in places as diverse as Papua New Guinea, Kazakhstan, and even the Amazon River in South America. In some cases, the Japanese live better than the locals due to their different lifestyle, while in other areas they are shunned and persecuted.

The remaining Japanese government has created a new plan to reunify their people. It is called the Megafloat—huge artificial islands that can hold 1 million people each are to be set in the ocean where Japan once stood. Developed alongside this is the "Earth Simulator" which can predict the future of the environment and the future looks grim. According to the simulator, a new ice age will soon devastate agriculture in the Northern Hemisphere. The simulator predicts that a billion people will die in the next thirty years. When Japan warns the world, the U.S. and China try to manipulate Japan's Megafloat project to their own ends. A conflict then emerges between the Prime Minister, who feels the Japanese should keep the technology to themselves, and the Foreign Minister, who feels Japan should use this as a way to further integrate with the rest of the world. The book ends with the Foreign Minister becoming Prime Minister and Japan helps the rest of the world. Then, there is a final epilogue showing a descendant of one of the main characters living on a space station. As they look down upon the earth, as predicted the Northern Hemisphere is covered in ice, while numerous Megafloats populate the equator.

Actually, from this concept, Komatsu even had ideas of a third part of the story which he shared on the radio program *Suntory, Saturday, and Waiting Bar* in 2006, "If I make the third part, the Japanese who lived in the second part can only go to space."

Of course, the above story was not how *After Japan Sinks* would have unfolded as it would be set only a short time after the first film. Furthermore, it's unknown just when Komatsu got his ideas for the sequel to the novel. That being said, surely Komatsu and the other writers, whoever they may have been, would have concocted some more natural disasters to befall the world in the sequel. That was, after all, a big part of what had made the original a hit.

Chapter Notes

[1] In some of my old, uncited notes I found a description that claimed the sequel would have partially dealt with Onodera and Reiko (the two romantic leads of the first film) reuniting with one another in Geneva, Switzerland.
[2] Komatsu had, however, always intended to do a sequel as the first novel ends stating, "Part One, The End".

JAPAN SINKS ON TV!

It's possible that one of the reasons that a sequel to *Submersion of Japan* never materialized was the lukewarm reception to the companion TV series that aired on the Tokyo Broadcasting System.

Though many Americans saw *Submersion of Japan* through its U.S. release as *Tidal Wave* in 1975, most have never seen, and are unaware of the accompanying TV series. Supposedly shot simultaneously with the movie, the series isn't a sequel but a TV version of the concept and different actors portray the roles such as Takenori Murano as Onodera now. The series was produced by Tomoyuki Tanaka, and Jun Fukuda even directed the first episode "Scattering Sea". Koichi Kawakita was also one of the special effects staff but not the main director. Each episode of the series more or less focused on seeing a new location or Japanese city sink beneath the waves and was preceded with an announcement that what the viewer was seeing was not newsreel footage, but a dramatization. Famous landmarks destroyed in the series included Kamakura's famous Buddha statue, the temples and castles of Kyoto, and Osaka Castle, which literally floats away during one episode's end. The novel's author, Sakyo Komatsu, even joked about the format of the series telling *Science Fiction Studies* that, "The novel described this gradual submergence of Japan by focusing on a few different areas, but in the television series, different locales would go under every week. As if they were telling people, 'Stay tuned for the destruction of YOUR city!' (Laughs)." [1]

The series premiered on October 6, 1974 to fairly healthy ratings that had dwindled by the time the finale aired on March 30, 1975.[2] It was a 55-minute program that aired Sunday nights at 8:00 PM. Ironically airing at the same time in completion was another Sakyo Komatsu-inspired series, Tsuburaya Production's *Ape Corps* (*Time of the Apes* in the U.S.).

Though it occasionally utilized footage from the movie, new effects scenes were shot for the series. Hiroshi Itsuki sang the theme song "Tomorrow's Love." While the series contained guest appearances by well-known Toho actors Katsuhiko Sasaki, Yoshio Tsuchiya, Yu Fujiki, Kenji Sahara, Kunie Tanaka, and Mie Hama, it starred Keiju Kobayashi, Kaoru Yumi[3], and Takenori Murano. Shin Kishida (the INTERPOL agent in *Godzilla vs. Mechagodzilla*) did the voiceover narration for the "next episode" teasers.

The TV series had several notable differences from both the novel and the film. For instance, while in the film Onodera and Reiko are

139

separated, in the TV series it is revealed they both escape to Australia. Also, the big Tokyo earthquake that takes place in the middle of the film serves instead as the series finale. The final scene of the series saw a pair of lovers clasping their hands for the last time inside of a Christian church, the only structure in Japan still standing as the last of the island nation sinks beneath the waves. Komatsu himself was not overly impressed with this adaptation, and didn't even bother watching it until many years later. "I didn't get a chance to see the television version when it aired, but I was able to see it for the first time recently on DVD. It wasn't very good."[4]

The series started re-airing in 1995 until the Southern Hyogo Prefecture earthquake occurred and the broadcast was halted after episode two.

Section Notes

[1] *Science Fiction Studies* #88, "An Interview with Komatsu Sakyo"

[2] The series started with an 18% ratings share, but had dwindled to 13% by the time of the finale. This could have also soured Toho on a *Submersion of Japan* sequel even though the idea was still discussed as late as 1978.

[3] Sakyo Komatsu wanted her cast in the movie as Reiko, so perhaps her role on the series was something of a consolation prize?

[4] [4] *Science Fiction Studies* #88, "An Interview with Komatsu Sakyo"

23.
BLUE CHRISTMAS

Alternate Titles: *Blood Type: Blue*; *The Blue Stigma*;
UFO Blue Christmas
Release Date: November 23, 1978

Directed by: Kihachi Okamoto **Screenplay by:** So Kuramoto **Music by:** Masaru Sato **Cast:** Hiroshi Katsuno (Oki), Keiko Takeshita (Saeko Nishida), Nakadai Tatsuya (Minami Ichiya), Eiji Okada (Dr. Hyodo), Kaoru Yachigusa (Mrs. Hyodo), Kuni Tanaka (Kazuo Nishida)

Widescreen, Eastmancolor, 133 Minutes

SYNOPSIS During the Christmas season of 1977, the earth witnesses a rash of strange U.F.O. sightings. The blood of those who witnesses these U.F.O.s turns blue in color. A prominent researcher of the phenomena, Dr. Hyodo, goes missing in America. Journalist Minami goes to New York where he tracks down Dr. Hyodo. However, he is advised to let the matter of what is happening to the blue-blooded people drop before Dr. Hyodo is escorted away by mysterious men. Upon returning to Japan, Minami is transferred to Paris. Meanwhile, Special Forces operative Oki keeps tabs upon the blue bloods as the government decides what to do about them as the year progresses. Oki falls in love with a lonely woman named Saeko, whom he only later discovers has blue blood. He is soon given orders from the government that on Christmas Day, 1978, all blue bloods are to be executed. Oki kills Saeko, and then turns his gun in anger at his fellow soldiers who proceed to murder him in cold blood. Elsewhere around the world, everyone with blue blood is murdered in a horrendous genocide.

COMMENTARY By now, most western tokusatsu fans have heard of all of Toho's many sci-fi and fantasy films, but there are a few that occasionally slip through the cracks. One such film that many western fans have never heard of is Toho's 1978 *Close Encounters of the Third Kind*-inspired *Blue Christmas*.

    Blue Christmas not only features no special effects scenes[1] despite its premise, but was also one of the few Toho sci-fi films not

141

produced by Tomoyuki Tanaka, who had recently transitioned to the President of Toho Co., Ltd.[2] That said, Tanaka was still responsible for the production. In 1977, he saw So Kuramoto's original story in *Kinema Junpo* and decided to make a movie out of it. Like the film, the story centered on government/media paranoia over people recently abducted by U.F.O.s.[3]

Tanaka wisely chose a director who had an affinity for U.F.O.s, the famed Kihachi Okamoto (*Sword of Doom*, *Kill!*), to helm the film adaptation. Okamoto was wise enough to begin filming some exterior location shots during the Christmas season of 1977 since the film obviously could not shoot the larger exterior Christmas scenes during the holiday season of 1978 when it would be released. Apparently, there was some friction between writer Kuramoto and Okamoto because Kuramoto insisted his script be 100% unaltered and adapted as it was written. The main problem with Kuramoto's script was that it was "as thick as a phonebook" so presumably some scenes were cut in order to bring it to a still lengthy runtime of 133 minutes.[4] There was at least one scene that was cut involving the White House in America. An outtake from this scene appears in the movie's trailer with an actor playing the U.S. president, who otherwise does not appear in the film, remarking "Must I do what Hitler did?" Another deleted scene showed the special forces attacking a large group of people in Hokkaido and supposedly stills of this scene existed in an issue of *Kinema Junpo*.

The film was widely released at the onset of the Christmas season in late November. Though clearly inspired by 1977's *Close Encounters of the Third Kind*, this film is far more downbeat, and may be the most depressing movie Toho's ever made. The story plays out over the span of one year, starting with the aftermath of Christmas 1977 where people across the world report not only having seen U.F.O.s, but their blood changing color to blue. A famous Japanese pop singer commits suicide when she discovers that her blood has turned blue.

Actually, we never do learn why the U.F.O. viewers' blood has turned blue or what the world's governments' problems with them are. Nor do we ever see the U.F.O.s, but truth be told, we don't need to and they would add nothing to the story. Ironically, not seeing the U.F.O.s almost adds to the real world feel of the story. After all, how many things do we hear about reported in the news which we do not ever see personally? Although some may find this tactic disappointing, it really only enhances the film and its pervading sense of paranoia.

The film's real merits exist in its mood and how the mystery is unraveled. This is aided along by the music by Masaru Sato, which is creepy and atmospheric. A particularly good example of this is a

142

scene where headlines about the U.F.O.s play over Christmas music. This otherwise excellent 70s conspiracy thriller is unfortunately marred by a segment wherein Minami travels to New York in search of Dr. Hyodo. While the Caucasian actors in these scenes are actually quite good compared to similar gaijin actors in other films, here it is the situation itself that is ludicrous as Minami wanders New York asking random passersby—even bums—if they have seen the doctor! Eventually, Minami does find the doctor, and in a scene made popular in many of the era's conspiracy thrillers, Dr. Hyodo is escorted away by mysterious black clad men in a cemetery.

The film shifts its lead characters in the last act from Minami to military man Oki. It's debatable whether or not this really detracts from the film, but it is somewhat strange the two character's portions of the film aren't better intercut. In fact, Minami's last significant moment is seeing a lobotomized Dr. Hyodo in Paris, a rather large coincidence all things considered (though a rather disturbing end to the mystery). The love story between Oki and Saeko manages to be quite intriguing. The audience and Oki only discover that Saeko is one of the blue bloods after they have made love for the first time and at the film's end, Oki and a regiment of soldiers are ordered to gun down all of them.

To make matters more tragic, Saeko tells Oki how she was supposed to have a special date with her boyfriend on Christmas night in her home several years ago but he stood her up. Saeko asks Oki then if he will come to her home on Christmas night. In a heartbreaking turn, Oki is soon thereafter informed that on Christmas night, all blue bloods will be ambushed in their homes and executed. From there the tension mounts, as we wonder just what choice Oki will make—and unfortunately, this ending is spoiled in the film's trailer. Still, the scenes leading up to the inevitable are well done, as they cut back and forth between an excited Saeko decorating her home for the night and Oki preparing for his mission.

Shockingly, Oki chooses not to save Saeko and is instead the very man to gun her down in her home. Naturally, Saeko merely thinks he's keeping his promise to spend Christmas night with her as he walks in the door. They lock eyes and he shoots her. Oki then goes outside to turn his gun on his fellow soldiers who gun him down. If this is a spur of the moment reaction or if Oki had planned this as a double-suicide all along, is unknown to the viewer. From there, we witness a montage of all the blue-blooded people of the world being graphically gunned down to Christmas music. The film then ends with a shot of Saeko's blue blood running down through the snow until it mixes in with Oki's red, implying that the color of people's blood never really mattered in the end.

Though it's frustrating the film ends with the viewer not knowing the governments' motives for committing a worldwide genocide, questions are always more alluring than answers. Though not terribly well remembered today, among this film's fans were Hideaki Anno who integrated elements of the film into his *Evangelion* series.

Chapter Notes

[1] Or rather, there are no scenes of the U.F.O.s or miniatures of them. Technically the blue-blood effects still qualify as "effects". Whilst Teruyoshi Nakano has no credit in the movie, the "Toho Special Effects department" is given a special thanks credit.

[2] Previously, he was the head of Toho Eizo, which produced Toho's tokusatsu efforts from 1972 to 1977.

[3] Kuramoto had previously touched upon the public's distrust and manipulation by the media in the dark comedy TV series *6 Kamome* in 1976.

[4] Okamoto said he thought Kuramoto's script would have been better adapted as a TV series or mini-series, instead.

24.
GUNDAM

Developed: 1983-1984

Screenplay by: Chip Proser **Producers:** Lion's Gate **Proposed Director:** Chip Proser **Proposed Cast/Characters:** Amaru Ray [GUNDAM pilot, son of Tim Ray], Sha Ray [ZAK pilot/Amaru's brother], Sara [Gundam pilot], Camilla Ray [Amaru and Sha's mother], Tim Ray [GUNDAM creator], Ziong [Legion Leader] **Proposed Monsters:** GUNDAM, ZAK

SYNOPSIS A pair of brothers, Amaru and Sha, are caught up in an intergalactic conflict on opposite sides. Amaru pilots the Gundam, a robot built by his father, while Sha pilots a giant ZAK for the evil Legion. The two brothers come to blows as the fate of the galaxy hangs in the balance.

COMMENTARY Another Japanese property that is nearly as well-known as Godzilla worldwide is the robot anime *Gundam*. It debuted in 1979 as *Mobile Suit Gundam*, an anime created by Sunrise. The series defined the "mecha" genre, and focused on pilots who board large, mechanical suits called Gundam.[1] Ironically, initial ratings for the series were low, and it didn't become a hit until the year 1980 when Bandai began producing models of the robots. After this, episodes from the TV series were edited into a trilogy of movies released theatrically in Japan.

Gundam wouldn't revive until the sequel TV series *Mobile Suit Zeta Gundam* in 1985, but before that, there was actually plans for a big-budget American live-action film adaptation from Lion's Gate in 1983.[2] Amazingly, the only reason many people even know about this lost project is through some conceptual artwork done by famous *Alien* designer Syd Mead.

Mead was asked about the aborted project by Jonah Morgan of Anime News Service:

> **Morgan:** Around 1983 you worked on an American film design project based on an anime property that was eventually aborted for legal reasons. That was a film for Lions Gate based on adapting the mobile suit Gundam mecha for domestic audience

film style. Can you tell us more on this project? Did you ever complete your original designs for Gundam?

Mead: No. I worked first on the ZAK character because for whatever reason, the director thought that would be more mechanically interesting as a demo. The character of GUNDAM was started after I drafted the ZAK character for computer vector plotting and modeling. (The computer being used at the time was a supercomputer CRAY.) Lion's Gate had failed to get license approval from Sunrise! The Sunrise New York office sent a cease and desist court order and the project was shelved, never to be resurrected. My job was to first, draft the ZAK character for plot input, and then I started on 'de-kabuki-izng' the GUNDAM character for the American market. I finished the head first, and was starting on the body when the project was discontinued.[3]

In 2017, intrepid fan Tom Winnicki decided to research the mysterious project and contacted Syd Mead's manager, Roger Servick, the film's proposed writer/director Chip Proser, and CGI animation pioneer John Whitney Jr. Thanks to his research, additional details on the project came to life…

As *Gundam* mania took over Japan in the early 1980s thanks to successful toy sales, some Bandai executives flew to Hollywood to try and find a bankroller for a major *Gundam* movie. Somehow they connected to Robert Altman's Lion's Gate production company, which in turn hired script doctor Chip Proser to write the film.[4] Proser boldly negotiated to write the script only if he would also be allowed to direct, a concession that Lion's Gate agreed to. Proser was then flown to Japan to have a better look at the source material.

Like *Tron* (1982), a pioneer film in the world of CGI effects, the producers had ideas of using CGI to bring the robots to life. To do so, Lion's Gate approached Digital Production, the team currently rendering CGI effects for *The Last Starfighter* (released in 1984). In hindsight, though, it is likely for the best the film wasn't made with this method, as CGI was still ineffective at the time.

The script begins deceptively, crafting visuals that suggest an earth setting (a French Village in Japan) that actually turns out to be a recreation of Earth within a large space station. Also, what the audience would first think to be a bird turns out to be a young girl, Nora, gliding on futuristic wings. Flying with her is her pal Sha, and below both of them on the ground, Japanese boy Amaru. This, of course, is meant to be Amuro Ray/Rei, the lead of the series. It's thought this wasn't a conscious decision to change the name, but an innocent typo or mistake upon the part of Proser. Proser's other changes weren't so subtle, though. Char Aznable, originally a masked antagonist in *Mobile Suit Gundam* turned protagonist in *Mobile Suit Zeta Gundam*, is here retconned to become Sha, Amaru's younger brother!

Anyhow, as the children play, evil Legion ZAK suits fly towards the space station and break into it. They are described as "100-meter tall GREEN MONSTERS." The giant ZAK suits cause some fun destruction within the space station while the three youthful protagonists do their best to evade them. Amaru, for instance, uses a futuristic motorcycle to deliver an important computer to his father, Tim Ray (Tem Rei in the series), amongst the chaos.

Amidst the attack, Tim Ray is killed and Amaru is able to pilot a Gundam to fight off the ZAK suits. The battle is certainly amusing, with the Gundam grabbing one of the ZAK's where its "metal balls would be," causing the robot's crotchular region to shoot flames! The flames propel it into the air, where it then explodes.

During the battle, the surviving colonists of the space station, called O'Neill 7, join with the ship White Base. The dialogue within O'Neil 7 reveals that this apparently would've been an R-rated affair as the F-bomb is dropped.

Back within the space station, Camilla Ray has collected her young son Sha. The duo is then cornered by a gigantic ZAK suit, which stops in front of them. Instead of killing them, the commander steps out of the gigantic robot to speak with them. This leads to the mother and son being kidnaped, which has interesting ramifications later in the story when Sha is brainwashed into becoming a Legion pilot. This was presumably a nod to the original character of Char Aznable as an antagonist.

Back to the story, Amaru pilots the Gundam in space to fight off the remaining ZAKs. To deliver the final blow, he utilizes his laser sword. The White Base is then able to warp away to safety to an asteroid that they hide away in. As the story progresses, the Legion tracks them there (with Sha). A battle commences which the Legion wins. In the chaos, Amaru and another character aboard the Gundam are separated from the main group in a massive explosion. This explosion propels the Gundam suit to crash through the atmosphere of an alien planet, leaving Amaru stranded there. With him is the character of Sara, basically meant to be this script's version of the *Gundam* character Sayla. Naturally, while stranded on the planet, they form a romantic bond.

Eventually, the two are rescued and head for this script's own quasi version of Tatooine from *Star Wars*, in this case a binary moon of the planet Nightside. The duo is looking for mercenaries to join their fight against the Legion, and the scene is definitely reminiscent of the Mos Eisley cantina scene from *Star Wars*. It also pulls from

The Magnificent Seven (1960), and Proser even describes one character as "a young Steve McQueen." The two are successful in recruiting a few mercenaries to join their cause and bring them back to the White Base where the Gundam is being repaired.

Actually, new weapons have been built too, one of which is the Guntank from the anime. The other two creations are unique to the script, however, and are named the Gunfighter and Gungrenadier. The ragtag group attacks the Legion base, but only Amaru is able to get inside. There he discovers that the face of the Legion group, known as Ziong, isn't even real. He's just a computer program! Brainwashed brother Sha comes along, and he and Amaru do battle across various levels of the base (though Amaru is unaware that Sha is piloting the red ZAK!). It is at this point that a famous scene from the finale of the anime called the "Last Shooting" is recreated. In the scene, Amaru finally learns that Sha was the pilot in command of the ZAK. The two fight, and intriguingly we never learn the winner.

Instead, in an epilogue, we see the two brothers return home to their mother, who reveals she allowed Sha to be taken because she knew in the end he would eventually turn on the Legion. This is effectively true, by the way. It is actually Sha who destroys the Ziong program before he begins battling Amaru. The battle was more about jealousy between brothers than it was the fate of the galaxy after the "death" of Ziong.

The very final scene is set on O'Neill 7, with the surviving characters mourning the fallen ones. The Gundam has been rebuilt into a monument of sorts. The final line reads: "[The Gundam is] a memorial and a reminder and he'd be content to stand there forever...if they never, ever again, need GUNDAM."[5]

Unfortunately, this solid first draft script never got to a second draft because production was soon cancelled. As it turned out, Bandai didn't have the official go-ahead from the show's various rights holders. Some sources claimed Sunrise was to blame, while others said it was the Nippon Herald. A few years later, Bandai would buy out Sunrise, which would have eliminated part of the problem, but this wasn't until the 1990s, long after the 1983 proposed film was dead.

Ironically, Syd Mead would eventually cross paths with *Gundam* again in 1998 when Sunrise and *Gundam* director Yoshiyuki Tomino invited him to work on the 49 episode run for *Turn-A Gundam* on TV. Mead's artwork for the Gundam movie can be found in his Japanese book for Kodansha, *Oblagon*.

Chapter Notes

[1] The name comes from "gun" combined with "freedom" initially to be Gundom, but the creator felt that Gundam had a better sound to it. He also felt like the word "dam" implied the restraint of great power.

[2] This is not to be confused with today's Lionsgate, they are separate companies, Lion's Gate now defunct.

[3] http://web.archive.org/web/20150709210633/http://www.animenewsservice.com/archives/sydmead.htm Original source from Anime News Service, published July 29, 2004.

[4] Proser would later be best known for doing rewrites for *Top Gun* (1986) and *Innerspace* (1987).

[5] archive.org/details/Gundam1983MovieScript/page/n117

25.
TOKYO BLACKOUT

Japanese Title: *Disappearance of the Capital*
Release Date: January 17, 1987

Directed by: Toshio Masuda **Screenplay by:** Toshio Masuda, Hiroyasu Yamamura & Sakyo Komatsu (novel) **Special Effects by:** Teruyoshi Nakano **Music by:** Maurice Jarre **Cast:** Tsunehiko Watase (Tatsuya Asakura), Yuko Natori (Mariko Koide), Shinji Yamashita (Yosuke), Hideji Otaki (Seichiro Outawara), Osamu Sakuma (Isao Natsuyagi), Tetsuro Tamba (Nakata), Midori Ebina (Keiko Yasuhara), Eimei Esumi (Takeda), Yoko Ishino (Mieko Matsunaga), Haruko Kato (Umeko Koide), Ittoku Kishibe (Yasuhara)

Widescreen, Color, 120 Minutes

SYNOPSIS When Tokyo is unexpectedly enveloped by a mysterious electromagnetic cloud, the world is stunned. All communication is lost within the city, and the U.S. pressures Japan to form a new government. In the middle of the investigation are reporters Asakura and Mariko who desperately want to get back inside the city so Mariko can see her daughter. A scientific means of breaching the cloud is developed through a new machine. Two of the machines are mounted to military vehicles but when they attempt to breach the cloud, it begins to draw them in and so they retreat. A brave general drives one of the trucks back into the cloud and seems to cause some effect. Asakura boards the second truck and barrels into the cloud. Finally, it begins to open and dissipate. Asakura and Mariko walk into Tokyo for the first time, hoping to find survivors. When they find a lost dog, the cloud lifts entirely....

COMMENTARY After *Submersion of Japan* (1973) and *ESPY* (1974) became back-to-back big hits, the stories' creator, Sakyo Komatsu, became a hot property in the Japan film industry. The year 1980 saw his novel *Resurrection Day* (U.S. title, *Virus*) adapted as the most expensive Japanese film up to that time. His next work, *Sayonara Jupiter*, which began in 1978 but wasn't completed until 1984, was a bit too expensive to make much of a profit. So Komatsu's next adapted work, *Capital City Disappears*, would end up being something of a gamble. The story was initially serialized from December of 1983 to December of 1984 in the *Hokkaido Shimbun, Chunichi Shimbun,* and the *West Japan Newspaper.* The story was well received and even won the 6th Japan SF Award. Naturally, Komatsu's story was optioned for film a few years later. Rather than Toho alone, it would be a co-production between Toho and Tokuma Shoten (which had purchased Daiei in the late 70s) along with Kansai Telecasting (KTV).[1]

Even though it's set in the late 1980s, *Tokyo Blackout* still has all the usual tropes of a Japanese science fiction film of the 1950s and 60s. As usual, a pair of reporters anchor the film and are surrounded by various scientists and military men. The film's problem is also solved by the creation of a scientifically advanced mech. The ending is as well done as it can be, with a good deal of suspense being generated by the machines trying to breach the wall. After two failed attempts, it is finally the film's hero Asakura who breaches the wall. Asakura and the female lead, Mariko (who has a daughter trapped in the city) tepidly enter the city for the first time since the cloud appeared. At first, it seems that the film is going to end on a depressing note much like 2007's *The Mist.* But, Asakura finds a puppy amongst the wreckage. If a puppy can survive, perhaps so too did the residents of Tokyo.[2] The couple walk into the dissipating cloud hopefully and the film comes to a close revealing that Tokyo still stands, and only the outskirts were charred by the cloud.

The film more or less follows the novel for the first half, but begins to deviate in the second half which is more proactive than the book regarding the rescue of those stuck inside Tokyo. In the book, things more or less resolve themselves, with the cloud mysteriously dissipating after a few months. The film, naturally requiring a sense of urgency for the audience, implies that manmade technology plays a role in getting the cloud to dissipate—or retreat as it is said to be an alien device of some sort. Like *Blue Christmas,* no aliens are ever seen and nor are their mysterious motives ever revealed.

Where the novel is different concerns the story's timetable. The movie takes place over a relatively short period of time, whereas in the book the cloud lingers over Tokyo for around four months before disappearing. The book is also much more political, with the U.S. pressuring Japan to set up a new government being one of the focal points. A Soviet fleet also approaches Japan to investigate when an earthquake occurs and a tsunami hits. Apparently, Komatsu also envisioned the book ending with the cloud survivors developing enhanced intelligence and abilities but the idea was scrapped in favor of a more tidy end.

The book was also very similar to the 1964 story *Object O* where a ring-like object envelops Osaka which Komatsu also had a hand in writing. In *Tokyo Blackout*, there is even a scene where the cloud is referred to as Object O. The film's screenplay was written by director Toshio Masuda and Hiroyasu Yamamura, who had written many scripts for Tsuburaya Production's TV series like *Mirrorman*, *Ultraseven*, and *Dinosaur War Izenborg*. One of Yamamura's few motion picture credits included helping Jun Fukuda with the script for 1974's *Godzilla vs. Mechagodzilla*. As for Toshio Masuda, he was the director of 1974's controversial disaster film *Great Prophecies of Nostradamus*. Reuniting with Masuda was Toho's main special effects director Teruyoshi Nakano, who handled the effects work. This would be one of Nakano's last films, and he would retire (though, some feel he was pushed out by Toho in favor of the younger Koichi Kawakita) after the release of that same year's *Princess from the Moon*.

As for Nakano's work on this film it is naturally mostly devoted to the strange cloud itself. The cloud appears early in the film, enveloping Tokyo in a dark storm pulsing with lightning. A large aircraft carrier is destroyed when it tries to breach the cloud, so fans of miniature destruction don't have to wait too long to get their fix. Compared to the tidal waves, earthquakes, and other assorted natural or nuclear disasters from previous Japanese disaster films, a giant cloud can't offer much by comparison. But what it lacks for in destructive capability, it makes up for in mystery. That being said, there are a few instances of lightning causing some miniature destruction and Nakano does get to blow up a few buildings and oil tanks—though it really isn't much compared to his previous works.

The effects highlight of the film may well be when a U.S. air force plane flies over the cloud trying to breach it from above.[3] Instead, the cloud attacks it with lightning and the plane begins to streak with green fire. Another great scene (which has a spooky *Ghostbusters* quality to it) concerns Asakura, Mariko, and the scientific team trying to enter the cloud from the ground. To their shock, nothing—not even bullets—can penetrate it. In all, about 100 tons of dry ice was used for the cloud effects. Teruyoshi Nakano even won a Japanese Academy Award for his effects work on the film.

If the film has one weak spot, it is ironically the score. The film's music composer was the famed French film composer Maurice Jarre who scored *Dr. Zhivago*, *Ghost*, and many other famous films. Unfortunately, one would be hard pressed to think that the composer of this film was the same man who composed classics like *Lawrence of Arabia*. Like many of Jarre's other scores, it is heavy on piano, but is very forgettable. His only fitting music cues are a few he uses for the cloud, which themselves sound suspiciously similar to music and sound effects used for the storm-causing alien probe in *Star Trek IV: The Voyage Home* (1986).

Earning ¥760,000,000, the film probably wasn't as big a hit as was hoped for. In some respects, this was also Sakyo Komatsu's last major film adaptation or rather, the last one he was involved with. After this would be the 1989 TV series *Sakyo Komatsu's Anime Theater* and the remake of *Submersion of Japan* in 2006.[4]

Chapter Notes

[1] Though Toho contributed to the production and distributed, the film is considered to be more of a Daiei picture, and when released on home video is often through Daiei.

[2] The movie seems to strongly—and ridiculously—imply that the dog in distress caused the cloud to appear!

[3] Sharp-eyed fans will notice this scene features actor Dennis Falt, the Russian sub commander from *The Return of Godzilla* (1984). In an interview with Patrick Galvan, Falt remembered that the scene was filmed on a Toei soundstage.

[4] Entitled *The Sinking of Japan* for English markets to avoid confusion with the original. In their homeland, both movies are merely entitled *Japan Sinks*.

THE BLACK HORROR (1957) Announced alongside *The Mysterians* was *The Black Horror*, Ken Kuronuma's follow-up project to his popular *Rodan*. Despite the dark title, it was to have been a Superman-inspired superhero story filmed in color. Actually, it would be a series of serials not unlike Shintoho's *Starman*. In the story, a young man is given great power. Though the script is lost to this day, scholars believe one can guess its contents thanks to a novel Kuronuma published entitled *Black Fire* not long after. In *Black Fire*, 200 million years in the past, aliens attack a super advanced benevolent earth society and try to steal the power of the earth's core. This advanced civilization fends off the aliens and then goes to live underwater. In the present, a boy named Goro is gifted by them with the power to defend earth against the returning aliens. As to why *Black Horror* was never produced, that is anyone's guess.

THOSE MAGNIFICENT MEN IN THEIR FLYING MACHINES (c.1960s) One of the dream projects of Ishiro Honda and Eiji Tsuburaya both was to create a Japanese version of *Those Magnificent Men in Their Flying Machines*. Ishiro Honda said of the film to David Milner that, "I interviewed many of the pioneers of Japanese aviation, and a script was completed. I'm not sure if the project was canceled for financial reasons, or if it was canceled simply because Toho decided against producing the film."

ISHIRO HONDA'S TODAY I AM IN THE SKIES (1960) Likely the same film as what Honda called a "Japanese version of *Those Magnificent Men in Their Flying Machines*" was *Today I Am in the Skies*. Honda envisioned the film as a semi-documentary on the history of Japan's pioneer aviators including Kokichi Ukita, Chuhachi Ninomiya, and Yoshito Tokugawa. The film was written by Honda with Katsuhito Inomata and Eiji Tsuburaya, of course, lined up to do the effects. Just as the film was nearing production, Honda was taken off to go film *The Human Vapor* (1960) instead. The aviation film was made in 1964 by Kengo Furusawa, as Honda was by then too intertwined with the kaiju genre for Toho to let him do the film. In *Ishiro Honda: A Life in Film, From Godzilla to Kurosawa*, Honda is quoted as saying, "I had a lot of things I wanted to say to [Tomoyuki Tanaka] about that. My version was nothing like the film that was made."

EIJI TSUBURAYA'S TALE OF THE BAMBOO CUTTER (mid-1960's-1970) One of Eiji Tsuburaya's dream projects had been to realize a film adaptation of the folktale *The Bamboo Cutter's Daughter/The Tale of the Bamboo Cutter*, about a young girl from the skies who is adopted by a simple bamboo cutter. Tsuburaya wrote down various notes on the film over the years, right up to his death in 1970. The film was produced many years later as *Princess from the Moon* (1987; known as *Tale of the Bamboo Cutter* in Japan).

SPACE GUARDIAN BASE NO. 7 (1965) *Space Guardian Base No. 7* was among several planned co-productions between Toho and UPA initially announced in 1965. Unlike the five feature films, this was to be a 30 minute, color, TV movie to be shown in 26 territories. It was planned in November of 1965 in conjunction with Tsuburaya Productions and would be produced by Tomoyuki Tanaka.

UNMADE TOEI/WILLIAM ROSS COPRODUCTIONS (1966) During the production of 1966's *Water Cyborg* (*Terror Beneath the Sea* in the U.S.) William Ross, a bigwig at RAM Films, stated that if the film proved successful, he would sign an agreement with Toei to produce "13 more similar films in Japan, probably at the rate of four a year." The film was not a success and the proposed deal was struck.

100 SHOT/100 KILLED: BIG DUEL IN THE SOUTH SEAS (1966) Initially, this was to be the sequel to 1965's Akira Takarada spy thriller *100 Shot, 100 Killed* (*Ironfinger* in international markets). Nothing is known of the plot, but the subtitle was lifted to become the subtitle for *Godzilla, Ebirah, Mothra: Big Duel in the South Seas/Godzilla vs. the Sea Monster* (1966). Considering Jun Fukuda directed the original *100 Shot, 100 Killed* and was slated to do the sequel, it's possible that the 1966 Godzilla film killed the *100 Shot, 100 Killed* sequel in more ways than one. In any case, Jun Fukuda and Takarada did reteam to film *100 Shot, 100 Killed: Golden Eyes* (*Booted Babe, Busted Boss* internationally) in 1968.

NIPPON HIKOKI YARO (1970) Tied to Ishiro Honda's dreamed-of film about Japanese aviation pioneers eventually realized by another director as *Today I Am in the Skies* (1964); Eiji Tsuburaya also worked on a treatment for such a film. In fact, he was working on the project right before he passed away on January 25, 1970. Apparently, he wrote notes for the proposed film every day, and had planned to pitch it to Toho upon his return to the studio, planned for January 26th, the day after he ended up passing away in his sleep. Tsuburaya consulted with Ishiro Honda on this film. In fact, it was the last thing they spoke to one another about. *Ishiro Honda:*

A Life in Film, From Godzilla to Kurosawa quotes from a *Bungei Shinju* article from April of 1970 regarding the conversation. In November of 1969, Tsuburaya told Honda, "Let's... make special-effects films not just about monsters destroying buildings but more fantastic and entertaining. Something to give children a sense of dreams and hope." The duo agreed to begin working on the project in March of 1970. Sadly, the project died with Tsuburaya and Honda was never able to realize his dream project.

INVISIBLE BEAUTIES (1970) Before deciding to produce *The Invisible Swordsman* for children, Daiei had ideas of producing a serious tokusatsu film aimed at adults. Judging by the title, perhaps it would have focused on an invisible woman or women.

THE SINKING OF THE JAPANESE ARCHIPELAGO (1971) Before Sakyo Komatsu could publish his book, *Submersion of Japan*, and before Toho could adapt it for film, Daiei almost adapted the concept for screens. The sequence of events given by Japanese website cyberkids1954 states that in early 1971, Daiei was toying with making a film about the Great Tokyo Earthquake. Then in the fall of 1971, Daiei caught wind of Sakyo Komatsu's novel and wanted to adapt it. Prematurely, or without a written agreement with Sakyo Komatsu, Daiei President Masaichi Nagata announced that the company would produce *The Sinking of the Japanese Archipelago*. Also announced alongside of this film was *Gamera vs. Two Headed Monster W*. Daiei declared its official bankruptcy in December of 1971 (though had been bankrupt since 1970), and neither film was made.

GLORY OF THE UNION FLEET (1973) In 1967, Toho released *Japan's Longest Day*, which turned out to be the first of six war films that they produced up until 1972's *Navy Special Soldier*. Many of these films had special effects by Teruyoshi Nakano. The script for the seventh entry in this series (for some reason called the "Toho 8.15 series") was written in October of 1972 but never went before cameras for its planned summer 1973 release date.

NEW WORLD RAIDERS (1974) This script was proposed to Tomoyuki Tanaka by Kunmei Takahashi, who was a planner for *Zone Fighter*. The screenplay was by Yuji Amemiya of *Spectreman* and one of the writers of *Zone Fighter*. The film was to be directed by Jun Fukuda with special effects by Teruyoshi Nakano. Just what it was about is a mystery.

DEEP SEA CRISIS (1974) In the Autumn of 1973, Toho smelled a hit in the form of their *Submersion of Japan* about to be released that December. They began making plans for their next great disaster film, and among the candidates were Sakyo Komatsu's *Resurrection Day* (adapted by Kadokawa in 1980 and titled *Virus* for English markets), and another novel, *Deep Sea Crisis* by Takahiro Yoshimatsu. A review script for *Deep Sea Crisis* was written by Yoshimatsu and Shinichi Sekizawa by December of 1974, but the project was shelved.

GREAT PROPHECIES OF NOSTRADAMUS II: FEAR OF THE GREAT DEVIL (1975) This sequel to *Great Prophecies of Nostradamus*, the most successful film of 1974, was initially set for release in 1975. Meant to be comprised of the same production crew as the first film, it was likely cancelled due to trouble caused by the "No Nukes" group in regard to the first film. The unfinished story treatment (the story concept of which was said to be created by Tomoyuki Tanaka) tells of reporter Tsutomu Goto (named after the real writer of the book which the screenplay for *Great Prophecies of Nostradamus* was based upon) investigating an experiment in East Asia using spirit mediums in an attempt to contact the long dead Nostradamus about his predictions concerning the end of the world. As seen in the previous film, the world is consumed in a global conflict, with the battles taking place on land, at sea, under the sea, and even in outer space. At the end, a huge U.F.O. appears over Japan, the one nation to stay neutral while the rest of the world was at war. Though the U.F.O. is regarded as the great King of Terror that falls from the sky in Nostradamus's prophecies, the U.F.O. takes the Japanese people into space to begin a new future while the world burns. Also attached to this project was writer Masato Ide, author of screenplays for Akira Kurosawa films such as *Red Beard* (1965). Fourteen pages were written for this treatment in all. On a related note, in 1991, Tsutomu Goto finally published a sequel to his original book entitled *Predictions of Nostradamus: Middle East Chapter.*

GREAT EVACUATION (1976) Based upon a 1975 novel by Koji Tanaka, the film adaptation had a screenplay by Shuichi Nagahara (1977's *The War in Space*) and was to be directed by Toshio Masuda (1974's *Great Prophecies of Nostradamus*). The film was to be the second entry in Toho's "Special Effects Panic Movie" series to follow 1975's *Conflagration,* about terrorists exploding an oil tanker in Tokyo Bay. *Great Evacuation* would have seen a passenger plane crash land on a deserted island. However, the island is a secret testing ground for biological weapons. Eventually, the main character (a photographer named Ryuzaki) is the only survivor and is pursued by a faction of the Japanese government that wants to keep the island a secret. Had the film been made, it would have predated movies such as *Virus* (1980) and *Outbreak* (1995). In 1983, the script was adapted into a manga.

BATTLE OF THE GALACTIC EMPIRE (1977) Though one may assume that this was some sort of precursor to 1977's *The War in Space*, there may be more than that to this abandoned film. A logline in the 1978 Toho line-up proclaimed, "When the earth cannot live by itself alone, the planets of the Galactic Universe have created a large empire with a diameter of 80,000 light years!" It is believed that this was to have been an adaptation of Isaac Asimov's Foundation Series. However, Sakyo Komatsu and several other of Japan's leading science fiction writers were working on this story in a group. The first meeting of the writers group was held at Otani Hotel on September 8, 1977 and included 12 writers. Among some of the other writers were Masahiro Noda and a few illustrators also participated in the process. A first draft of the story was scheduled to be completed by the end of January 1978 and Shuichi Nagahara was tasked with turning the writers' notes into a screenplay and did so by March of 1978. The storyline involved peaceful people from earth fed up with warfare that leave to find a new planet. They establish the Galactic Federation and set up a new home on the planet Shangri-La. The violent Terrans (earthlings) soon take to space to take over Shangri-La and a battle for the peaceful planet ensues. The preparation period for this film was to last at least five months and Koichi Kawakita was the proposed effects director. The film was announced for 1978 at one point but Toho eventually dropped it. Though sources are conflicting, it would seem *Sayonara Jupiter* also came out of Sakyo Komatsu's writers group that birthed *Battle of the Galactic Empire*.

MOLK: DICTATOR OF 2051 (1977) In 1977, when Tomoyuki Tanaka found himself president of Toho, one of the films slated for development was the sci-fi film *Molk: Dictator of 2051*. It was an adaptation of the novel *Mysterious Frozen Human: Adventure of Space Ship Super Nova 2* a story by British science fiction writer Angus MacVicar. It had been published in Japan by Kadokawa Bunko and translated by Mamoru Nakagami. The film was planned by none other than *Godzilla vs. Hedorah* director Yoshimitsu Banno (who presumably hoped to direct) and Kenichiro Tsunoda, an executive producer on *The War of the Gargantuas*. The story concerned a "superman" called Molk, who is found frozen in suspended animation in a special capsule on an asteroid. When he is revived by the crew of the spacecraft Super Nova, it is revealed that he has been asleep for 100,000 years. Molk soon takes over lunar base 2051 and chaos ensues. MacVicar had also written a sequel, *The Mystery of Pluto—Adventure 1* (also published by Kadokawa Bunko) so perhaps Toho hoped for a franchise. As to why the film was abandoned, budget woes were probably to blame.

MARTIAN ARMY (1978) The story contents of this sci-fi script are unknown, but it was written by author Mitsutoshi Ishigami and considered for a time by Tomoyuki Tanaka. Ishigami was an actor who appeared in such films as *House* (1997) and was the future writer of Toho's *Princess from the Moon* (1987).

NOBORU TSUBURAYA'S UNTITLED DISASTER MOVIE (1978) More of a desire than an actual, bonafide project; Noboru Tsuburaya stated that one day he dreamed of doing a disaster movie similar to Irwin Allen films such as *The Poseidon Adventure* (1972) or *The Towering Inferno* (1974). Specifically, Tsuburaya was speaking about the success of working on *The Last Dinosaur* for ABC in 1978: "We've reached the top of Mont-Blanc (the ABC television network), now we'd like to climb Everest (Irwin Allen disaster films)." This statement was taken from the *Japanese Fantasy Film Journal* #12, which itself is quoting from a February 6, 1977 article from the *San Francisco Examiner and Chronicle*.

SHOGO TOMIYAMA'S DO ANDROIDS DREAM OF ELECTRIC SHEEP (mid-1980s) Unaware of the movie *Blade Runner* (1982), Toho producer Shogo Tomiyama at one point wanted to adapt Phillip K. Dick's *Do Androids Dream of Electronic Sheep*.

ISHIRO HONDA'S GHOST (1992) In an interview with David Milner, Ishiro Honda mentioned a film that he had always longed to make about a Japanese soldier. Specifically he said, "A third movie I originally was going to work on was a Japanese version of *Ghost*. A dead soldier comes back to Japan from a foreign war. He wanders around...This is highly classified information!" Though this may sound like "The Tunnel" sequence in *Akira Kurosawa's Dreams* (1990), the interview was conducted in 1992. As such, this must be a different—albeit similar—idea.

NOSTRADAMUS HORRIFYING REVALATION: TRAVELER TO THE UNKNOWN (1994) This film, mentioned in a letter in *G-Force* (later *G-Fan*) #8 in March 1994 by Hikari Takeda, says that it was a Toei film. The only other known details were that Tomokazu Miura of *Sayonara Jupiter* would star in it. If this was in some way related to

Tsutomu Goto's 1991 bestseller *Predictions of Nostradamus: Middle East Chapter* is unknown.

JAPAN SINKS 1999 (1998) In 1998, Shochiku announced plans to remake *Submersion of Japan* with Kazuki Omori directing and possibly writing. The production was formally announced on September 30, 1998, at the Ginza Tokyo Hotel stating that the film would be a New Year's movie for 2000 released in December of 1999. Things got serious enough that there was an advance trailer made that ran in theaters. Supposedly, the film was budgeted at ¥1.2 million with a hoped for gross of ¥3 billion. Omori, along with Sakyo Komatsu, was a victim of the Great Hanshin-Awaji Earthquake of 1995. Omori hoped to use the film to promote earthquake awareness amongst the younger generation. Shochiku hoped to utilize CGI for the film's special effects, though presumably miniatures would be used as well. However, Shochiku was not able to secure the funds to produce the film, and on March 5, 1999, Shochiku president Nobuyoshi Otani announced at a press conference that the production was cancelled.

UNTITLED KOICHI KAWAKITA EARTHQUAKE FILM (2002) In 2002, *G-Fan* reported that Koichi Kawakita would make a film about the 1994 Kobe Earthquake for the Kobe Museum. Yoshikazu Ishii was to have been the second unit director.

STEVEN SODERBERGH'S MATANGO (2016) As odd as it sounds, *Erin Brockovitch* and *Magic Mike* director Steven Soderbergh at one point wished to remake Toho's *Matango*, which he had seen as a kid. Reportedly, he couldn't bring himself to eat a mushroom until he was 30 years old. In an interview with *Little White Lies* he said, "I wanted to remake that. [But] I couldn't come to terms with the studio... it was a movie I saw as a kid and it scared the shit out of me. I wanted to remake it but I couldn't figure out a deal with Toho, so it didn't happen." The interview was conducted in 2017, but he is referring to the year 2016 when this happened. Ed Godziszewski, also aware of the project, said on Twitter that, "In the course of our research on the Honda biography, we found that when there was interest expressed in remaking *Matango* in the late 2000's, Toho quickly moved to renew the rights to the original story to prevent that project from happening. So this is no surprise."

APPENDIX II
ALTERNATE VERSIONS
OF EXISTING FILMS

THE H-MAN (1958) In the original draft, Masuda volunteers to turn himself into an H-Man as a means of better understanding and defeating the enemy. Also, there was no fiery climax as in the finished film. The film was also originally envisioned as being in black and white, but after the success of *Rodan* (1956) and *The Mysterians* (1957) in color, it was decided to film *The H-Man* in color as well.

BATTLE IN OUTER SPACE (1958) The original draft for this film included a scene where, on the moon, the Earth Defense Force battles Natal tanks that resemble pillbugs. Early designs for the Natals were also insectoid, as they had six tentacle-like arms and only one eye. *Toho Special Effects Movie Complete Works* (2012) says that in the second draft script, a Natal appears during an earth conference meeting and has an epidermis like tree bark, and would have plant-like attributes. In the final film, there is mention of an attack on a ship in the Panama Canal when it is pulled from the ocean into the air and destroyed. In early drafts it was meant to be a fairly major effects scene. Though the characters of Dr. Adachi, Dr. Immerman, and Etsuko (the same names of characters that appear prominently in *The Mysterians*) exist in the finished *Battle in Outer Space* film, it is believed in the first draft they were to be those exact same characters carried over. This element was likely present in the story pitch by Jojiro Okami, who had gotten the ball rolling with *The Mysterians* as well. Apparently, the final script just kept the names and they are not meant to be the same characters. Furthermore, this film was to begin shooting in August, but problems with *The Birth of Japan* bumped shooting back to November.

THE SECRET OF THE TELEGIAN (1960) Ishiro Honda was the original director of this film and reportedly had a hand in its development. Due to scheduling conflicts that began due to *The Birth of Japan* and *Battle in Outer Space*, Jun Fukuda directed this film in Honda's place.

THE HUMAN VAPOR (1960) Reportedly, earlier versions of the script are similar to the finished film except for one scene Ishiro Honda insisted be cut. In the scene, Mizuno the Vapor Man would have murdered the wife and child of a policeman!

THE LAST WAR (1961) The first draft explicitly identified the U.S. and the Soviet Union, and subsequent drafts changed the names to make the film easier to market internationally. The project went through six drafts, whereas most went through four at the most. As for differences, Tamura's daughter Saeko was a nurse, as was the female love interest in Toei's *The Final War*. The Tamura family would have also fled from Tokyo to escape the bomb. Takano (Akira Takarada's character) was to try and convince Saeko to leave with him but she wouldn't abandon her patient. The script was then overhauled to change the similarities between it and Toei's film. The original director was also to have been Hiromichi Horikawa (the man whom almost directed *Inter Ice Age 4*), but he was taken off of the project because he kept campaigning to remove as many effects scenes as possible. Yumi Shirakawa's role as the kindergarten teacher was also originally slated for Japanese singer Izumi Yukimura.

THE GREAT THIEF/THE LOST WORLD OF SINBAD (1963) Though this film doesn't contain any giant monsters, storyboards seem to show Hideyo Amamoto's witch Granny growing to gigantic proportions to battle Toshiro Mifune's Luzon/Sinbad. The giant kite was originally supposed to be a bird disguise for Luzon/Sinbad.

MATANGO (1963) As this story was partially inspired by a real life incident wherein some rich kids took their father's yacht out to sea and had to be rescued, the first draft of *Matango* centered around more youthful, spoiled characters. Furthermore, Masami Fukushima had written a Japanese version of William Hope Hodgson's "The Voice in the Night" story. In Fukushima's story, it is clear that inhaling the spores can also turn one into a Mushroom Person (this is implied in the climax of the finished film). Kumi Mizuno's transformation scene was also different. Originally, she was to sport the same keloid scars as the other Mushroom People, but Honda felt it would be more effective if she instead became more beautiful—to heighten the temptation to eat the mushrooms. According to actor Yoshio Tsuchiya, the film has an alternate ending where Akira Kubo's face is still normal. This is not meant to convey that he wasn't affected by the mushrooms, but to leave the picture on an ambiguous note where the audience wonders if Kubo's character is just crazy. And indeed, *Toho Complete Works* states that

162

the first draft ends with the face of Kubo's character being normal and unscarred.

GOKE, BODY SNATCHER FROM HELL (1968) Amongst P-Productions' other failures of 1967 was this proto-version of *Goke, Body Snatcher from Hell* from Shochiku. As it turned out, the Hajime Sato cult classic began as a potential TV series from P-Productions. Filmed with puppets, the series focused on good aliens trying to recapture an alien monster that escaped from their craft over earth. In this version, Gokemidoro is a furry monster with multiple arms. The concept was somehow acquired by Shochiku, which teamed with P-Productions (who would handle the special effects) to turn the concept into a much more serious horror film. Writer Susumu Takaku suggested Toei's Hajime Sato as director and off the film went. Initially, Sato came up with an idea wherein invisible alien monsters ran amuck in a mental ward until he came up with the idea of instead opening the film on an airliner that crashes. Some sources indicate that the multi-armed Gokemidoro was considered to appear in the film as a giant monster, but was dropped. Images of this incarnation have been included in a series of Japanese trading cards featuring kaiju and associated characters.

SUBMERSION OF JAPAN (1973) Reportedly, drafts for *Submersion of Japan* went through a few changes. The first draft, which was said to be relatively short, had Onodera and Dr. Tadokoro witnessing an underwater volcano erupting which was soon cut and exists only in the first treatment. Deleted scenes in other scripts aren't terribly exciting, a good example being Prime Minister Yamamoto and secretary Mimura discussing the crisis on a golf course (a concept that would work its way into *Deathquake*). On the other hand, scenes such as Onodera looking for Reiko in the volcanic ash after Mt. Fuji erupts and the Sanriku Coast sinking are not included at all. Remarkably, the very final scene of the epilogue featuring the train isn't in the final script. Author Sakyo Komatsu also lamented to *Science Fiction Studies* about a few scenes in the novel excised from the film he was sad to lose:

...there were still two little things left out of the film that disappointed me. In the novel, the old man Watari has the ear of the Prime Minister, but he also has a rapport with a man everyone regards as a "mad scientist," Dr. Tadokoro. There's a scene that takes place in a teahouse, where Watari asks Tadokoro, "Is Japan's destruction really upon us?" and as Tadokoro is explaining his conclusions, there is a small earthquake. Just before the tremor, the birds outside take flight

163

and Tadokoro says "It's coming." After the quake has passed in the novel, the teahouse flower arrangement drops a single camellia blossom. That detail was left out of the film. The other omission was a scene at the very end in which Watari says to a young woman, "Would you let me see you?" and she slips out of her kimono. I wanted that in the movie, even if they had to film it from behind. [Laughs]

THE BLOODSUCKING CLAW (1974) Before *Bloodsucking Rose*, Ei Ogawa turned in *The Bloodsucking Claw*. How different it was from *Bloodsucking Rose* is unknown, but Cyberkids1954 considers it different enough to label it as "unproduced". A 2014 book, *Godzilla: Toho SPFX Movies*, also lists this as a lost project (rather than a proto-version of *Bloodsucking Rose*) so it must have been a different conclusion to the Bloodthirsty trilogy.

THE WAR IN SPACE (1977) Though it does contain the human-sized "Space Beastman," this film was also supposed to contain some giant, slug-like monsters on Venus. Additionally, the planet was to be covered in lush jungle life with moving plants and vines that attack in a manner similar to the one in *Mothra* (1961). The characters all had different names in early drafts, including the Hell Commander who hailed from "Hercules Zero." Takigawa's secret bomb weapon was not present in the first draft either. Apparently there was no Space Beastman either, just a taller, bigger humanoid alien to contend with. Though the translation could be wrong, it would seem the aliens have a fortress on Venus, though the fortress could be the same as the ship in the finished film.

SAYONARA JUPITER (1984) Like many films, *Sayonara Jupiter* originally started out as a much more ambitious film. Had the film been made as originally envisioned, it would have ran nearly four hours long, though. As such, characters were compressed and combined, and numerous scenes were cut out. Sakyo Komatsu reported, "Due to the limited time and budget, the scenes which were set on the moon were all cut out [though, the film opens with a scene on the moon]. Also, scenes on Earth were cut out except for the Jupiter Beach sequence. As for the story, the past of Eiji and Maria, political struggles, were all cut out." When Komatsu handed over the script to director Koji Hashimoto who drastically cut it, he changed the character of Carlos into that of a boy rather than a man, and the final version of the story was completed.

164

APPENDIX III
MORE TOKUSATSU FILMS
UNRELEASED IN THE U.S.

THE RAINBOW MAN (1949) Daiei B&W (with color sequences), 80m. *Director:* Kiyohiko Ushihara *Screenplay:* Hajime Takanoshi *Special Effects Director:* Eiji Tsuburaya *Music:* Akira Ifukube *Cast:* Teruko Akatsuki, Keiju Kobayashi, and Katsuko Wakasugi.

Notes: Based on a 1947 novel by Kikuo Tsunoda, this film isn't so much a sci-fi story as much as a regular murder mystery. The effects scenes by Eiji Tsuburaya only come into play whenever one of the victims takes a drug that makes them hallucinate a rainbow. As this happens, the black and white film suddenly switches to a color pattern similar to a rainbow. Since there were no color films in Japan at this time, the effect was rather shocking—especially on the big screen.

Basically, the film is a typical noir/spooky house mystery notable for having a female lead. The main plot concerns the Maya family, whose mad scientist patriarch has created a drug that causes people to hallucinate a rainbow before they die.

GHOST TRAIN (1949) Daiei B&W, 81m. *Director:* Kazuo Miyakawa *Screenplay:* Hideo Oguni *Special Effects Director:* Eiji Tsuburaya *Music:* unknown *Cast:* Kinjiro Yanagi and Hanabu Akacho.

Notes: The film, which began as a radio drama, begins with a group of passengers set to go on a bus tour. When the tour is cancelled due to bad weather, the station manager tells them the tale of a ghost train that crashed years ago but is still occasionally seen. Supposedly, anyone who sees the train will die. Eiji Tsuburaya did the effects for the train crash scene.

BEAUTY OF THE ICE PILLAR (1950) Daiei B&W, 86m. *Director:* Seiji Hisamatsu *Screenplay:* Rampo Edogawa *Special Effects Director:* unknown *Music:* Yuji Koseki *Cast:* Joji Oka, Chieko Soma, and Michitaro Mizushima.

Notes: This film is based on a vampire story by Rampo Edogawa written back in 1930. The story was changed drastically when adapted for film. It concerns two men fighting a duel over a woman. One of the men is presumed dead, but he soon returns disfigured to keep pursuing the girl. The music is done by future *Mothra* (1961) composer Yuji Koseki.

IRON CLAW (1951) Daiei B&W, 82m. *Director:* Nobuo Adachi *Screenplay:* Nobuo Adachi and Joji Oka *Special Effects Director:* Joji Oka *Music:* Yoshinobu Shiraki *Cast:* Joji Oka, Sumiko Hidaka, and Ryosuke Kagawa.

Notes: Basically Daiei's version of *Dr. Jekyll and Mr. Hyde*, it begins with an investigation into a murder committed by a man resembling a gorilla. As it turns out, a peaceful man (Joji Oka's character Tashiro) who cares for orphans at a local church is the culprit. The man doesn't transform because of a serum, but is a sort of were-gorilla (he was bitten by a gorilla during the war, and whenever he experiences what we today would call PTSD, he transforms into an ape-like human). The film climaxes with Tashiro transforming into his ape-man persona, abducting a female showgirl, and climbing to a rooftop with her a la King Kong. He falls from the rooftop, and his spirit, now at peace, walks from his dead body across the Ginza skyline back to the Christian church where he worked.

Appropriately, this film was directed by the same man who helmed *Invisible Man Appears* (1949). The film was also said to be inspired by *Murders in the Rue Morgue* (1932) and *King Kong* (1933). Actor Joji Oka apparently did his own makeup for the role. Photographs of the film don't show much of a monster though, just some crude fangs protruding through Oka's mouth that look like they could be bought from a Dollar Store in today's world. The tagline on the poster read: "A devil person? A monster? A shiver of the foggy night! The appearance of the ferocious gorilla human being!"

JOURNEY TO THE WEST (1952) Daiei B&W, 84m. *Director:* Yasuzo Fuyushima *Screenplay:* Fushi Hakka *Cast:* Kotaro Bando.

Notes: Daiei's adaptation of the famous Chinese tale of Sun Wukong, the "Monkey King."

LEGEND OF THE WHITE SERPENT (1956) Toho Color, 103m. *Director:* Shiro Toyoda *Screenplay:* Toshio Yasumi *Special Effects Director:* Eiji Tsuburaya *Music:* Ikuma Dan *Cast:* Ryo Ikebe, Shirley Yamaguchi, and Makoto Kobori.

Notes: Also known as *Madame White Snake*, this was a co-production between Toho and the Shaw Brothers of Hong Kong. It is a combined adaptation of both the Chinese tale *The Legend of the White Snake* as well as Fusao Hayashi's story, "Madam White's Witchcraft". The film features very limited effects scenes of a tsunami destroying a feudal Japanese coastal village and also contained scenes of Madame White Snake transforming into a snake.

VAMPIRE BRIDE (1960) Shintoho B&W, 80m. *Director:* Kyotaro Namiki *Cast:* Junko Ikeuchi, Yasuko Mita, and Reiko Seto.

Notes: When the beautiful Fujiko is pushed off a cliff and disfigured by jealous women, she comes back to haunt them with the newfound ability to change herself into a hairy, killer beast. Supposedly when lead actress Junko Ikeuchi rose to stardom in the later 1960s, she purchased all existing prints of the film and had them destroyed! (Not to be confused with 1959's *Woman Vampire*)

INVISIBLE TENGU (1960) Daiei B&W, 73m. *Director:* Mitsuo Hirotsu *Screenplay:* Tetsuro Yoshida *Special Effects Director:* unknown *Music:* Takeo Watanabe *Cast:* Yutaka Nakamura, Chitose Maki, and Ryuzo Shimada.

Notes: This Daiei production features an invisible swordsman is out to avenge his father. The titular invisible tengu is a type of yokai, so even before Daiei's yokai trilogy of the late 1960s, they were playing around with the spooks.

THE DEMON OF MT. OE (1960) Daiei Color, 114m. *Director:* Tokuzo Tanaka *Screenplay:* Fuji Yahiro *Special Effects Director:* Daiei Special Effects Dept. *Music:* Takeo Watanabe *Cast:* Kazuo Hasegawa, Kojiro Hongo, and Fujiko Yamamoto.

Notes: This samurai film about a popular Japanese legend may well contain Daiei's first real monsters before the creation of Gamera. The film includes a giant spider marionette that looks nearly as convincing as the Kumonga marionette from 1967's *Son of Godzilla* and the bull-like monster is comparable to the Peplum monsters of Italian cinema.

WIND VELOCITY 75 METERS (1963) Daiei B&W, 88m. *Director:* Shigeo Tanaka *Screenplay:* Hajime Takasui & Kozo Taguchi *Special Effects Director:* Yonesaburo Tsukiji *Music:* Tadashi Kinoshita *Cast:* Ken Utsui, Jiro Tamiya, and Junko Kano.

Notes: Directed by Shigeo Tanaka (who would go on to direct *Gamera vs. Barugon* in 1966), this film covered an oncoming typhoon. Naturally, the climax was an effects spectacular directed by Yonesaburo Tsukiji wherein Tokyo is partially destroyed by the typhoon. Tsukiji had just cancelled work on *Giant Horde Beast Nezura* when this film began filming. An entire miniature set of Ginza was built for the typhoon scene. 15 tons of water was dropped onto the miniature set and ended up damaging the soundstage.

Obviously, for a non-Japanese speaker, this film isn't really of any interest until the final act when the titular typhoon hits. Actually, the typhoon doesn't hit until 71 minutes in and considering that the film runs at 88 minutes, there's not much to see. The effects shots that are shown are very well done, though, there just aren't many of them.

ADVENTURE IN KIGAN CASTLE/ADVENTURES OF TAKLA MAKAN (1966) Toho Color, 105m. *Director:* Senkichi Taniguchi *Screenplay:* Kaoru Mabuchi (Takeshi Kimura) *Special Effects Director:* Eiji Tsuburaya (uncredited) *Music:* Akira Ifukube *Cast:* Toshiro Mifune, Mie Hama, Yumi Shirakawa, Akiko Wakabayashi, Akihiko Hirata, Jun Tazaki, and Ichiro Arishima.

Notes: Toshiro Mifune, who also produced the film alongside Tomoyuki Tanaka, stars as Osami, a soldier of fortune out to collect the ashes of Buddha. The journey takes him to the Middle East where he battles giant birds and wizards as far as fantastical aspects go. The picture was actually filmed in Iran. Considering this film reunited most of the cast and crew of 1963's *The Great Thief/Lost World of Sinbad* (and is almost a beat-for-beat remake of it), it's a shame AIP didn't snatch this picture up as a sequel to the aforementioned film. Being set in the Middle East, this film is even more Sinbad-like. Some of the sets from this movie were also used on episode seven (with Antlar) of *Ultraman*.

KONTO 55: GREAT OUTER SPACE ADVENTURE (1969) Toho Color, 72m. *Director:* Jun Fukuda *Screenplay:* James Miki *Special Effects Director:* Yoichi Manoda and Shoji Okawa *Music:* Kenjiro Hirose *Cast:* Kinichi Hagimoto, Jiro Sakagami, Hiroshi Kawaguchi, Keiko Sawai, and Midori Uchiyama.

Notes: This *Konto 55* comedy film was written by James Miki, who around this same time was also working on *Adam of the Stars* for Toho. From what this author can gather, the film actually begins in the Edo (feudal) period and has the two comedy leads abducted by a U.F.O. and taken to another planet. There they endure a series of challenges, and then return to earth where more than 100 years have passed. The film was double-billed with *All Monsters Attack* (aka *Godzilla's Revenge*). The film also borrowed footage from *The Last War* (1961) and *Latitude Zero* (1969). It also features stock footage (or possibly new footage) of the P-1 from *Invasion of Astro-Monster* (aka *Monster Zero*, 1965).

The Konto 55 duo was formed in 1966 and starred in several other Toho comedies and were comprised of comedians Kinichi Hagimoto and Jiro Sakagami. This ended up being the final Konto 55 movie, but was supposed to be followed by *Konto 55: Strong Heart Expo Campaign*. The story would have been set around the Osaka Expo '70 (famous to kaiju eiga fans as the setting of *Gamera vs. Jiger*) where a rich American corporation owner needs a new heart and targets one of the comedy duo believing their heart is a good match.

PINK LADY'S BIG MOVING PICTURE/PINK LADY'S MOTION PICTURE (1978) Toho Color, 83m. *Director:* Tom Kotani *Screenplay:* James Miki *Special Effects Director:* Unknown *Music:* Shunichi Tokura *Cast:* Pink Lady (Keiko Masuda and Mitsuyo Nemuro), Masumi Harukawa, Kunie Tanaka, Ken Tanaka, and William Ross.

Notes: A comedy like *Konto 55: Great Outer Space Adventure*, this film was primarily a musical vehicle for the musical duo, Pink Lady. They are mostly known in the west for the infamous *Pink Lady and Jeff*, a variety show that ran for all of three episodes before being cancelled (*Tidal Wave's* Lorne Greene made an appearance on the show as well). Needless to say, they were far more popular in Japan.

The nonsensical film features a special effects sequence with a giant dog, invisibility, and an alien monster. As an aside, the next year Pink Lady would appear on the variety program *Yanyan Singing Studio* where they guested alongside the Titanosaurus suit from *Terror of Mechagodzilla*, marking its last onscreen appearance in a caveman spoof

LUSTY TRANSPARENT MAN (1979) Nikkatsu Color, running time unknown. *Director:* Isao "Ko" Hayashi *Screenplay:* Chiko Katsura

Notes: After going bankrupt, Nikkatsu became notorious for making soft-core porn films. One of them was this invisible man spoof which also had a sequel that same year.

GREAT TOKYO EARTHQUAKE MAGNITUDE 8.1 (1980) Yomiuri Television/Toho Eizo Color, 96m. *Director:* Kiyoshi Nishimura *Screenplay:* Kiyomi Shimokazaka & Kazuo Kasahara *Special Effects Director:* Koichi Kawakita *Music:* Masanori Sasaseji *Cast:* Sonny Chiba, Keiko Takeshita, and Toshio Shiba

Notes: This movie has the distinction of being the only major TV movie produced by Tomoyuki Tanaka (according to the film's Japanese Wikipedia page). It had a budget of ¥150,000,000 and ¥30,000,000 went to special effects alone. The film had the cooperation of the self-defense forces and utilized a large number of extras to portray refugees. It starred Sonny Chiba and also featured Toshio Shiba (*Silver Mask, Godzilla vs. Hedorah*). It would seem the film was broadcast only once until 2015 when this "phantom TV movie"—as the Japanese call it—resurfaced. When initially broadcast, the movie won an audience share of 18.3%.

APPENDIX IV
LOST U.S. VERSIONS
OF TOKUSATSU FILMS

HALF HUMAN (1958) B&W, 70m. *Director:* Kenneth G. Krane *Cast:* John Carradine, Russel Thorson, Robert Karnes, and Morris Ankrum.

Notes: The 1958 Americanization of Toho's *Abominable Snowman* is quite poor when compared to 1956's *Godzilla, King of the Monsters!* starring Raymond Burr. For this film, new footage of John Carradine and other actors was shot. Though one might assume the new footage featured the storied actor on the trail of the Yeti in the Japanese Alps, Carradine's Dr. Rayburn does little more than sit behind a desk and narrate the original Japanese footage—so little of which is shown that the scenes weren't even dubbed into English. The film would have fared much better had it simply been dubbed into English as was done with its predecessor, *Gigantis, the Fire Monster.*

The new footage was directed by one-time director Kenneth Krane, though the assistant director, Hal Klein had served as an assistant director on such distinguished films as *All About Eve* (1950). The film's opening credits do their best to hide the fact that the film was a Japanese production, though the closing credits state, "The segments of this picture depicting Japanese people and locales were written and filmed in Japan. Special credit is due to the artists and technicians there who contributed much to the authenticity of this picture." The American version, which runs a scant 70 minutes, also completely excised Masaru Sato's score. Ironically though, the film does feature some new effects scenes regarding the autopsy of the infant snowman. Toho shipped the original suit to America for filming of the new footage.

The film was peddled to theaters throughout 1958 by Distributors Corporation of America which operated from 1952-1959 and unleashed such turkeys onto the public as *Plan 9 From Outer Space* (1959). *Half Human* was released on a double bill with two alternating features: *Monster from Green Hell* (about giant wasps) and *The Man Without a Body* (self-explanatory). The film was released onto VHS in the U.S. in 1990 by Rhino Home Video and remains one of the only ways to see the film today.

THE FINAL WAR (1965) B&W, 76m. *Director:* William Ross

Notes: After a limited theatrical release, Toei's *The Final War* played on U.S. television throughout the 1960s—and possibly as late as 1974. It was distributed to U.S. theaters by Sam Lake Enterprises in 1962 and to television by Medallion TV. Oddly, footage from Toei's other 1961 effects film, *Invasion of the Neptune Men,* was edited into the TV version of *The Final War.* These aren't mere destruction shots, but clips of the film's U.F.O.s! To explain this, the dubbing states that these are new Soviet Union weapons! Obviously, the distributor wanted to beef up the film's effects shots, and ironically, Toei themselves had used footage from *The Final War* in *Invasion of the Neptune Men!* William Ross, who would later produce *The Green Slime* and distribute *The Super Inframan* in the U.S., directed the U.S. version. In the credits, the cast is credited as "Tatsuo Umemiya and the Toei players".

THE SECRET OF THE TELEGIAN (1964) B&W, 85m.

Notes: The Secret of the Telegian was the only of Toho's mutant trilogy not to see a theatrical release in the states. It was acquired for theatrical release by Herts-Lion International Corp. in January of 1964 and was announced as both *The Telegians* and *Secret File of the Telegian.* For whatever reason, the theatrical release was cancelled and instead went to television in a cropped, black and white version. If Herts-Lion International had plans of doing their own dub or not is unknown, but the TV version utilized Toho's international dub recorded in Hong Kong and featured Ted Thomas as Detective Kobayashi. Alternative sources say the TV version was uncut, while others say it excised five minutes' worth of footage. In his *Japanese Science Fiction, Fantasy and Horror Films* book, Stuart Galbraith reported that as the book was going to press that "an obscure distributor began selling English-dubbed, color videocassettes of the picture." If this was a bootleg release or a legitimate one, is unknown. Otherwise, it doesn't seem that *The Secret of the Telegian* ever saw a VHS release in the U.S. However, as this book's editor, Ted Johnson, has in his collection the VHS master of the U.S. edit of *The Secret of the Telegian,* it seems that it did, in fact, have a VHS release in the States at some point.

GORATH (1964) Color, 83m. *Producers:* Edward L. Alperson & Stanley Meyer *Editor:* Kenneth Wannberg

Notes: Brenco Pictures Corporation secured the rights to release *Gorath* theatrically in the U.S. in late 1962 and spent more than a year and half editing the film for release. It was announced as *Gorath, the Mysterious Star* and another title played with was *Astronaut 1980.* It was released on a double-bill with *The Human*

Vapor on May 15, 1964 through Allied Artists and again in 1968 in an attempt to save a struggling Brenco.

Brenco's version notoriously cut out the giant monster Magma, which they jokingly called Wally the Walrus. However, initially Brenco made attempts to doctor the footage of Magma rather than excising it completely. To do so, they used an optical printer to add fog to the sequence to partially obscure the monster. They also redubbed his original shrieks with Rodan's more menacing roar. A version of this film was screened for test audiences who still laughed at the monster, and so at the last minute, Brenco decided to edit out all footage of Magma and revise certain bits of dialogue concerning him (conflicting sources say Magma was in the theatrical cut, just never the TV or VHS versions). These weren't the only alterations, actually, most of Tsuburaya's effects footage of Tokyo being flooded, which Brenco deemed inferior, was obscured by a layer of fog via an optical printer! Some sources say six minutes of footage was cut while others say four.

As for dubbing, the English language script was done by John Meredith Lucas, future *Star Trek* writer and alleged idea man behind *Frankenstein vs. the Human Vapor*. Sadly, only four actors total (including Paul Frees who oversaw dubbing) dubbed all of the characters into English! A whining sound effect was also added to the Gorath star itself, and the ending with the destruction of the moon was reedited to occur just as the Earth moves out of Gorath's orbit. A few new sequences of star charts were filmed for the U.S. release, but no new actors were used. *Gorath* had a VHS release first through Congress Video and later Prism Entertainment in the mid-1980s, but it has yet to see a DVD release in the States. That said, this film, in its edited Brenco cut, does air from time to time on the TV network Comet, so it's not entirely lost.

THE HUMAN VAPOR (1964) Color, 81m. *Producers:* Edward L. Alperson & Stanley Meyer *Editor:* Kenneth Wannberg

Notes: Another Brenco release from the same team that worked on *Gorath*, which this film was double-billed with on May 20, 1964. Like *Gorath, The Human Vapor* was heavily re-edited, cutting out 11 minutes worth of footage and adding in a few bits of new footage distinct to the U.S. version. The biggest change is the fact that Mizuno narrates the whole film and thus survives the end explosion (supposedly Yoshio Tsuchiya actually prefers this edit of the film!). This version even has end credits, and a narrator gives the actors' names as footage of each character replays. Prism Entertainment Corporation released the film to VHS in 1986 and presumably this was the last licensed home video release for the film in the U.S.

172

THE LAST WAR (1964) Color, 79m. *Producers:* Edward L. Alperson & Stanley Meyer *Editor:* Kenneth Wannberg

Notes: Part of what was a three-picture purchase from Brenco, *The Last War* was cut down to only 79 minutes for its American version. This version contains the song *It's a Small World After All* and audio of President John Kennedy's anti-nuclear weapons speech. The dubbing was headed by Paul Frees. It saw at least one VHS release through Video Gems in 1985 featuring a bear and an eagle (meant to represent the U.S. and Soviet Union) facing each other down on the cover.

Even more obscure, though, is Toho's international version of the film, which presumably is the full 110 minute version with its own English dub.

THE LOST WORLD OF SINBAD (1965) Color, 95m. *Notes:* Though Toho's non giant monster films weren't often acquired for distribution by AIP, they took a liking to Toho's *The Great Thief* and decided to rebrand it as a Japanese version of Sinbad, popular from *The 7ᵗʰ Voyage of Sinbad* (1958). AIP cut the film by two minutes and initially announced it as *The 7ᵗʰ Wonder of Sinbad* until it was changed to the current title. It was released in March of 1965 with *War of the Zombies*. The English language credits notoriously misidentify Shinichi Sekizawa as the Director of Photography! *The Lost World of Sinbad* never secured a VHS release in the U.S.

ATTACK OF THE MUSHROOM PEOPLE (1965) Color, 88m.

Notes: The U.S. version of this film utilized Toho's international dub and cut only 1 minute's worth of footage. It aired on television through AIP-TV in 1965.

TIDAL WAVE (1975) Color, 80m. *Director:* Andrew Meyer *Screenplay:* Andrew Meyer *Producer:* Max Youngstein *Cast:* Lorne Greene, Rhonda Leigh Hopkins, and John Fujioka.

Notes: With disaster movies like *Earthquake* (1974) having proven themselves as big hits, Roger Corman's New World Pictures acquired the rights to *Submersion of Japan* which they retitled *Tidal Wave* (the movie was likely retitled *Tidal Wave* because *Earthquake* had already been taken, and apparently there weren't any tidal wave disaster films yet. In reality, almost none of the film revolves around a tidal wave, and the tidal wave sequence is small potatoes compared to the Kanto earthquake scene).

For the first time in years, a *Godzilla, King of the Monsters!*-style makeover was given to a Japanese effects film. The U.S. version adds in Lorne Greene (*Bonanza*) as Ambassador Warren Richards. In other roles are actors Susan Sennett, Clifford A. Pellow, Marvin

Miller, Ralph James and Philip Roth. Future director Joe Dante did some of the dubbing. Eric Saarinen (Ron Howard's *Eat My Dust*) did the cinematography for the new scenes. Nearly an hour's worth of footage from the original version was cut out. The *Japanese Fantasy Film Journal* hilariously described the new footage as a "buffer zone to deaden the mounting tension."

Roger Ebert (who liked *Super Inframan* by the way) panned the film mercilessly writing in his review that, "It is purely and simply a wretched failure, a feeble attempt to paste together inept special effects (filmed in Japan) and Lorne Greene (filmed in America to his everlasting regret, I'll bet)." The *New York Times'* review was only slightly nicer stating, "Andrew Meyer, a young American director ("Night of the Cobra Women") with some cult following, is credited as the director of the American version, the focal point of which is Lorne Greene, who plays the United States representative at the United Nations. Mr. Greene isn't on screen much. He appears from time to time to urge his United Nations colleagues to provide homes for the Japanese population, whose islands are sinking into the sea in the other part of the movie. Mr. Greene's voice is getting so sonorous these days you suspect he'd prefer to sing his lines."

HIGH SEAS HIJACK (1977) Color, 95m. *Director:* John A. Bushelman *Screenplay:* Uncredited *Editor:* Jeff Bushelman *Cast:* Peter Graves & Patricia Haber.

Notes: Presumably due to the relative success of *Tidal Wave*, Pine-Thomas Productions picked up Toho's 1975 *Conflagration* and decided to do the same thing by adding in new footage of Peter Graves as Elliott Rhoades. One source also says that Henry G. Saperstein and UPA played a part in distributing it in U.S. Whatever the case, it was released October 21, 1977 (however, the end credits features a copyright notice of 1976). It never secured a U.S. VHS release, though did have a Dutch VHS release. The last time it was publically seen was a mid-afternoon broadcast on AMC in 2007.

THE IVORY APE (1980) Color, 96m. *Director:* Tom Kotani *Screenplay:* William Overgard & Arthur Rankin Jr. (story) *Special Effects Director:* Tsuburaya Productions *Music:* Bernard Hoffer & Maury Laws *Cast:* Jack Palance, Steven Keats, Cindy Pickett, and Celine Lomez.

Notes: Happy with the results for *The Last Dinosaur* (1977) and *The Bermuda Depths* (1978), Rankin/Bass decided to do one more co-production with the crew of Tsuburaya Productions. On location filming was once again done in Bermuda and other scenes were shot at Tsuburaya Productions in Tokyo. The plot focuses on the hunt for an albino gorilla with Jack Palance in the lead. *The Last*

174

Dinosaur's Steven Keats also returns. The film premiered on ABC on April 18, 1980, and like the other two Tsuburaya/ Rankin/Bass co-productions was released theatrically in Japan with four extra minutes worth of footage.

Unlike *The Last Dinosaur* and *The Bermuda Depths*, Warner Archive has yet to release *The Ivory Ape*. It isn't clear whether this film was ever released onto VHS in the U.S. but it was released on VHS in the Netherlands.

THE LAKE OF DRACULA (1980) Color, 79m.

Notes: Since Dracula is mentioned in *Bloodsucking Eyes* (1971), Toho titled the film *Lake of Dracula* for international export, because of the integral lake setting. Henry G. Saperstein re-retitled the film *The Lake of Dracula* for its early 80s television release. Several of the more gory moments of the ending were cut, which was strange considering Hammer's Dracula films of the 1960s like *Dracula Has Risen from the Grave* were airing on television relatively uncut. Three minutes in all were cut, and the edits mostly applied to the climax, where Shin Kishida tries to wrench a stair post from his chest after being impaled on it. Kishida is also awkwardly dubbed with a European accent. Some sources say this film was considered under the title of *Japula* in a nod to *Blacula* (1972). It was released to home video through Paramount Gateway in 1994, where the box cover identified it by its international title, *Lake of Dracula.*

EVIL OF DRACULA (1980) Color, 81m.

Notes: Tying in with the previous film, Toho invoked the Dracula name once again for overseas distribution. UPA released *Evil of Dracula* to television the same year as *Lake of Dracula*. This time, the climax is left intact (it's not terribly gruesome to begin with) but an earlier scene is severely edited for TV where the principal's wife cuts off a girl's face so that she can wear it as her own. Bits of nudity were naturally also edited out. It was released to home video through Paramount Gateway in 1994.

ESPY (1981) Color, 86m.

Notes: ESPY saw a limited release through Toho International in subtitled form in 1975. At a later date, the film was released to U.S. TV as *E.S.P./Spy* through Henry G. Saperstein's UPA. This version cuts out the psychedelic credits and instead overlays the English title *E.S.P./Spy* over the mountains of Switzerland and the credits roll over what is the pre-credits assassination scene in the Japanese version.

The film cuts out moments of gore too intense for TV. It also cut out the rather racy scene set in the Turkish nightclub where Tamura psychically rips out the tongue of one of the villains! The striptease still exists, but all footage of Abdul, the villainous henchman, is excised and therefore there is no nudity from Kaoru Yumi. Instead, the scene lasts very briefly, and it appears as though Tamura is shocked unconscious in the chair he is strapped to. After this, a brief snippet of dialogue from Ulrov regarding Tamura ripping Abdul's tongue out is cut on the following boat scene.

Other, more curious cuts, included the deletion of a telephone call between the Japanese head of ESPY and International head of ESPY early on in the film. There are more curious deletions of dialogue as well, such as a few short snippets in the Paris scene between Maria and Tamura, and also when Salabad dies aboard the plane. It almost seems as if they are trying to mask the fact that Salabad is dead, as a scene of Ulrov mentioning his death is also removed. Also, in the Japanese version, Miki's dog is named Caesar but here it is curiously changed to Cheetah. This version was released to home video through Paramount Gateway in 1994 through UPA.

THE LAST DAYS OF PLANET EARTH (1981) Color, 88m.

Notes: This version of *Great Prophecies of Nostradamus* was released to VHS, and as such is the only licensed Home Video release of the film in America (it was never released to VHS in Japan). It was released through UPA and features Toho's international dubbing recognizable in the 70s Godzilla films (notably *Terror of Mechagodzilla*). At 88 minutes, it is two minutes shorter than Toho's international version, though is a completely different cut entirely and lacks 26 minutes from the full *Great Prophecies of Nostradamus*. It was released to home video through Paramount Gateway in 1994. Unlike the two "Dracula" films and *ESPY*, this release was packaged to match Paramount's releases of the Godzilla films at the same time.

DEATHQUAKE (1982) Color, 80/102m. *Cast:* Hal Linden (narrator)

Notes: Deathquake was released to U.S. television editing out 24 minutes of footage. It was supposedly narrated by Hal Linden (*Barney Miller*) who had previously dubbed Akira Takarada's character in *Godzilla vs. the Sea Monster*. There are reportedly two U.S. edits of the film, one is a VHS release which utilized the 102 minute Toho international cut, and the TV version is much shorter at 80 minutes.

FUGITIVE ALIEN (1986) Color, 102m. *Directors:* Minoru Kanaya & Kiyosumi Kuzakawa *Screenplay:* Keiichi Abe, Bunzo Wakatsuki, Hideyoshi Nagasaki, Toyohiro Ando, Yoshihisa Araki, and Hiroyasu Yamamura *Special Effects Director:* Kazuo Sagawa *Music:* Norio

176

Maeda *Cast:* Jo Shishido, Tatsuya Azuma, Miyuki Tanigawa, and Akihiko Hirata.

Notes: This was one of several Tsuburaya TV series compiled into movie format for U.S. television by King Features Entertainment produced by Sandy Frank. The television series was actually called *Star Wolf* and aired in 1978. Naturally, it was inspired by *Star Wars'* success, but the TV series was also a loose adaptation of three American novels from the late 1960s by Edmond Hamilton: *The Weapon from Beyond, The Closed Worlds,* and *World of the Starwolves.*

TIME OF THE APES (1987) Color, 94m. *Director:* Kiyo Sumi Fukuzawa and Atsuo Okuana *Screenplay:* Koji Tonaka, Aritsune Toyota, and Keiichi Abe *Special Effects Director:* Kazuo Sagawa *Music:* Toshiaki Tsushima *Cast:* Reiko Tokunaga, Masaaki Kaji, Hiroko Saito, Tetsuya Ushio, Kazue Takita, Baku Hatakeyama, and Kin Omae.

Notes: One of the better King Features/Sandy Frank compilation films, this one is made up from Tsuburaya Productions' 1974 series *Monkey Army*, written by Sakyo Komatsu among others. The direct-to-video movie takes footage from the first and last episodes to make for a complete, if disjointed, story compared to their other compilation movies.

STAR FORCE: FUGITIVE ALIEN II (1987) Color, 75m. *Directors:* Minoru Kanaya and Kiyosumi Kuzakawa *Screenplay:* Keiichi Abe, Bunzo Wakatsuki, and Hiroyasu Yamamura *Special Effects Director:* Kazuo Sagawa *Music:* Norio Maeda *Cast:* Jo Shishido, Tatsuya Azuma, Miyuki Tanigawa, Choei Takahashi, and Akihiko Hirata.

Notes: Comprised of two back-to-back episodes from Tsuburaya's *Star Wolf* TV series, this was King Features only "sequel" they made out of their direct-to-video compilation movies.

SWORDS OF THE SPACE ARK (1987) Color, 94m. *Director:* Minoru Yamada *Screenplay:* Masaru Igami *Special Effects Director:* Nobuo Yajima *Music:* Shunsuke Kikuchi *American Director/Writer:* Bunker Jenkins *Editors:* Michael Part and Floyd Ingram *Cast:* Hiroyuki Sanada, Akira Oda, Ryo Nishida, Yoko Akitani, and Ritsuko Fujiyama.

Notes: After the success of *Message from Space* (1978), Toei created this TV series follow-up *Message from Space: Galactic Battle.* In America, a TV compilation film was made and titled *Swords of the Space Ark.* It was released through New Hope Entertainment in 1981.

MIGHTY JACK (1988) Color, 95m. *Director:* Kazuo Mitsuta *Screenplay:* Shinichi Sekizawa and Eizaburo Shiba *Special Effects Director:* Kazuo Sagawa *Music:* Isao Tomita *Cast:* Hideaki Nitani, Naoko Kubo, Hiroshi Minami, and Hideyo Amamoto.

Notes: Fans of Tsuburaya Productions and James Bond/spy films will find this compilation movie of the 1968 TV series *Mighty Jack* of interest. Footage is taken from the first episode, "The Man Who Vanished from Paris" and the thirteenth, "The Mysterious Dirigible."

LOST...ALMOST
ESSAYS ON NON-DAIKAIJU JAPANESE TOKUSATSU
FANTASIES BY MIKE BOGUE

English dubbing–the bane of many serious Japanese science fiction fans. After all, dubbing had brought Western scorn on the Land of the Rising Sun's fantasies in the fifties, sixties, and seventies. Critics and laymen alike ridiculed the mismatch of dialogue and lip movements–how many times did we hear, "A blind man could do better"?

Inane phrases such as "Banana oil!" supposedly epitomized the absurdity of English dubbing, but 21st century American tokusatsu fans can sigh in relief for now the majority of Japanese genre films are available in the West in English subtitled editions that preserve the dignity of the original Japanese language track.[1] English dubs–who needs 'em?

Believe it or not, *we* do. And by "we," I mean right-thinking kaiju eiga fans–and yes, that means you!

The English dubs heard in the fifties, sixties, and seventies have historical significance by putting 20th century Japanese fantasy fandom in perspective; for Westerners, the dubs provided virtually our entire vocabulary for Japanese genre films. Dubs were all baby boomer fans had, and they weren't all disasters; paging the intelligent and generally effective dubbing of 1964's *Godzilla vs. the Thing*.

However, the dubs don't just have historical importance for giant Japanese monster movies, but also for the non-giant Land of the Rising Sun genre efforts such as *The Secret of the Telegian*, *Warning from Space*, and *The Last War*. While baby boomers are still alive and possess functioning memories, it's important to document fan instances of catching the English dubs of Japanese science fiction efforts, particularly those with either human-sized monsters or no monsters at all.

Also of importance to the history of Japanese tokusatsu movies on American TV screens from the sixties through the eighties are two factors: pan-and-scan and who-knows-when.

Now, I think we all know what pan-and-scan means; this was the standard manner in which fans and non-fans saw all movies on American TV for the better part of the 20th century (and even into the 21st!). Major prestige films such as 1959's *Ben-Hur* and 1962's *Lawrence of Arabia* aired on network TV in pan-and-scan versions, just as Japanese fantasy films such as *The Secret of the Telegian* and *The Human Vapor* did on local stations. No widescreen film, no matter how esteemed or humble, got to strut its scope on the tube.

My point is, except for Japanese fantasy movies seen in movie theaters, all American kaiju fans shared the experience of having seen Land of the Rising Sun genre flicks in 16mm pan-and-scan (some might call it chop-and-crop) format. For example, Gamera's second-through-fifth movies bypassed American theatrical distribution completely, instead released to Stateside television courtesy AIP-TV.[2] Consequently, the only way an American kaiju fan saw these films was in the pan-and-scan mode, and that held true from the sixties through the eighties.

"Okay," I hear some of you saying, "I get pan-and-scan, but what the heck is 'who-knows-when?'"

Who-knows-when describes the way kaiju fans saw all genre movies on TV from the fifties through the seventies. The heyday of the VCR didn't hit until the eighties, so in the three prior decades, fans had to trust blind fate as to whether they would catch this or that monster or sci-fi movie. For example, I first became aware of 1961's *Mothra* in 1963 via a positive movie review in *Castle of Frankenstein* #4, and latter ooh-ed and aah-ed over a photo-laden three-page photo layout from the film in *Famous Monsters* #49–but I didn't actually see the movie until 1980 (On TV, natch)!

Every week monster fans like me would peruse the local Sunday newspaper TV listings, if not the nationwide *TV Guide*, in the hopes that a Japanese fantasy movie might appear in print. For example, throughout the sixties, I had longed to catch *Godzilla, King of the Monsters!*, but to no avail–none of the local stations showed it. So I still recall in the fall of 1972 scanning the Sunday paper TV listings and... dare my eyes believe it? There was *Godzilla, King of the Monsters!* slated to appear on Saturday night's local "Boo Theater" at 10:30 p.m. Oh, joy! Rapture!

Now for American Japanese genre fans, the trio of dubbing, pan-and-scanning, and who-knows-when-ing held true for both kaiju and non-kaiju-centric Japanese fantasies from the sixties through the seventies and even (to an extent) into the eighties. But in keeping with the theme of John's book, this essay comprises an oral history of one fan's experience of encountering ten *non*-giant monster Japanese genre movies in the sixties, seventies, and eighties –and in my case, I saw all but one of them on TV. [In the entries below, first I will give the title, the year released in Japan, the year released in America, the year I saw it, and my age at the time.]

WARNING FROM SPACE (aka THE MYSTERIOUS SATELLITE released in Japan as SPACEMEN APPEAR IN TOKYO). Released in

Japan 1956; to American TV in 1965; seen on local TV in 1968 at the age of 12.

I will never forget the bizarre and even outrageous aliens in this Daiei effort–upright starfish sporting large, cyclopean eyes. One commentator said they looked like actors stuffed in pillowcases. Named Pairans, the aliens have come to warn us that a runaway planet is on a collision course with Earth.

Other than the "pajama" costumed aliens, most of the special effects and miniatures are proficient. One of the best sequences shows one of the starfish aliens transformed into a human; I wondered why the rest of the footage with the aliens couldn't have been as effective. AIP released this entry to American TV around 1965 and as usual, the English dub job produced at Titra Sound Studios was competent.

As was often the case during my childhood years, my older brother Frank (2 ½ years my senior) watched this movie with me; suffice to say, Frank was not a Japanese fantasy fan. Indeed, he generally found Japanese genre films more painful than being forced to binge watch every episode of *Here Comes Honey Boo-Boo*. For example, in one scene after the presence of the Pairans in Japan has been established, Japanese picnickers by a lake start derisively yelling "Pairans! Hey, Pairans!" as they laugh.

My brother rolled his eyes.

"'Pairans,'" he aped the film actors in a sarcastic voice, "'hey, Pairans!' That is *so stu*pid!" (when critiquing Japanese genre movies, "stupid" was his favorite adjective.)

THE SECRET OF THE TELEGIAN (released in Japan as THE ELECTRONICALLY TRANSMITTED MAN). Released in Japan 1960; to American TV in mid-1960's; seen on local TV in 1969 at the age of 13.

In retrospect, I feel fortunate to have viewed this generally obscure Toho sci-fi film when I was young. Then, I had no idea it was a rarity for any American fan to catch this film, and for that, I can thank Amarillo, Texas's Channel 7, KVII, who aired several Japanese fantasies in the sixties and early seventies, including *Atragon, Frankenstein Conquers the World*, and this oddity (to their discredit, they also announced they would be showing *Godzilla vs. the Thing* and *Majin, the Monster of Terror*, but showed neither. Such was the unpredictability of free TV).

Telegian's plot concerns a lance corporal who, in World War II, was betrayed by his fellow soldiers; in present-day, he uses a matter teleportation device (think 1958's *The Fly*) to begin killing the still-living members of his unit. The special effects were quite inventive, basically showing Sudo as a living, humanoid television signal. The dubbing[3] seemed reasonable enough–I always understood what was going on and to me, the film seemed grown-up in a way Toho's monster opuses did not (now this no doubt had a lot to do with my age–13, just starting to feel the strain between the supposedly childish and the supposedly mature, and often opting for the more superficial of the two choices–pseudo-sophistication. But to be sure, inside, I never forsook the unabashed child-like pleasures of Japanese fantasy).

Many of you have read that though a color film, *Telegian* was released in the U.S. in black and white. So, did I see a color version or the black and white version? Well, I'm afraid at the time, the Bogue family only had a black-and-white TV, so we saw *everything* in black and white, even *The Wizard of Oz*!

Another aside–my brother actually thought *Telegian* was pretty good, an amazing and unexpected admission on his part. No doubt this had to do with the film's low-key manner, plus the absence of crowds fleeing in panic (my brother loved to mimic what he saw as "hysterically overacting extras" in Japanese monster movies–he would wave his hands in the air and scream while waggling his tongue from side to side).

LATITUDE ZERO (released in Japan as LATITUDE ZERO: GREAT STRATEGY). Released in Japan 1969; to American movie theaters in 1970 co-billed with *Tarzan's Jungle Rebellion*; seen at local movie theater in 1970 at the age of 14.

At this stage of my life, I was heavily into rock and pop music and rapidly collecting a cache of record singles ranging from the Moody Blues' *Question* to Sly & The Family Stones' *Thank You (Fallettin Me Be Mice Elf Again)* to the Archies' *Sugar, Sugar* (a bold true confession, that one). Japanese fantasies were still on my radar screen but now that I was in ninth grade, I was wary about my teenage peers knowing anything about my kaiju connections.

Consequently, it was with fear and trembling that I decided to catch *Latitude Zero* on a Saturday afternoon in 1970 with a "safe" friend (he was one of the few who knew about my Japanese genre fixation) whom I'll call "Dale". Dale went to a different junior high than I, so there was no chance of him spilling the beans to **my** junior high peers that I had actually gone to the Western Plaza movie theater to see a *gulp* Japanese science fiction movie.

But while we milled about the theater foyer, there was Chuck, a peer from **my** junior high (ack!!!) getting in line with a little kid (probably a nine-year-old) to see *Latitude Zero*! He asked me what I was doing and since Dale and I were undeniably there to see a movie, all I could say was that we were going to see the Tarzan film that was double-billed with *Latitude Zero*. Yeah, that was my story and I was sticking to it!

My friend Dale knew better, but didn't give me away (good ol' Dale).

But after that angst-ridden episode, it was a relief to sink into my theater seat, kick back, and relax with this new Toho science-fiction movie about which *Castle of Frankenstein* #14 had said the following: "Eiji Tsuburaya's special effects should put some plasma in this effort." Well, they did and they didn't. When they did, as with several spectacular pyrotechnics, they were great, but when they didn't, as with close-ups of obvious miniatures of the heroes using rocket belts to fly atop a steep bluff, they were spectacle-challenged.

The plot proved equally erratic, a tossed salad of comic book, spy movie, and cliffhanger serial ingredients. Meanwhile, the acting varied from Joseph Cotten's restrained thesping to Cesar Romero's hammy, over-the-top villainy. But yes, there were also monsters–giant rats (guys in suits), and winged bat-men (not to be confused with Adam West of course). And then there was the lion. Oh, my.

When I first saw this cloth-textured feline, I was stunned, because it was obviously a guy in a totally unconvincing lion suit. But hey, later, the crazed Romero grafts vulture wings onto the feline, plops a human brain into its skull, and presto! Kroiga, the instant griffin, gets the jumbo treatment courtesy Romero's growth serum. This was something of a relief–unlike the lion it had supposedly been, as a griffin, the creature was passable and even kind of cool in medium and long shots.

Overall, I found the movie okay and I was glad I'd seen it–but I was also glad Dale and I sat through (most of) the uninspired Tarzan co-feature *Tarzan's Jungle Rebellion*. After all, that was my "cover story" for Chuck and the guys at school. At least when I watched one of these things at home nowadays, no one knew except my older brother Frank, who was now a senior in high school.

The English in *Latitude Zero* sounded fine, as it was obvious the Western actors were not dubbed, but speaking in their actual voices; not only that, but these were pretty good actors. After all, in 1971, Richard Jaeckel would be nominated for a Best Supporting Actor Academy Award for Paul Newman's *Sometimes a Great Notion*.

All in all, *Latitude Zero* was one mixed bag and also one of the last Toho fantasies I would see in a movie theater.

THE LAST DINOSAUR (released in Japan as POLAR PROBE SHIP POLAR-BORER). Released in Japan 1977; to American TV on February 11, 1977; seen on ABC-TV in 1977 at the age of 22.

I couldn't help it–when I saw the ad for *The Last Dinosaur* in a February 1977 *TV Guide*, I did a happy dance inside, but my feet remained cool, calm, and collected outside, of course. I was in college, but only lived twenty-two miles from home. Consequently, I was parked in front of the Bogue family's portable Sony color TV on the night of February 11, 1977. Why? To catch *The Last Dinosaur* in all its hoped-for glory, of course! Certainly the ad showing the big Tyrannosaurus looked cool enough.

An important aside: at this point, I did not know *The Last Dinosaur* was a Japanese-American co-production. I just assumed it was a regular movie-of-the-week that ABC planned to air on its *ABC Friday Night Movie* (they had done so the same year with Dan Curtis's *Curse of the Black Widow*).

Another important aside: at this point, my older brother Frank was living at home, so he was my viewing companion for *The Last Dinosaur*. Unlike me, he was skeptical about the movie's probable quality. A voracious reader of science fiction novels and short stories, he found most sci-fi movie presentations to be second, third, fourth, or nth-rate. I, on the other hand, was a staunch genre film completist long before I had even heard the term.

There we were, two brothers already at odds over a movie we hadn't even seen yet. Within the first few minutes, we see a helicopter land at an Arctic base and the chopper had a familiar look to it. It reminded me of—

Pointing at the chopper, my brother cried "A-ha!" as though he'd just solved the riddle of the ages. "That helicopter is the same kind of obvious model you see in Japanese monster movies! This movie is *Japanese!*"

Well, I guess the cat–or in this case the dinosaur–was out of the bag.

Frank found the movie's dinosaurs–especially the Tyrannosaurus–to be less than convincing. "Those are *so* bloody *fake*," he complained (subtlety was not his strong suit).

But I thought the monsters fared well enough and I thoroughly enjoyed the battle between the Tyrannosaurus and Triceratops in the former's bone yard lair–an inspired idea. Though these prehistoric critters were clearly men in monster suits, I found them decently articulated; I also thought it interesting that the Tyrannosaurus bellowed with Godzilla's trademark roar.[4]

Frank was not only a non-fan of the movie's dinosaurs, but also derided the movie's dialogue and plot. "Richard Boone is such a jerk! And the dialogue is terrible!"

Frank's favorite body language that signified his disdain for Japanese monster movies was the rolling of his eyes. For example, I estimate that during *Frankenstein Conquers the World*, he probably rolled his eyes nine or ten times. But for *The Last Dinosaur*, he rolled his eyes at the rate of a slot machine spinning every five seconds.

Indeed, I feared that at some point his eyes would roll up into his head altogether and never again see the light of day.

Somehow, we made it to the end of the two-hour (with commercials) movie. Frank shook his head (his second favorite piece of disdainful body language) and said, "That was pretty awful."

"Well, *I* liked it," I replied.

He just shook his head and–what else?–rolled his eyes.

THE HUMAN VAPOR (released in Japan as GAS HUMAN BEING NO.1). Released in Japan 1960; to American theaters in 1964 on a double bill with *Gorath*; seen on local TV in 1979 at the age of 24.

Unlike many of the other entries in this essay, this Toho entry did enjoy an American theatrical release on a double bill with *Gorath* in 1964, and what a great drive-in double bill that would have been! But alas, I saw it on TV only. It aired, unannounced, on a local afternoon movie program on Channel 24, the local NBC affiliate. By this time, I was living at home and going to school, and the Bogue family had a color TV, so I did see *The Human Vapor* in color, although the screen kept "bleeding." I found the film sometimes poetic, sometimes slow, but almost always intriguing.

A scientist conducts an experiment that allows the protagonist to turn himself into a swirl of gas at will, a state in which he can imaginatively rob banks and suffocate unlucky humans. He turns to crime to help his beloved fulfill her traditional dancing career but it all comes to a bad end. The dubbing was decent, but not up to the standards of AIP (Brenco had released the English dubbed and heavily-altered *The Human Vapor* to the States). However, I felt lucky to have happened upon this unannounced film just a few minutes after it had started. I wouldn't see the movie again until the 1990s (Also, by this time, my older brother Frank had moved and was living and working almost a hundred miles away, hence his absence of commentary during the film)!

THE H-MAN (released in Japan as BEAUTY AND THE LIQUID PEOPLE). Released in Japan 1958; to American theaters in 1959 on a double bill with 1958's *The Woman Eater*; seen on local TV in 1981 at the age of 26.

In the late seventies, eighties, and early nineties, the self-proclaimed Superstation TBS aired numerous genre movies, many of them Japanese and many of which I'd never seen. *The H-Man* was one of the latter. I thought it grand that I was finally getting to see this movie, since all I knew of it were curious Toho publicity stills that had appeared in American monster magazines, one showing a man and woman cringing from a strange being with a huge eye, and a normal human-sized hand reaching up from the weird quasi-human thingies. I was disappointed that no such scene occurred in the film but was pleased with the special effects for the H-Men, especially their blue-green wraith forms, not to mention their penchant for melting human victims. Yech!

However, I found the main cops-and-robbers plot boring. At times, it was as though the H-Men were guest stars instead of the main attraction. For example, I found a long car chase about two-thirds through the film to be exasperating. I was surprised by the seedy night club dancers and they seemed to detract from the movie's sci-fi angle. Still, one major plus was that I was seeing the film in color! However, I wonder what my impressions of *The H-Man* would have been if I had first seen the film in black-and-white?

The dubbing fared well, though not up to the level of the AIP dubs. I recall the scene aboard the abandoned ghost ship when sailors search the vessel for the crew and instead find one of their own melting in the captain's cabin. One of the actors goes almost hysterical and my Mom, who was ironing at the time, thought the guy was overacting. "What's wrong with him?" she quipped (like my older brother Frank, Mom was not a fan of Japanese fantasy movies).

THE LOST WORLD OF SINBAD (released in Japan as THE GREAT THEIF). Released in Japan 1963; to American theaters in 1965 on a double bill with *War of the Zombies*; seen on local TV in 1981 at the age of 26.

I caught trailers for this AIP release in a walk-in movie theater circa 1965. The reason I didn't try to talk Mom or Dad into letting me see it? The previews were 100% monster-free and I thought a Sinbad fantasy film without monsters was like a Godzilla movie without atomic breath. But I was a Japanese fantasy movie completist and I was pleased that a local TV station, Fort Smith's not-always-dependable Channel 24, was airing the film at midnight on a Saturday night.

From competent Titra Sound Studios' dubbing to the appealing settings, everything was going fine for about fifteen minutes as Toshiro Mifune, the ersatz Sinbad, set sail on the sea and then the film stopped.

"Oh, well," I thought, "they're just having a little technical problem."

But after a few more seconds, the station logo popped up on the screen, followed by the station sign-off... and then nothing.

I couldn't believe it. Incensed, I called the station. Nobody answered. I next wrote an indignant letter that I mailed on Monday asking what had happened to the rest of the movie. I never got a reply and the station didn't rebroadcast the film. To this day, I have

186

never seen the entirety of *The Lost World of Sinbad* and perhaps I never will (cue weepy violins, or should that be an eye-roll from my brother?).

THE LAKE OF DRACULA (aka LAKE OF DRACULA released in Japan as THE BLOODSUCKING EYES). Released in Japan 1971; to American TV in 1980; seen on local TV in 1981 at the age of 25.

Toho and vampires? An unexpected combination, to say the least, but I approached *The Lake of Dracula* with an open mind. However, I confess I recall very little of the film. Yes, you saw fangs and yes, you saw blood and yes again, the movie appeared to be straining for a Hammer horror feel. But it just didn't make it, and I found myself underwhelmed. Where was Christopher Lee when you really needed him?

THE LAST WAR (released in Japan as GREAT WORLD WAR). Released in Japan 1961; to American theaters in 1965; seen on local TV in 1984 at the age of 29.

This Toho nuclear war drama played in a severely edited version (the original Japanese film ran 110 minutes but the American version clocked in at only 79 minutes). I saw the unannounced film on a Saturday afternoon on local Channel 24, which in the early eighties played several Japanese fantasies, including *Atragon, Majin, the Monster of Terror*, and *Godzilla vs. the Smog Monster.*

When I started watching, the film had already been on maybe twenty minutes, and it alternately frustrated and fascinated me. At this stage of my life, I was floundering in my uncertain twenties and struggling with finding a job, which may partially explain my cross attitude with the film. For example, some of the effects I thought were quite good; others I found deplorable. Some of the military hardware passed muster but some of it was clearly unreal. Because *The Last War* aspired to be a serious film, I was more critical of it than I was with Japanese giant monster films in which I didn't expect photorealism.

While the heroine reads Scripture, I found the model of Moscow that we see to be an outrageously unconvincing tabletop miniature. Also, I thought the effects during the final nuclear destruction sequence uneven; however, the burgeoning red mushroom cloud billowing over Tokyo was undeniably ominous. Much of the city destruction likewise captivated, including the realistic destruction of a Japanese house, but again, many scenes involved obvious miniatures (the ship churning in Tokyo Bay and the airliners scooting across the runway).

Overall, *The Last War* disappointed me. I didn't think it lived up to Greg Shoemaker's rave review in *The Japanese Fantasy Film Journal*

#13 (1981 issue), which called the movie "a personal film of incredible power."

As for the dubbing, I thought that it, like the visuals, ran hot and cold. The inclusion of the Disney song *It's a Small World* playing over the scenes of the merchant ship crew sailing back to the now bomb-blasted Tokyo was completely inappropriate. The excerpt of a John F. Kennedy speech also seemed ill-advised.

[Timewarp to the 21st century. I now realize that many of the problems I had with *The Last War* could be laid at the feet of the Americanization, which chopped up the movie, cut major portions, and added the Kennedy speech and *It's a Small World* to the final scenes. But still, I now appreciate the American version better than I did back in 1984. However, more importantly, I have had a chance to view the original widescreen Japanese language version of *The Last War* several times and I have a much higher opinion of the movie today than I did in 1984. For one thing, the scope of the effects Eiji Tsuburaya and his crew attempted were formidable and no Western studio attempted such large-scale nuclear devastation at the time, so it's little wonder that all the effects don't work. The script and acting, however, work almost too well.]

THE LAST DAYS OF PLANET EARTH (aka PROPHECIES OF NOSTRADAMUS released in Japan as GREAT PROPHECIES OF NOSTRADAMUS). Released in Japan 1974; to American TV in 1981; seen on local TV in 1987 at the age of 32.

Then–and now–this is one of the most inconsistent apocalyptic dramas I've ever seen. Some of the effects, such as the flooding, are awful whereas others, such as the earthquake, are quite good. This episodic entry tosses in everything from giant slugs to zombified scientists to nuclear holocausts as it supposedly relates how Nostradamus's cryptic prophecies are bearing fruit in modern times. But the film's most disquieting sequence occurs near the end... two starving, post-holocaust humanoids–their heads bulbous, their faces deformed, their bodies misshapen–fight over which one gets to eat a snake. The mutants' makeup is so chilling, their movements so quasi-human, that had the whole film been this effective, *The Last Days of Planet Earth* might have been hailed as an apocalyptic masterpiece.

But next we find out–surprise!–this was all only a what-if scenario. The overwrought scientist at the beginning of the film had actually been relaying the film's ending events to listeners in the Diet Building. The scientist has only browbeaten us with a future that *might* be–and probably *will* be–unless we get our act together. A very unsatisfying finale for a very unsatisfying end-of-the-world movie. And yes, perhaps I was a bit harsh in my appraisal at the time, but

188

today I still think the movie promises much but delivers little. As for the dubbing? Well, Titra Sound Studios need not fear the competition from Toho's international dubbers.

The late movie critic Gene Siskel said you can only see a movie for the first time once. That may mean little to younger readers but for baby boomers who grew up during the age of dubbing, pan-and-scanning, and who-knows-when-ing, that reality completely colored their perceptions of Japanese fantasy movies seen on TV. For example, in the 1960's, on TV I saw every Japanese genre movie in black-and-white, including *Rodan*, which I was to find out much later actually sports vibrant color. Ditto for *Warning from Space* and several others.

In some ways, non-kaiju Japanese fantasies were more amazing to see than their giant monster brethren, for while Godzilla did get moderate coverage in 1960's and 1970's monster magazines, the same couldn't be said for the Human Vapor, the Pairans, and a host of others. Consequently, they were often fresh discoveries when they'd pop up on the tube unannounced.

Yes, we need to historically preserve all the American 16mm TV prints[5] of Japanese fantasies–particularly those that *didn't* feature giant monsters–while they still exist. Otherwise, what are the memories of the elders (that's you, baby boomers) other than the legends of tomorrow? And Frank, if you're reading this, no eye rolling allowed.

END

Section Notes

---

[1] Though many of those translations are of dubious quality.
[2] The seventh and eighth films went direct to television as well. *Gamera vs. Zigra* didn't make it to U.S. shores until 1987, courtesy of Sandy Frank! *Gamera Super Monster* jumped across the Pacific in record time, showing up on American television in 1980, released by Filmways–the company that AIP became briefly.
[3] *The Secret of the Telegian* was one of the first Japanese releases to make it to America using an international export dub, rather than being dubbed here in America by the American distributors themselves.
[4] it's a mix of Godzilla and Toho's Kong, with a little of Tsuburaya's Red King thrown in.
[5] UPA's releases of *The Lake of Dracula* and *The Last Days of Planet Earth* were not sent to TV in 16mm format. They were mastered on videotape.

BIBLIOGRAPHY

Articles

Franklin, Garth. "Soderbergh Wanted To Remake 'Matango'." (August 28, 2017) www.darkhorizons.com/soderbergh-wanted-to-remake-matango/

Ide, Kazuko. "Japan Sinking? Sequel to 1970s Novel finds Japan Sunk and the Japanese Scattered." *Asahi Shimbun*, September 16, 2006.

Kiss, Robert James. "Shut Your Venus Flytrap!" *MAT* #8, Vol. 2 (2010)

Scanlon, Hayley. "*The Rainbow Man* (Kiyohiko Ushihara, 1949)." windowsonworlds.com/2016/06/10/the-rainbow-man虹男-kiyohiko-ushihara-1949/

Shimomura, Kenju. "*Sayonara Jupiter:* Art or Entertainment?" *G-Fan* #80 (Summer 2007)

Schultz, Mark A. "Horror—Toho Style." *G-Fan* #19 (Jan/Feb 1996)

Tsuburaya, Hideyo. "*Gorath:* A Retrospective." *Japanese Fantasy Film Journal* #15 (1983)

Winnicki, Tom. "When Gundam Came to Hollywood." http://www.zimmerit.moe/when-gundam-came-to-hollywood/ (January 09, 2017)

Books

Abe, Kobo. *Inter Ice Age 4*. Alfred A. Knopf: New York, 1970.

Bogue, Mike. *Apocalypse Then: American and Japanese Atomic Cinema, 1951-1967*. McFarland, 2018.

Brothers, Peter H. *Mushroom Clouds and Mushroom Men: The Fantastic Cinema of Ishiro Honda* (2nd Edition). Seattle, WA: Createspace, 2013.

Galbraith, Stuart IV. *Japanese Science Fiction, Fantasy and Horror Films*. London: McFarland, 1994.

Galbraith, Stuart IV. *Monsters Are Attacking Tokyo*. Venice, CA: Feral House, 1998.

Godziszewski, Ed. *The Illustrated Encyclopedia of Godzilla*. By the Author, 1998.

Macias, Patrick. *TokyoScope: The Japanese Cult Film Companion*. San Francisco: Cadence Books, 2001.

Ragone, August. *Eiji Tsuburaya: Master of Monsters*. San Francisco: Chronicle Books, 2007.

Ryfle, Steve. *Japan's Favorite Mon-Star: The Unauthorized Biography of "The Big G"*. Chicago: ECW Press, 1998.

Ryfle, Steve & Ed Godziszewski. *Ishiro Honda: A Life in Film, From Godzilla to Kurosawa*. Middletown: Wesleyan University Press, 2017.

Japanese Sources

1973 "Japan Sinking" Complete Documentation (Film Hidden Collection) Tomio Tomii, Editor. (Yosensha, 2018)

Godzilla: Toho Tokusatsu Unpublished Material Archive: The Era of Producer Tomoyuki Tanaka. Shinichiro Kobayashi, Editor. (Kadokawa Shoten, 2010)

Toho Special Effects Movie Complete Works (Village Books, 2012)

Godzilla: Toho SPFX Movie (Kodansha, 2014)

Tokusatsu Hiho vol. 2 (Yosensha, 2015)

Websites

www.davmil.org/www.kaijuconversations.com

http://www.tohokingdom.com/cutting_room.htm

https://vantagepointinterviews.com

Index

194

THE BIG BOOK OF JAPANESE GIANT MONSTER MOVIES SERIES

VOLUME 1: 1954-1982

VOLUME 2: 1984-2017

THE LOST FILMS

TERROR OF THE LOST TOKUSATSU FILMS

WRITING JAPANESE MONSTERS

EDITING JAPANESE MONSTERS

Be sure to read these other great books!

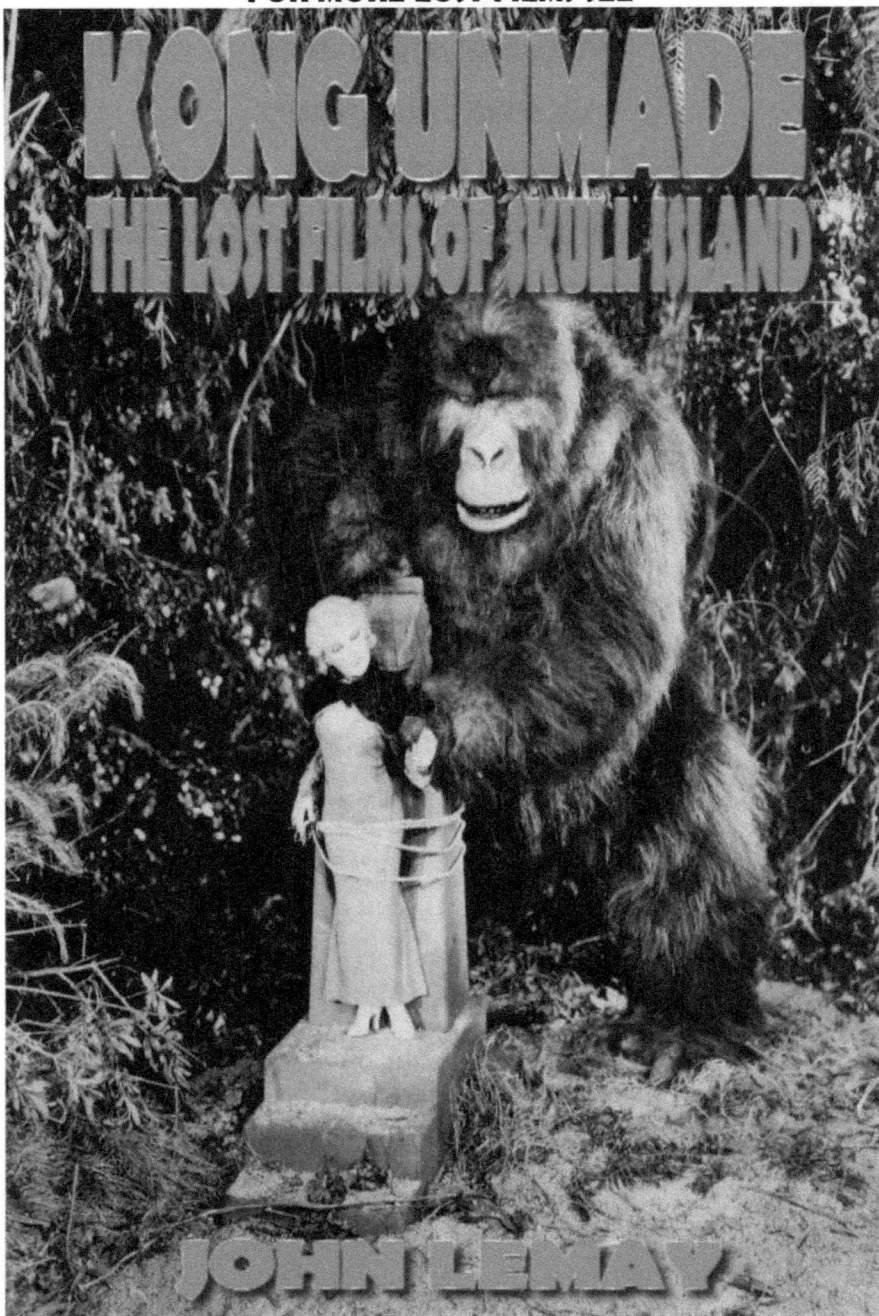

About the Authors

John LeMay is the author of over a dozen books that include three entries in *The Big Book of Japanese Giant Monster Movies* series including *Volume 1: 1954-1982*; *Volume 2: 1984-2016*; and *The Lost Films*. LeMay is also the author of books such as *The Real Cowboys and Aliens: UFO Encounters of the Old West* with Noe Torres, *Tall Tales and Half Truths of Billy the Kid*, and *Cowboys & Saurians: Dinosaurs and Prehistoric Beasts as Seen by the Pioneers*. He is a frequent contributor to magazines such as *G-Fan*, *Mad Scientist*, *Xenorama*, *True West* and *Cinema Retro*.

Colin McMahon is a writer living in Massachusettes and is the author of the novel *The Dreamcatchers* (2018). For more information, see colinmcmahonauthor.com.

Peter H. Brothers is the author of *Mushroom Clouds and Mushroom Men: the Fantastic Cinema of Ishiro Honda*, and *Atomic Dreams and the Nuclear Nightmare: the Making of Godzilla (1954)*.

Allen A. Debus has written numerous articles, several for journals and many more for a variety of fanzines—the latter including *Prehistoric Times, G-Fan, FilmFax, Mad Scientist* and *Scary Monsters*—usually intertwining the subjects of science fiction and paleontology. Allen has also authored eight books, the two most recent being *Dinosaurs Ever Evolving: The Changing Face of Prehistoric Animals in Popular Culture* (2016) for McFarland Publishers, and *Dinosaur Memories II: Pop-Cultural Reflections on Dino-Daikaiju & Paleoimagery* (2017 – Createspace). He is a self-taught dinosaur sculptor and a retired environmental chemist.

Mike Bogue is a community college educator who regularly writes for *G-FAN* and *Scary Monsters Magazine*. He has also written for *Mad Scientist, Castle of Frankenstein, Journal of Frankenstein, Wonder,* and *Monster Bash Magazine*. He lives in Ozark, Arkansas, and the author of several books, the best known one being *Apocalypse Then: American and Japanese Atomic Cinema, 1951-1967*.

www.ingramcontent.com/pod-product-compliance
Lightning Source LLC
Chambersburg PA
CBHW031930090426
42811CB00002B/140